Praise for Zen & Psychotherapy

"Often the most interesting places in our lives are found where two contrasting spheres of influence meet—those warm tidepools of the littoral zone that bristle with all sorts of fertile surprises. Joseph Bobrow's book embodies just such a rich encounter in the interfacing of Zen and psychotherapy. His several decades of experience have enabled him to draw knowledgeably and freely from both disciplines. His narrative coaxes insights as often from academic papers, encounters, and dreams, as it does from koans and dialogues of the ancients, poems, and song lyrics. All of these he has brewed together in the fecund pool of his own wisdom and thoughtful analysis, and what has emerged from that crucible is a fine book, brimming with life, and resonant with integrity and heart. It would be no surprise if people were quoting from it long into the future."

—AJAHN AMARO, author of *Small Boat, Great Mountain*; *Silent Rain*; and *Rugged Interdependency*

"Zen master and psychoanalyst Joseph Bobrow has a rare depth and subtlety of experience in both disciplines and ways of life. After nearly forty years of practice and teaching in each, he has written a definitive, clear, and compassionate book that argues persuasively that Zen and psychotherapy are complementary traditions. Each challenges and enriches the other. Even enlightened Buddhist practitioners can expand themselves as individuals and in their relationships. Therapists and their patients can become more meaningfully aware of the depth of experience that lies beyond individuality and individuation. Mindful of differences, but also indivisible links, Bobrow challenges us to realize the integration of the personal and the universal in our daily lives. Anyone interested in psychological or spiritual ideas or practice will find much of value in this deeply gratifying and informative work."

—GERALD I. Fo⟨⟩ ⟨⟩alyst
and form⟨⟩ ⟨⟩nter

"This is a quiet book that works you, ⟨⟩ ⟨⟩dies unconscious affective communicatio⟨⟩ ⟨⟩ism. He's lived it. The book carries it. The reader experiences it."

—CHARLES SPEZZANO, PhD, author of *Affect in Psychoanalysis* and co-editor of *Soul on the Couch*

Zen & Psychotherapy

Partners in Liberation

JOSEPH BOBROW

FOREWORD BY NORMAN FISCHER

Wisdom

Wisdom Publications
199 Elm Street
Somerville, MA 02144 USA
wisdomexperience.org

Originally published in 2010 by W. W. Norton.

Library of Congress Cataloging-in-Publication Data
Names: Bobrow, Joseph, author.
Title: Zen and psychotherapy: partners in liberation / Joseph Bobrow.
Description: Second edition. | Somerville, MA: Wisdom Publications, 2020. |
    Originally published: New York: W. W. Norton & Co., c2010. |
    Includes bibliographical references and index.
Identifiers: LCCN 2019044499 (print) | LCCN 2019044500 (ebook) |
    ISBN 9781614296805 (paperback) | ISBN 9781614296812 (ebook)
Subjects: LCSH: Buddhism and psychoanalysis. | Zen Buddhism—Psychology. |
    Psychotherapy—Religious aspects—Zen Buddhism.
Classification: LCC BQ4570.P755 B63 2020 (print) | LCC BQ4570.P755 (ebook) |
    DDC 294.3/3615—dc23
LC record available at https://lccn.loc.gov/2019044499
LC ebook record available at https://lccn.loc.gov/2019044500

ISBN 978-1-61429-680-5   ebook ISBN 978-1-61429-681-2

24 23 22 21 20   5 4 3 2 1

Cover design by Phil Pascuzzo. Interior design by James D. Skatges.

"Sleep" by D. W. Winnicott used by permission of Paterson Marsh Ltd on behalf
    of the Winnicott Trust.
"Break the Mirror" by Nanao Sakaki used by permission of Blackberry Books. Originally
    published in Sakaki, N. (1996). *Break the Mirror*. Blackberry Books.
"To be of use" from CIRCLES IN THE WATER by Marge Piercy, copyright © 1982 by
    Marge Piercy. Used by permission of Alfred A. Knopf, a division of Random House,
    Inc.

Printed on acid-free paper that meets the guidelines for permanence and durability of
the Production Guidelines for Book Longevity of the Council on Library Resources.

Printed in the United States of America.

MIX
Paper from
responsible sources
FSC® C005010

Please visit fscus.org.

To my father, Robert Bobrow,

and my mother, Helen Krieger,
for the gift of life

To Aitken Gyoun Roshi, Yamada Koun Roshi,
and Ven. Thich Nhat Hanh for helping reveal
its essential nature

To Joseph Caston, for helping me learn to live it fully

Contents

Foreword

I've known Joe Bobrow for a long time. He is, as you will soon sense from the pages you are about to read, an intensely questioning person whose feeling for life and for others runs deep—which is why it was perhaps inevitable that he would devote himself to a lifetime of study of both psychoanalysis and Zen Buddhism.

Many of us (like Joe) who seriously undertook Buddhist practice in the 1960s and 1970s came to it out of great need. We were fleeing a world that had ceased to make sense to us, and were searching for ultimate experiences that would somehow catapult us out of that unworkable world, remaking our lives in the process. Having gone to great lengths to have such experiences, we were surprised, shocked, and disappointed to realize that our lives were not remade: that what we thought we had left behind was still there, inside us—that our conditioned selves, formed by our families and the sufferings of our time, painfully remained, despite our Buddhist practice, indelible as ever.

Here is where we needed Buddhism—a religion, the repository of such ultimacy and depth—to encounter psychology, the humanistic science and art of discovering who we are as persons among others. For us this encounter was not a matter of mere interest of curiosity; it was something we needed to understand in order to live the lives we had embarked on.

Psychology's realm, as you will learn from this book, is the realm of self-awareness, of character formation, of interpersonality and social interaction, of being a person in the world in which one finds one's self. Buddhism's realm is in a sense otherworldly; it references the beyond-human context of being human, the cosmos, the eternal, the nature of consciousness and reality, and engages questions of ultimate meaning. Why are we alive? What is death? What is the meaning of human suffering? Buddhism naturally takes us to places where such questions are engaged, offering us methods and teachings to help.

It may seem at first glance that these two realms are distinct. Perhaps they were a few hundred years ago. But we are living in the post-Jungian era of depth psychology, which sees religious experience as a human phenomenon, and in the era of Buddhist modernism, when religion in general, and Buddhism in particular, have been remade in the light of science, personal autonomy and interiority, and mass culture. Buddhist modernism isn't just a Western phenomenon: as scholars have been pointing out for some decades now, the Buddhisms that came to the West from Asia were transmitted not by traditionalists who were espousing ancient wisdom but by modern teachers (though many of them were clerics wearing traditional garb), well aware of the era in which they were living. In other words, Buddhism and psychology have had, for some time now, tremendous overlap. It would not be too much to say that each has revolutionized the other.

This long process has been mostly, to use a psychological word, *unconscious*. That is, most psychologists who have been influenced by Buddhism may well not realize this, and most Buddhist practitioners whose practice stands on modern psychological assumptions may not recognize that this is so.

Here is where what we call theory helps—and this book is to a large extent a masterful and subtle exploration of theory. If you want to practice as a psychotherapist or a psychotherapeutic patient or as a Buddhist practitioner or teacher, your practice will be well served by contemplation of the process you are engaged in. Thinking about what you are doing doesn't excuse you from the necessity of doing it, but it may shed some light on how you will do it and how you will feel about the doing of it. And if, like me, you are committed to your practice, some theory about what it is and how it works in the human heart is, simply, delightfully and usefully interesting.

The straightforward title of this book is a signal that between its covers you will read a clear—if nuanced, sensitive, perhaps poetic, and certainly nonreductive—account of both these great disciplines, and how they might impact and expand one another: indeed how they have impacted and expanded one another in the life and practice of Joe Bobrow. Joe tells plenty of engaging stories about his own life and the lives of some of his patients in these pages, but what is important for me here is his probing reflections on the key ideas of psychology and Buddhism and how he has seen them inform and inflect each other in crucial ways, in a lifetime of dual practice. These days there are many Buddhist teachers who have trained in and practiced psychotherapy, but I am not aware of another book that plunges so deeply into theory, with equal respect and appreciation for both disciplines.

As a person whose study has been mostly in the Buddhist realm, I appreciate this book for its clear and soulful explication of works of key psychoanalysts like D. W. Winnicott and W. R. Bion, who took the original insights of the founders of psychology to new depths and subtleties. I assume that readers well versed in psychology will have a similar appreciation for the book's clear grasp of Zen Buddhism's purpose and methodology as it translates into psychological process.

This book was written for psychologists interested in Buddhism, so throughout most of it Joe speaks as a psychologist who is also a Buddhist teacher. In the afterword the reader will hear Joe's voice from the Zen teaching seat, clear, compassionate, encouraging, deep, yet modest. Those adjectives apply to the book in its entirety, which you are about to enjoy.

—Norman Fischer

Introduction

Gateless is the great Tao,
There are thousands of ways to it.
If you pass through this barrier,
You may walk freely in the universe.

—Zenkei Shibayama

Oh freedom! Oh freedom! Oh freedom over me!
And before I'll be a slave I'll be buried in my grave
And go home to my Lord and be free.

—Negro spiritual

My Zen teacher, Robert Aitken Rōshi, once asked me, "Are you a thera-pist who teaches Zen or a Zen master who practices psychotherapy?" He was not checking my understanding as Zen masters are wont to do. Rather, he was gauging my devotion to the Zen Buddhist path. From the other side, some of my psychoanalytic colleagues were no doubt also wondering where my true allegiance lay. The truth is: I did not want to choose; both paths were important to me. Now, in answer to my teach-er's question, I would reply, "I won't say! I won't say!"[1]

Despite my intuition that for me the two paths were inseparably linked, for all practical purposes I actually kept them separate for thirty-five years, resisting the temptation to construct a premature hybrid. Now I see that this allowed each of them plenty of time to sink in, take root, and cross-fertilize in an organic way. Once, when someone asked how I combined psychotherapy and Zen, I stopped and had to think. "I don't," I replied, "except that in my inner development they are always intertwining." Gradually, this outward separation has dissolved, as I've developed multidisciplinary community programs for incarcerated youth and, most recently, for veterans and their families and caregivers. However, these are secular *adaptations* of Zen-informed, and humanistic *adaptations* of, psychotherapeutic principles and practices. At a Buddhist teachers' conference with the Dalai Lama a number of years ago, His Holiness listened to reports about a wide range of programs making use of meditation, and he was uniformly encouraging. Someone then asked why—since he supported all these programs that enabled people to practice meditation independently of Buddhism—it was necessary to wear robes, do all the rituals, and be a Buddhist. He laughed and replied, "Oh, that's *applied* Buddhism. If you want to study Tibetan Buddhism, you have to do everything I say." His comments affirmed my intuition to "let a thousand (applied) flowers bloom" while maintaining the integrity of Zen practice and psychotherapy and allowing inevitable changes to occur deliberately and thoughtfully.

Similarities with a Difference

Human life is of a piece. We can't "get it together"; it *is* together. We divide it—distinguishing material reality from psychic reality, relationships from drives, psychology from physiology, and conscious from unconscious. We divide the intrapsychic and intersubjective, internal reality from external reality, the spiritual from the psychological, self from other, and personal life from cultural life. Such distinctions, however important, cannot capture the rich interwoven fabric of our humanity. Spiritual and emotional experience and growth evolve in concert, and, when functioning harmoniously, their interplay is seamless. In Zen, we say that our own true nature and the world around us are "not two." Seeing through duality is not the final aim, and lest we get stuck in a concept of unity, they are "not even one."

In this book, I propose that liberation, while inseparable into discrete elements, simultaneously unfolds in practice on two interconnected tracks, represented here by Zen and psychotherapy. Although they contain elements of each other and address similar concerns, Zen and psychotherapy are distinctive paths that challenge and, by virtue of their differences, enrich one another. Zen practice helps us to cut through the subject—object and self—other dichotomies that are such entrenched characteristics of our experience and to open to, realize, and put our-selves in accord with our essential nature. Psychotherapy promotes emotional growth, integration, resilience, and psychological freedom. While acknowledging the wide range of current psychotherapies, some informed by derived Eastern meditation practices, I use the word *psychotherapy* to refer to the psychodynamic psychotherapies, including psychoanalysis.

The Hungarian child psychiatrist René Spitz writes that life begins in dialogue, and that all psychopathology (or anguish) can be seen as derailment of dialogue. Each of the paths I explore—each set of principles and practices—is a full partner in the evolution of a broader, more inclusive narrative. "Similarities with a difference" characterizes their relationship: same and different and interpenetrating. They potentiate one another and, taken together, they help us think in a truly integral way about our human potential. Zen and psychotherapy each bring to this dialogue their own vision, dream, purpose, gifts, flavors, implicit values, privileged elements, and blind spots.

The fruits of their interplay enrich each without compromising their distinctiveness. Through their intimate conversation, each changes gradually and is enriched without compromising its integrity. Their interplay evolves, deepens, expands, and refines, benefiting each practice as it benefits the people who walk each path. It makes each better at its own project: variations on the theme of healing and transforming human suffering and liberating the deepest human potentials. How? By creating a more experience-near, deeper, comprehensive, and representative framework that helps people become freer, wiser, more peaceful, more alive, and more compassionate. While new blueprints are a dime a dozen and guarantee nothing—one must still walk the land and build the house—the integrative vision that I will trace may open the realm of the possible in new ways. Furthermore, I believe that this integrative vision may well provide medicine for a certain kind of suffering that has afflicted many contemporary spiritual communities, which I explore more fully.

Interplay of the Universal and the Personal

This book is about the integration of the universal and personal dimensions and why they each need the other. As its author, I want to "walk the talk." So, as part of introducing this book to you, I weave stories from my own personal, professional, and spiritual development as I trace the book's themes. I choose to do this because I learn best when information is personally and affectively embedded, and I know that the same holds true for many readers. Also, in sharing my experience, I want to help dispel two notions: that a Zen master has transcended, once and for all, and that enlightenment, as pivotal an experience as it is, provides a lifetime exemption from human suffering and growth. The experience of *kensho* (*satori*, enlightenment, awakening) conveys by direct experience that all beings by nature are awakened from the beginning and the other is none other than oneself. It brings in its wake a deep sense of compassion for all beings. In Zen, it is a beginning, a glimpse. Yamada Koun *Rōshi* ("old teacher") described kensho as standing in a glassed-in room with windows so steamed we cannot see out and wiping clear a little spot from one part of one window. Zen is a lifetime path of deepening, tempering, refining, and personalizing.

Interplay of the Universal and the Particular

The interplay of this universal dimension and the realm of the particular is another prism for our exploration of Zen and psychotherapy. The universal is not undifferentiated in the psychological sense. Rather, in Zen the universal and the particular "inter-are." The poet William Blake presents this when he writes in his "Auguries of Innocence":

> To see a World in a Grain of Sand
> And a Heaven in a Wildflower,
> Hold Infinity in the palm of your hand,
> And Eternity in an hour.

The grain of sand, the sound of the rain, or a child crying is the whole universe. It does not represent the universe, it does not symbolize or condense the universe, and it is neither a transmutation nor a derivative of the universe. It is the universe, the whole universe. This is difficult for us to wrap our dualistic Western minds around. Why? It is like a cat chasing its tail or a fish asking what water is. It is our mind, but the self-absorbed small self has to slough off for it to be experienced. In Zen, each and every phenomena presents the universe. Yamada Rōshi represents this with the metaphor of a fraction. Each moment has as the denominator the infinity symbol within a circle, empty infinity. This is our boundless essential nature, void of any permanent or separate (as in isolated and self-perpetuating) essence. Because there is no such essential "stuff," we call it essential nature. In the numerator we can place anything: a boy, a girl, the wind, a thought, a piece of cake, a state of mind, a dying person. A subset of the particular is the personal, and the interplay of the universal and the personal realms is the fertile field of Zen and psychotherapy,

> All beings by nature are Buddha,
> As ice by nature is water
> Apart from Buddha there are no beings
> Apart from beings no Buddha.
>
> —HAKUIN

In Zen, we need a person, a fully functioning human being, to embody our essential nature. To connect with and actualize our deepest human potential and to be in alignment with our true nature are not mutually exclusive enterprises; rather, they go hand in hand. Just as we are, we are already doing it. It is only through the personal that the impersonal and the universal can find expression. Psychotherapy is a bit like a midwife in helping us develop the requisite personal "container" such that we can give expression to our essential nature and the spiritual qualities that are said to evolve after and as we continue to awaken.

The Streams of Zen and Psychotherapy: What I Hold Dear

I have had my feet in the streams of Zen Buddhism and psychology for some time. As a boy, I had no interest in either and instead enjoyed playing sports. Although my family is Jewish by birth, our household religion was progressive politics. While walking my dog in my diverse working-class neighborhood in the Bronx, I would pass the Orthodox synagogue around the corner from where we lived and occasionally peek in and glimpse the goings on—old men rocking from side to side, chanting, singing, praying. My grandmother, with whom I spent quite a bit of time, was Orthodox, but my mother rebelled against her strictures. The needs of the oppressed, marginalized, underserved—those without a voice—were our core values, and organizing and helping them was paramount. Building community was a stream that ran through me from my earliest days. It should not be surprising then, although it was to me, that after founding Deep Streams Zen Institute in 2000, Deep Streams began offering, in addition to Zen practice, education for mental health professionals on the interplay of Buddhism and psychotherapy, and soon thereafter community-based programs that brought together elements of each to create healing and transformative environments. I later realized that a core value of mine was that the fruits of Zen practice, psychotherapy, and their interplay, should be made available not only to the relative few who practice or partake directly but also to the many in the wider social commons. Spiritual practice, multidisciplinary education, and service became the foundations of Deep Streams. They bear a resemblance to another trio—*dhyana*, *prajna*, and *sila*, which mean meditation, wisdom, and precepts in Sanskrit. *Dhyana* also means concentration or absorption and is the root of the word *Zen*. Taking liberties, I also use *dhyana* to mean practice or attention; *prajna* as insight, enlightenment, and (non-conceptual) understanding; and *sila* as ethical behavior or awakened action. These in turn reflect yet another trio—absorption, realization, and personalization—that our old Japanese master, Yamada Rōshi employed as an *upaya* (skillful means) to describe the process of Zen training. They will serve as organizing threads throughout the book.

When I was a teenager, a distant uncle by marriage, who was a psychoanalyst, came over to our apartment a few times for supper. He was well liked, smart, and decent. As I was readying excitedly to move to Europe to finish college and follow my heart, anxiety reared its head, and he gave me a referral to a wise colleague. We met for a few sessions, and as we engaged I would ask him about how the process worked. His dignified manner, the smell of his pipe, his way of listening, and a question he asked about a dream that continues to bear fruit to this day were helpful. He also planted a seed when he said, "You'd make a good psychologist." I had begun my first year at the City College of New York and was taking a class in psychopathology from a Freudian psychoanalyst with a thick Bronx accent, who would enthrall a lecture hall filled with wet-behind-the-ears girls and boys with tales of the unconscious and how it worked, seemingly miraculously, in ordinary life. The identifications deepened. The following year, I took an elective with him, "Contemporary Theories in Psychotherapy." On the list of optional readings was *The First and Last Freedom*, by the Indian sage Krishnamurti. It was as if Krishnamurti were speaking directly to me. "Truth is a pathless land," he wrote, and all conventional accrued knowledge must be relinquished if we wished to encounter it. His message resonated with the adventurous developmental urges of a young adult wanting to break free, internally and outwardly. Spiritual practice always takes place and is expressed in the context of a person with unique attributes and history, but there was more: intimations of a depth of reality I had not fathomed. Later, after much therapy and analysis, in which Zen-related relationships were occasionally the theme, something remained. Everything was not reducible to psychological conflicts, deficits, and personal problems.

Once, as a young adult, while playing tennis I saw in a flash that I was not really playing the game but rather playing to the crowd. What was tennis then? What was non-self-absorbed activity? It was a huge shock and an auspicious discovery. After a breakup with my girlfriend, I went into therapy again, three times a week. Relational troubles are a subset of human suffering that bring people not just to therapy but also to Zen practice. At one point in our work, the therapist told a Zen story. At another moment, as I was describing my impressions of how space and time felt in a Japanese film, I paused, searching for words. After a while he said, "Maybe there is no space and no time." From the mouth of a Western therapist, no less, this had a profound influence on me, partly because of the strong positive transference to him. He studied yoga, so I did, too. One day, at the end of a series of asanas, in the corpse pose, I relaxed to such a degree that I lost sensation in my body but remained aware. It was quite a revelation—awareness that was not dependent on sensory feedback. On another occasion, a phrase I had heard came to mind, something about thought creating the world. I wondered, "What about when thought was not operative? What was the world then?" For a few moments, the space opened wide, a wordless expanse. When we ended therapy, I set out on a pilgrimage of sorts through France and Spain, to Morocco, then into the Sahara. I spent three months in a small desert oasis and an abandoned fishing village on the sea. I knew nothing about meditation, and the only Buddhist book I had seen was the collection of koans and stories, *Zen Flesh, Zen Bones*.

When I arrived in the desert, I was consumed with terrible "what if" fears, certain that I had left the stove on or forgotten something dreadfully important. Gradually, I settled in, cooking food over a wood fire in the small adobe building with dirt floors where I slept. I practiced yoga, sat quietly, and found my way into long states of absorption, after which I would sometimes sleep, a dreamless sleep, vividly aware. Then one night, on a sand dune under a sky of pulsating stars that seemed to hover just above my head, there was a flood of tears, a sense of immanence and presence arose that cut through all thought. More tears flowed, tears of gratitude for this life, its wonder and beauty, for all of it.

After returning to the States and joining relatives in Maui for a family reunion, I tried to recapture the experiences I'd had. I read a bit more and sat *zazen* (Zen meditation, literally "sitting Zen"), one part of me meditating, one part waiting for the lightning bolt of kensho. Up the road from the valley where my relatives lived was an old moss-covered Japanese-style gate through which lay a simple path, bordered by daylilies, that led to a covered deck. There were cars parked outside periodically. I heard that it was a Zen temple. I didn't want any of "that formal stuff." But, one day as I ambled along the dusty roads of upcountry Maui, I saw an old man, dressed in jeans, weeding the lilies. I went up and asked him about the place. He responded in an informative way and invited me to come for zazen should I wish. The next week, I came to a daylong sitting, and there he was, in full robes, leading the chanting, the sitting, the walking meditation and giving instruction. In short order, I became a resident and inflicted my cooking skills on the group of mostly young men and women who lived and practiced at the temple.

My first formal meeting with Aitken Rōshi occurred in his library, located off a long wooden outdoor walkway in the back of the plantation house temple compound. In this space, permeated by the smell of books and tropical humidity, he would read introductory talks to each new student individually. A Gauguin print faded by the sunlight bore the tiny inscription by the painter, "Who are we, where do we come from, where are we going?"—existential questions that Rōshi often referred to in his talks. I entered dressed in crusty cutoff jeans and a tank top, somewhat redolent from a long walk. He suggested that when I came for part two of the orientation I consider wearing pants and a shirt that covered my shoulders, not fancy but clean. I responded, "But aren't all beings by nature Buddha?" He waited and responded, "Disorganized outside, maybe disorganized inside." If he only knew.

The practice side, *dhyana*, was difficult. I had injured my hip by overly ambitious yoga and had to sit Japanese style, straddling cushions, on a bench, or sometimes on a chair—not the best positions for long periods of meditation for a Westerner. My mind wandered a lot, and I continued to try to recapture the experiences in the desert. Eventually, I settled in, supported by my comrades in the deep silence. The prajna or insight side unfolded—the barest glimpse into true nature. In those early days, the teacher and the other retreat participants recognized each student who experienced kensho. I recall how, in the days after the experience was confirmed by Aitken Rōshi and Yamada Rōshi and recognized by the *sangha*, or community, a sense of having accomplished something gradually crept in, which was completely absent from the experience. Some weeks later, I got a lesson in *sila*, awakened activity. During evening meditation, while everyone was gathered for chanting and meditation in the *Zendo* (Zen meditation hall). I was upstairs in our tree house dormitory, solitary and absorbed in contemplation. There was a knock on the door that disoriented me, and Aitken Rōshi entered in his robes. He asked what I was doing, and I replied, "All things are flashing into the phenomenal world," a phrase from a Zen sutra. He said simply, "And we're missing you in the meditation hall." Any experience can be hijacked and placed at the service of ego aggrandizement.

Within three months of becoming a resident at the Maui Zendo, I accompanied my teacher to a conference of the Association of Humanistic Psychology in Honolulu at which he had been asked to present. I met an interpersonally oriented psychoanalyst, who later became my therapist and mentor. During his workshop, previously unconscious early feelings surged up. When he came to Maui to vacation, we did a

powerful and meaningful piece of work together that felt quite liberating. This personal emotional work came directly on the heels of my
modest initial Zen opening.

One day, while working in Aitken Rōshi's library, I discovered that
he and his wife Anne had worked and been part of the community at
Happy Valley School in Ojai, California; the school had been founded
by close associates of Krishnamurti. I found more information on
Krishnamurti and resolved to visit Ojai, meet my original inspiration
personally, and learn about a new school he was helping develop. There
was also a possibility of helping at a nursery school that the Zendo was
sponsoring. There had been an early rupture in my relationship with my
father, and I resolved to track him down and meet him. I think this
history sensitized me to issues of integrity and alignment of talk (teachings) and walk (action). Amid the teeming profusion of personal identity issues, I was also working on koans that plumbed our existential
origins, such as "Show me your face before your parents were born." I
was able eventually to respond to such koans, but this did not keep me
from wanting to see my father's face—to the contrary.

I did visit Ojai and enjoyed meeting Krishnamurti personally, but I
found his understanding of children wanting, so I declined to become
involved in his new school. During the same trip, I was visiting schools
in Southern California in preparation for restarting the nursery school
on Maui. I had an emotional and memorable reunion with my father,
and my relationship with him for the remaining four years of his life
until his death from leukemia meant the world to me. Within a few
years of his death, I had changed my adoptive surname back to my original name.

Living at the Zen temple provided a holding environment, a halfway
house of sorts, for a young man in search of home, in search of his father,
his identity, his origins, his professional calling—a lost boy in a sense.
Or, maybe we can think of it as a moratorium, as Erik Erikson describes
it, before leaping into adult life. Along the way, real Zen practice happened, and something profound stuck. I was extruding a personal identity, while simultaneously inquiring into spiritual reality and origins.
With a fellow Zendo resident, I created a new school, the Peahi Nursery
School, and became the director of this Zendo-sponsored community
project. I was twenty-four and—armed with a well-used copy of D. W.

Winnicott's *The Child, the Family, and the Outside World*, experience working in recreation and day care, a BA in psychology and French, inspiration from reading A. S. Neil and Maria Montessori on the natural learning instincts of children, and a few years studying Piaget and other developmentalists in France but without formal teacher training or teaching experience—I dived in. What, I wondered, would define a Zen-sponsored school? The qualities of compassion, considerateness, and creativity were the central pillars and remain relevant today. I eschewed formal religion. The closest we came to formal meditation was taking a few moments before lunch to quiet down, listen, and notice how many different sounds we could hear. Combining structure with free play and exploration, the school was a parent cooperative where parents shared their own special interests, passions, and expertise with the children. I began to notice that some parents had a way with children; their very presence seemed to sponsor a beneficial unfolding in the children. What was this facilitative ingredient? Chapter 4, "Presence of Mind," owes its roots to this ongoing question. I was not aware at the time that this educational work in the community represented something that would later be called *engaged Buddhism*—applying the principles and values of practice in the wider cultural commons. Aitken Rōshi and Thich Nhat Hahn each apparently coined the term independently. I agree with Bollas that we seek "objects" that help us release our own distinctive idiom. We learn about it après coup, as we live our life. We check our tracks and can see traces and impacts of what really matters to us, what infuses our activity, what we live by—based on what we hold dear.

Ten years later, I spent two summers at Plum Village, a community of Vietnamese refugees. I had attended a seminar with visiting Vietnamese Zen master and peace activist Thich Nhat Hanh at Tassajara Zen Mountain Monastery in California. Inspired by his presence, I decided to see more for myself. After a long trip, when I arrived at his community in the Dordogne region of France, Sister Phuong (now Chan Kong) greeted me and showed me around. Moved by the families and children, the simple, heartfelt sense of peace that permeated the place, and all the work that needed to be done on the buildings and in the fields of plum trees and sunflowers, I said, "If there's anything I can do to help, let me know." She replied, "Just to be is enough." Her response stopped me in my tracks and for two summers liberated me from the guilt I realized, with her comment, that I felt over our role in the Vietnam War. I did not have to serve because I received a high lottery number, and I spent parts of that period traveling, on "pilgrimage," and studying Zen. I took Chan Kong up on just being that summer and the next, enjoying the simple company of residents: weeding, walking, playing with children, cooking, meditating, laughing, translating, socializing. The polarities of being versus doing and personal benefit versus communal good fell away. The community held the residents, all survivors of trauma, with a light yet profound touch. The children were at the center, and their parents felt the supportive power of the village. This was clearly not psychological treatment, and there was relatively little formal Zen practice compared to what I was used to in our Japanese tradition. But, the compassionate embrace was palpable.

The seeds planted at Plum Village were among the inspirations twenty-five years later to begin the Coming Home Project and our residential retreats for veterans, their families, and caregivers. These workshops welcome people, without judgment, from all faiths, as well as atheists and agnostics, into a nondenominational community and create an environment of safety and trust in which to share stories and experiences and support one another, learn stress management and wellness skills derived from ancient meditation practices, use writing and other modes of creative expression to represent what cannot yet be spoken, enjoy the beauty of serene natural settings and outdoor recreation with others, and participate in secular rituals.

Liberation: Individual and Collective, Inner and Outer

What stands out now as I reflect on this trajectory is that liberation is of a piece: individual, familial, collective, national, international, inner, and outer. Not only has Buddhism emerged from the temple into the social commons, so has psychotherapy. Treatment does not end in the consulting room any more than meditation ends in the dojo. The consulting room and the culture, the temple, and the social commons are intimately connected. Taking liberties, we could say that dhyana, prajna, and sila correspond, on the cultural register, to peace, freedom, and justice.

In our Coming Home retreats for veterans and families, uncondi-
tional welcome and acceptance are perhaps the most catalytic qualities.
As in individual psychotherapy, they engender trust, belonging, and
safety, the conditions in which healing and transformation can unfold.
Radical inclusiveness is something I first encountered, paradoxically
some readers may find, at the Zen temple. In the early 1970s, visitors and
residents of the temple represented the culture of the day, and occasionally their unusual behavior showed it. Once during *kinhin* (walking
meditation), a student began doing 360-degree twirls while walking in
the line. Part of our practice is not to distract others—simple basic consideration. This individual's twirling, laughing, and smiling knowingly
to himself during formal talks not only distracted me and other residents, the irritation that it spawned became an even bigger distraction.
We lobbied our teacher to take action. He listened but held firm. Thirty
years later, I met up with this individual again at a retreat; he was married and worked as a counselor. We were happy to see one another; I
could not believe what good shape he was in, and I was shocked when he
thanked me of all people for hanging in there with him. I reminded him
that it was our teacher. Once, during *shosan* (public dharma exchange)
Aitken Rōshi was asked by a student how he would save (liberate) a qua-
dratic equation. He replied, "By including it." Animate or inanimate,
living or dead, wounded or whole, all are welcome, all are included.
Likewise, in this book, I want to bring together and explore the intrinsic
interpenetration of Zen and psychotherapy; spiritual and emotional
growth; attention, insight, and awakened action; and other elements—
without collapsing their differences, indeed by highlighting them, and
demonstrating why their interplay is important for both fields, especially for all who aspire to live more freely.

In and Out of Alignment

This is the stone
Drenched with rain
That marks the way.

—SANTOKA

In the early days of the Maui Zendo, after *sesshin* (Zen retreat) we would often pile into the Zendo van and drive to Baldwin Beach to swim, hang out, and eat junk food. Aitken Rōshi would usually accompany us. Once, after a swim, I sat next to him and asked him about something I had observed and was curious about: "Why is it that those who experience kensho often continue to treat others in the same thoughtless ways they did before their experience?" He replied, "They must not be really doing zazen." Over the years, I heard similar comments from my other respected teachers, Yamada Rōshi and Thich Nhat Hanh. I knew at the time from personal experience how easily attentional focus could drift during zazen to entertaining all manner of thoughts, feelings, and fantasies. I felt deep respect for my teacher, but even as a green student, his response raised questions for me. Was it simply a matter of practicing more diligently? Our senior Japanese teacher, Yamada Koun Rōshi, taught that Zen was "the perfection of character," but it didn't seem to be, at least for us mostly young Zen students. The *transfer of training*, a term I'd heard in an education class at CCNY, did not seem to be reliable. There was not an automatic alignment of dhyana, prajna, and sila. Although compassion did rise in the breasts of those who saw into their true nature, it did not seem to translate into mutually beneficial conduct or observable character change. Yamada Rōshi's schema for the Zen training process—meditation (absorption or *samadhi*), realization (kensho or enlightenment), and personalization (embodying the experience of awakening in the particulars of one's life while letting go of all trace of attachment)—seemed to get hung up as we made it our own and lived it.

The disconnects among dhyana, prajna, and sila—a lack of alignment among practice, understanding, and conduct—frequently present themselves in Buddhism, as they do in psychotherapy with patients and therapists alike. The centrality of understanding itself—formerly privileged as a transformative element in therapeutic change—has come into question in psychotherapy. I find these three dimensions and their interplay an elegant and useful lens in exploring the partnership of Zen and psychotherapy and the interplay of spiritual and emotional growth and integration. In Buddhism, ideally they intrinsically interpenetrate and co-arise. However, realizing their symbiosis in ourselves, and especially in our relationships, is challenging. There have been two additional sources for my ongoing interest in the interplay of Zen and psychotherapy. One is the ethical misconduct and boundary violations on the part of Zen teachers, other spiritual teachers, and religious leaders from other faiths. It has been a difficult and ongoing education to learn of teachers, respected for their insight, practice, and virtue, acting in ways detrimental and harmful to their students. Tumultuous, conflictual interpersonal and group dynamics, accompanied by organizational upheaval, have also provided grist for the mill and strengthened my conviction about the importance of contributions from Western psychotherapy.

Enlightenment, Practice, and the Unconscious

Yamada Rōshi was once asked how a renowned leader in the Rinzai sect could have committed suicide; he replied that the master must have not been fully enlightened. I do not agree. The difficulty is not solely in the practitioner: The path itself can stand some examination. At the end of his life, concerned about growing international conflict and longing for world peace (and perhaps aware of discord in his community regarding his eventual succession), Yamada Rōshi made what I find to be a remarkable turnaround and integration. Given his own dramatic and profound enlightenment experience, he had always emphatically taught the importance of developing and refining the enlightened eye, our insight into essential nature. Compassion and awakened activity, "the perfection of character," would ensue naturally. However, in his later years he wrote that just as important—perhaps even more important than enlightenment and its refinement—was the cultivation of simple spiritual qualities like kindness, compassion, mutual respect, and understanding.

Here is a story from *Taking the Path of Zen* :

Bird's Nest Rōshi was a teacher who lived in the T'ang period and did zazen in a tree. The governor of his province, Po Chu-i, heard about Bird's Nest Rōshi and went to see him. This Po Chu-i was no ordinary politician. He was one of China's greatest poets, well known for his expression of Zen Buddhism. Po Chu-i found Bird's Nest Rōshi sitting in a tree doing zazen. He called to him, saying, "Oh, Bird's Nest, you look very insecure to me up there." Bird's

Nest Rōshi looked down at Po Chu-i and replied, "Oh Governor, you look very insecure to me down there." All things are under the law of change and political position is the most ephemeral of all. Po Chu-i knew very well what Bird's Nest Rōshi was talking about. So he took a different tack. "Tell me," he said, "What is it that all Buddhas taught?" Bird's Nest Rōshi replied by quoting from the Dhammapada, "Always do good / Never do evil / keep your mind pure / thus all the Buddhas taught." So Po Chu-i said, "Always do good; never do evil; keep your mind pure—I knew that when I was three years old." "Yes," said Bird's Nest Rōshi, "A three-year-old may know it, but an eighty-year-old man cannot put it into practice."

In classical Zen meditation approaches, we become aware of somatic, emotional, and mental experience while meditating on the cushion and in daily life, and train our attention so that we return to our practice or to the task at hand, eschewing distraction and preoccupation while developing focus and stability of attention. In other Zen traditions, we focus closely on emotions as they arise in the body and on how we amplify some and reject others. Some Buddhist practitioners, aware of how motivation and intention create a chain reaction of effects, cultivate specific benevolent intentions in their practice. However beneficial these methods may be, we often fail to appreciate a simple fact: *If conscious introspection alone sufficed to transform the factors that engender individual and collective suffering, then we would have long ago achieved individual as well as universal peace, freedom, and justice.* Most of what produces anguish is outside conscious awareness. We become aware of how our activity, inner or outer, has slipped out of alignment with non-harming, or *ahimsa*, perhaps the most central Buddhist teaching, après coup, and then only if we are open to becoming aware of the resultant impacts. Although this is especially true in interpersonal relations and the relational field, it also contributes mightily to self-deception. We may check our motivation and practice awareness of body, mind, and heart, but we may be deluding ourselves regarding what is going on inside and in our relationships with others. We may do personal work to address trauma held deeply in the body, but even this, in my experience, does not always translate into awareness in action and awareness in relationship of the pervasive impacts of unconscious emotional communication. It is this capacity and appreciation for its ubiquitous moment-to-moment activity, as well as the use to which we put such awareness, that escape the purview of many Buddhist teachers and practitioners. I use the term *unconscious communication* rather than transference, countertransference, and projection because I do not think these convey the multi-directionality of unconscious emotional communication. I also think these terms have become saturated in spiritual circles and their meaning diluted and taken for granted.

Value of Unconscious Communication toward Psychological and Spiritual Development

An exchange with the Dalai Lama when I participated in a gathering of 250 Western and Asian Buddhist meditation teachers from various traditions around the world illustrates the value of unconscious emotional communication in the relational field to the development of Buddhist practice in contemporary culture and how this cross-fertilization can lead to a more integrated view of human psychological and spiritual development than is available just using one or the other practice and worldview. A conference coordinator, anxious it seemed over the Dalai Lama's imminent departure from the conference, posed a long question in what sounded like a plaintive manner, beseeching His Holiness for "suggestions, last words, and blessings" for the Western teachers gathered who were troubled by scandals and difficulties in their work with Western students. The Dalai Lama took it in, rocked from side to side breathing deeply, waited quite a while, and then responded: "When I'm uncertain or distressed, I look inside and check my motivation. Motivation is key. If I am motivated by afflictive emotions, I work on myself. If I am motivated by wholesome emotions, if that is clear after careful examination, I don't care what anybody thinks [about me]." This response could have come from a seasoned psychotherapist and was right on target in a number of ways. It also illustrates a key point—the limits of conscious introspection: Freud pointed out that motivations are multiple and mostly unconscious. When the Dalai Lama was asked about unconscious intention and motivation, he conveyed—speaking through two translators—one Tibetan and one a native English Tibetan

Buddhist teacher—that this was something difficult to translate accurately into Tibetan, but an analogue might be *alaya vijnana*, or seed consciousness, in Buddhism (the container for all experiential impressions, termed metaphorically *bija* or "seeds"). The Dalai Lama said that although he was interested, he did not know much about the concept of unconscious motivation or emotional communication in the relational field.

The "Gold" That Psychotherapy Brings

After nearly forty years immersed in Zen and psychotherapy, I believe that a key missing piece in Buddhist praxis is understanding and appreciation for *unconscious* emotional communication in the relational field. Since putting down roots in the West, Buddhist meditators have become quite aware of the wide range of human emotions, and *Theravada* and *Vajrayana* schools have honed methods for working with afflictive or destructive emotions. We have read about emotional intelligence and social intelligence and the neurobiological correlates of meditative states. We have become aware of the need to address interpersonal and group stresses and strains, harnessing "non-violent" communicational methods. In some contemporary Zen teachings, becoming aware of and working with emotions as they arise in the body, as well as the tendency to avert from and cling to certain emotional experiences, forms the very core of the practice. There are three treasures in Buddhism.[2] I think unconscious emotional communication in the relational field is the treasure, the "gold," that psychotherapy brings to the alchemy with Buddhism, to complement and enrich (and challenge) Buddhist practice and teaching.

Besides the gold of unconscious communication, there are two other important contributions psychotherapy can make to Zen and to an integrated narrative of freedom, which illuminate the personalization dimension of Zen training. (Remember that these training phases or dimensions of practice interpenetrate and continually dissolve in direct experience. I am using them as skillful means, or *upaya*, for purposes of discussion and expanding horizons and generating new understandings.) The second contribution is toward forging a differentiated person. What does it mean to be a fully functioning human being? I was listening recently to a presentation by a wise therapist and spiritual teacher. He spoke about the importance of the capacity to access regularly a state of unity where one is not separate. Although I think by "separate" he meant "alienated"—not belonging, apart from and isolated and disconnected from life—I couldn't help think of difference, otherness, and how liberating it can be to recognize and come to appreciate and embrace our differences. I thought, too, of the ongoing tasks of forging a person, a personal voice, of representing our idiom, and how critical that capacity is. This can be a fearsome task that involves mobilizing a certain aggression that spiritual practitioners tend to shy away from. My Zen teacher used to say that you needed a strong ego to practice Zen. I think he meant "strong ego capacities." We and other beings are the same and different and each presents the universal, *differently*.

The third contribution psychotherapy makes to an integrated narrative of liberation is the notion of psychic truth. The capacity for self-deception never ceases to amaze me. Awareness of psychic truth and how we turn, unconsciously as well as consciously, toward or away from it, can help us come to grips with a troubling fact: any human experience, no matter how uplifting, integrative, liberating, noble, or transcendent, can from one moment to the next be put (usually unconsciously) at the service of quite a variety of aims or "parts" of the personality, some of which serve emotional and spiritual growth and some of which do not. In Zen, many of us used to think that after one, maybe two or three *kensho*, we were home free—no more personal suffering or causing harm. In classical Buddhism many still adhere to the teachings of higher stages of development that are *permanently* resistant to afflictive experience and to the tendency to inflict it on others. I do not agree. We are all of us a moment away from self-delusion and from inflicting our "certain certainties," on others, not just while suffering but all the more so when feeling great. Beloved meditation teacher Sylvia Boorstein says that she is one word away from a meltdown. For her it involves picking up the ringing phone and hearing her daughter's voice on the other end: "Mom . . . ??"

The "Gold" That Zen Brings

What then is the "gold" that Zen brings to the alchemy with psychotherapy? In Buddhist circles, "unconscious" is often used to connote being unaware or not present and is not considered a skillful state. Consciousness, used here as attentiveness or conscious introspection, is privileged. In psychotherapy, however, an operative phrase might be, "let's get unconscious together." We value this dimension of our experience as a fertile source and ally and work toward helping our patients develop such acceptance. But, I believe that psychodynamic psychotherapists and psychoanalysts tend to privilege unconscious experience, internal and relational, and as a result miss what is closer to us than our own nose, what I take liberties in calling the "Bliss Body"[3] (according to a talk by Yasutani Haku'un Rōshi):

> Vividly clear, vividly clear, manifesting itself.
> The mountains, river, the great earth, the uncovered source
> There are the flowers, there is the moon—who is the Master!
> Spring, Autumn, Winter, and Summer compete with new garb.

There is a radical teaching in Zen: "Samsara is Nirvana, Nirvana is Samsara." Our ordinary world—doing the chores, laughing and weeping, eating and sleeping, living and dying; this world of 10,000 sorrows and 10,000 joys that flummoxes and exasperates and pains us; this daily grind we are seeking liberation *from*—is actually the world of Nirvana. We are already where we have been seeking to arrive. It does not require achieving a particular state of mind, believing in a set of esoteric teachings, or "transcending" these 10,000 sorrows. It involves awakening to what is intrinsically so, unobstructed by our dualistic and delusive thinking, in which actor, action, and the object acted on are experienced as separate entities; where the self, eternally dissatisfied, grasps out after an everreceding pot of gold at the end of the rainbow. When this activity sloughs off—usually through arduous and devoted practice—when, as Yamada Rōshi liked to say, we "forget our self in the action of uniting with something," the aim is not far at all. Aim, means, and agent fall away. What remains? Psychological disturbance can actually be seen in part as a retreat from this awareness. Blake wrote, "'We are put on earth a little space, that we may learn to bear the beams of love"—not sentimental love, but the plenitude of our existence. We say in Zen that here there is nothing missing and nothing left over, nothing to accomplish and nothing left undone. It cannot be seen with the eyes or heard with the ears or understood by the "mind," but its "marvelous functioning" never ceases: now happy, now sad, now young, now old, now reading, now talking, according with circumstances. Paradox seems at work here, but entertaining the concept *paradox* does not help us actually touch and make this Bliss Body our own and share it with those we meet for our mutual benefit. The term *bliss* may be misleading for it is not a matter of neverending happiness. But, most of us can imagine the relief of knowing beyond words that "we have arrived," that we are "arriving" in every moment, good, bad, or indifferent. The ordinary becomes extraordinary, and with ongoing practice, happily ordinary again. An old master, Fa-Yen, called it, "The fresh breeze that rises when the great burden is laid down."

This arrival is not in the register of arrivals and departures. It is not an individual experience, although an individual experiences it. It is a trans-subjective experience. As the subject returns home from chasing ghosts, phantoms, and mistaken identities, a universal, timeless, boundless dimension of life, usually hidden from our constricted view, becomes apparent.[4]

Subjectivity, Intersubjectivity, and Transubjectivity

Let us look at a Buddhist metaphor, the Jeweled Net of Indra, that illuminates another organizing construct for this book: subjectivity, intersubjectivity, and transubjectivity. Imagine a macramé sphere with a jewel at each knot. From the inside, each jewel reflects and contains every other jewel, yet shines with its own light. This may seem quite abstract but navigating between me and mine and the province of others—between personal benefit and collective good—is an issue for each of us individually, in our personal and family relationships as well as nationally and globally.

In Zen, each moment, each phenomenon, each being, not only presents the universe but also contains and interconnects with each and every other. In psychotherapy, an analogue might be how contingent we and our affective and relational experience are. In Buddhism, we call it *paticca samupaddha* or dependent co-arising. The interconnected whole needs each jewel to shine with its own light; each jewel contains and depends on all the others. Each is uniquely distinctive and simultaneously connected. Conflicts between individual and mutual benefit either do not arise here, or, if they do, they pass like clouds in the breeze. D. W. Winnicott's transitional experience might be an analogue, but it does not convey the simultaneous both-and element. Our current economic and ecological crises drive home the reality of interconnectedness, but realizing and living from an understanding of the simultaneity of individual and collective benefit is challenging.

Bodhisattva is a Sanskrit word that means "awakened being." It also means "awakening being"—a person who is in the process of waking up, and someone who helps others come to life. I used to believe the conventional wisdom that bodhisattvas forswore their own complete enlightenment until all beings were free. This postponement seemed frustrating, and now I see it is a mistaken belief. Someone who sees deeply, in this very moment, that his own happiness develops in concert with the happiness and liberation of others—and whose actions arise from the ground of this realization—such a person is an awakening being, a bodhisattva. As the other blossoms, I blossom and find joy. As I deepen, the other benefits. When we embrace the one who is different from us, he or she becomes family, part and parcel of the great community or net of beings. Time is short, and we are all in this together, more intimately connected than we ever imagined. This is the profound intersubjectivity of Buddhism.

With the concept of unconscious communication in the relational field, psychotherapy puts human flesh on the filaments of Indra's Jeweled Net, while Indra's Net provides psychotherapy a trans-subjective framework in which emotions and emotional relatedness find their place as a subset of a more fundamental and vaster mutual belonging. All of us desire to feel connected to our deepest nature, to one another, to our family, to our community, to grow beyond our small, self-preoccupied selves. We also desire to actualize our unique potentials, to represent our idiom, and contribute to the world.

The Chapters

As you read this book, remember that each chapter, like a jewel in Indra's Net, presents the whole but from a different perspective. Each develops an interconnected narrative while highlighting a specific element. In

Chapter 1, "Coming To Life," I describe and compare Zen and psychotherapy and explore the themes of awakening and aliveness. Using the
dimensions of coming forth and letting go, I examine the overlap and
differences between their practices, aims, and principles. Chapter 2,
"Fertile Mind," explores models of the mind and its activity in psychotherapy and Zen. I examine the blind spots and anxieties that plague
practitioners of both paths, the interplay of knowing and illusion, illumination and transcendence, and ordinary moment-to-moment
experience.

In Chapter 3, "Harvesting the Ordinary," I examine reverie, an
important subset of attention, or dhyana: its function, activity, and aims
in Zen, the psychotherapeutic process, and everyday life. Reverie—
mental, emotional, and somatic—is gleaned from just beneath the
threshold of consciousness and can serve as a pointer to subtle shifts in
developmental processes, as well as being transformational in its own
right. Chapter 4, "Presence of Mind," explores how models of the mind
affect the ways in which attention is deployed in psychotherapy and
Zen. I explore the meditative elements of each practice and, in particular, the experience of presence, as it is described in the concept of mentalization, the practice of mindfulness, and the teaching of no-mind.

In Chapter 5, "Singularity, Intersubjectivity, and the Immeasurable,"
I explore the basic ground of each path, using as a jumping-off point my
experience teaching Winnicott to candidates at a psychoanalytic institute. I challenge the view of the self as an isolate, which informs certain
psychological views on mysticism, and instead propose a relational view
of self and spirituality that reflects an implicit theory of suffering,
trauma, and its transformation. Chapter 6, "Knowing the Truth,"
explores the clinical, everyday, and existential iterations of truth in Zen
and psychotherapy. I examine truth as a motivational force with ethical
implications, in particular the turning toward or turning away from
truth, and the challenges of embodying the realization of true nature in
interpersonal and organizational life.

Chapter 7, "The Bliss Body and the Unconscious," pulls the threads
of the book together. I describe how the respective "treasures" of Zen
and psychotherapy partner in helping transform suffering and enhance
self-knowledge, aliveness, connection, and freedom. I begin with a brief
summary of theories of the unconscious, then move to a description of

the Bliss Body, which incorporates psychic fuels that are similar to but different from unconscious motivation. The final chapter, Chapter 8, "Forging Integrative Learning," uses as its starting point my experience in psychoanalytic training and a contemporaneous supervisor's training group. I explore the conditions for integrative learning and examine how the disavowal of the affective and the personal dimensions from psychotherapy and Zen training can eviscerate the learning process. I present integrative ideas differentiating the person and the personality, examining the work of Winnicott, Matte Blanco, Bion, as well as infant research and neuroscience. Finally, I use recent experiences of my own to place the personal in a wider context as I develop its centrality, and its limits, in an integrated narrative of liberation. As an afterword, I include "At the Heart of the Matter," based on a *teisho* (a non-discursive Zen presentation) I gave at a Zen sesshin about ten years ago.

Regarding quotations from Japanese, the reader is safe to assume that the translations I use come from Robert Aitken.

Anne Aitken, Robert Aitken Rōshi's wife and a loving wise teacher in her own right, used to make everyone she met feel like they were the only person in the world. Yamada Rōshi would encourage those gathered for teisho to listen as if his words were intended solely for them. I invite you to read in this spirit, open to awakening and to the liberation of all beings.

CHAPTER 1

Coming to Life

We shall not cease from exploration,
And the end of all our exploring
Will be to arrive where we started
And know the place for the first time.
　　　　　　　　—T. S. ELIOT, *Four Quartets*

Introduction

Religion and psychotherapy, with some exceptions, have been tradition-ally suspicious of one another, each tending to view the other as a pur-veyor of illusion. Psychotherapists' discomfort with religious or spiritual experience seems to have roots in a few key concerns: It can be an escape from unpleasant experience, a soothing balm that postpones coming to grips with reality, or worse, a self-deception. It kindles fears of a possible return to magic, to superstition. In turn, spiritual practitioners' discom-fort with psychotherapy is that it fosters self-centeredness. In this chap-ter, I contrast and compare Zen and psychotherapy and explore the themes of awakening and aliveness. Using the dimensions of coming forth and letting go, I examine the overlap and differences between their practices, aims, and principles.

Freud sees in religion a desperate turning to a powerful illusory authority as an antidote to human helplessness and a socially acceptable form of obsessive neurosis:

One might venture to regard obsessional neurosis as a pathological counterpart to the formation of religion, and to describe that neurosis as an individual religiosity and *religion as a universal neurosis* [italics added].

This view speaks to a narrowing of the range of experience and a diminution of personal awareness, discrimination, and agency. It reflects confinement within rigid rituals and prescriptions for what and how to think and be. So, it is both confinement and escape, not to mention the specter of sin that may be conjured up. The God one fears is just beneath the surface, a God who punishes for transgressions from the party line.

Religious objections to psychotherapy and psychoanalysis have been many and varied, but a central concern is that they build up or ignore the tendency toward self-centeredness rather than encourage its dissolution. This view sees psychological work as detrimental to the capacity to be in contact with and have concern for one's fellow humans and to know God.

Countering this polarization, Fromm and Symington describe a religious motivation characterized less by primitive psychological mechanisms than the search for fundamental self-knowledge, integrity, and core human values. Such a religious path views human beings as capable of responsibility, intention, and choice. Meditative practice can be part of such a path and, instead of imprisoning one in a rigid system of beliefs, can liberate rather than confine, reveal rather than obscure, and foster openness, resilience, the kind of loosening up that psychotherapists also look for. (Of course, meditation can also be put to other uses; it can have multiple functions.)

In fact, genuine meditative experience is quite subversive. It is subversive to the core of our beliefs about ourselves, our relations with others, and the very nature of reality and human existence. It challenges our most profound and unconscious assumptions about "the way it is" and "the way it's supposed to be"—the most cherished organizing concepts that give shape to who we take ourselves to be. Among these are our notions about the nature of mind, meaning, identity, and self. In so doing, meditative experience can facilitate a qualitatively different kind of exploration and deepen these dimensions of our lives.

In a spirit of respect for the distinctiveness of both psychotherapeutic and meditative traditions, I examine some of their similarities and differences with a view toward mutual enrichment. After all, both speak to the relief of suffering, emancipation from mental and emotional constraints, and the freeing of human potential to love and learn through self-knowledge. I suggest a way to think about their interaction and place it in the context of work by Mitchell, Ogden, Loewald, Erikson, Fromm, Symington, and Engler.

I suggest that two dimensions of human experience—which I call letting go and coming forth, or relinquishing and emerging—are common to both psychoanalysis and Zen, although each is privileged differently in the respective disciplines. These dimensions, which infuse our experience and development, are not simply sequentially related but are intrinsically synchronous. A vital human life—a coming to life—involves the capacity to both fall away and gather together, to be somebody and to be nothing at all, to know and to not know. It involves the ability to move between relinquishing and emerging, realizing moments when each activity is distinct, moments when they interpenetrate, and moments when (by virtue of being heuristic and fundamentally illusory organizing concepts) each falls away in direct, liberating, unmediated experience. I include a clinical vignette and discuss the notions of meaning, identity, self, and mind. I then explore the dynamic relation between psychotherapy and meditation and suggest a way to think about their interaction.

Zen

Zen Buddhism is not a religion in the traditional sense. The practice of Zen is not worship as it is commonly considered. There is no deity in the ordinary meaning of the word—no otherworldly, supranatural entity. Zen does not posit a soul, traditionally construed as an everlasting personal essence that changes form over time and space. Rather, through the practice of sitting meditation, or *zazen*, usually in the context of a mutually supportive community, or *sangha*, and usually through a relationship with a teacher, each person is capable, like the historical Buddha Shakyamuni, of coming to know (*gnosis*) for him- or herself the intersection of the sacred and the personal, the universal and the particular, through mindful awareness of one's own experience in the many moments of one's daily life.

Zen practice offers a path for addressing perennial human questions of identity, origin, meaning, and ethics: Who am I? Where do I come from? Where am I going? What is the meaning of my life? Why is there such suffering? What is it to live a good, wise life? The practice of Zen can productively help to engage what Mitchell called "the struggle of people at the end of the twentieth century for personal meaning and interpersonal connection." It offers an avenue for resolving what Loewald said is the "compulsive separation between self and other, inside and outside, on different levels of organization" (cited in Mitchell).

Complementary Paths

The intention of each path is, in a sense, quite different. Psychotherapy facilitates integration of the personality, a gathering together, particularly the integration of that which is unconscious—that which has been split off, dissociated, repressed, or otherwise excluded from awareness. Zen, on the other hand, offers the opportunity for fundamental ontological insight: What is the *essential* nature of the one who is born, lives and dies, loves and hates, laughs and weeps? Who is the subject? From this vantage point, humans exclude from awareness not only split-off affects, wishes, perceptions, memories, conflicts, parts of ourselves, and conflicting self-organizations, *we also keep unconscious our fundamental insubstantiality, interdependence, and, consequently, our own sacredness and that of our fellow beings—human and otherwise.*

The purposes of the two disciplines are not mutually exclusive or ultimately divergent. Rather, they are complementary and potentiating. In fact, psychoanalysis and Zen practice share various features. Each is a journey and a way of discovery—a process of inquiry, self-knowledge, and transformation. Each encourages the use, expansion, and ultimately the liberation of attention. Each recognizes the tendency toward self-deception and values truth, awareness, the depth dimension. Each acknowledges that things are not always what they seem, that indeed we ourselves and our fellows are not what we seem. What is not readily apparent does not lose value thereby; what does not make sense can be important and valuable. Ambiguity and uncertainty are not to be shied away from but can be a gateway. In each, knowing—understanding that is not discrepant from experience—leads to a kind of transformation. Each presumes that direct experiential understanding is not synonymous with being smart, that unlearning is important. So, each implies the activity of unknowing as well as deeper knowing. Curiosity activates, deepens, and energizes both processes, resulting in a richer understanding that leads to greater acceptance of oneself and one's experience, and to what might be called "a certain wisdom." This acceptance is contemporaneous with openness to others and the world, to activity for the good. Wisdom, compassion, and virtue go hand in hand. Each path leads to an expanded sense of meaning and aliveness and in so doing places value in this. Individual development and freedom (arising from expanded perspectives, from seeing oneself and one's activity as one actually experiences and constructs it) is not alien to deepening feelings of connection and responsibility. Each values a process of tolerating paradox, holding discrepant experiences, and letting things emerge, unravel, take shape, and give up their meanings.

Each situates its inquiry in, and values the cultivation of, the rich field of ordinary daily experience in its multifaceted dimensions. The lotus blooms in the mud; insight arises in the very field of pain, conflict, and confusion. It is from unhurried, gradually freed-up, skillful attention to *what is so* that understanding and growth emerge, not from chasing elsewhere, seeking to escape one's experiential and emotional field, or using willpower alone to forcefully make it other than it is. Another word for *buddha*, which means "awakened one" or "awakening," is *tathagata*, which means "thus come," the "one who thus appears," or "intimacy with that which arises." Nyogen Senzaki, an early Zen pioneer in America, left this message to his students:

Trust your own head. Do not put on any false heads above your own. Then, moment after moment, watch your steps closely. These are my last words to you.

Each setting involves stepping out of ordinary social norms of interaction. Fromm notes that people in our culture rarely speak truthfully and frankly to each other. Mitchell referred to "the protection and timelessness of the analytic situation" and how these conditions make "learning about and connecting with multiple self-configurations possible without having to account for oneself in the way one has to in ordinary life." Bion and others find the freedom to engage in reverie a central capacity of both patient and analyst in the unfolding of a deep, genuine psychoanalytic process, as it is in the mother–child relationship. At the outset of every Zen retreat or *sesshin*, participants are encouraged to leave behind social graces and habitual modes of interaction and let themselves settle deeply.

Each path, each discipline involves an intimate relationship over time with another person. The dyads of the analysand and the analyst on the one hand and the Zen student and Zen teacher on the other each struggle with and find some measure of experiential resolution to two key and apparently paradoxical dimensions of human existence—letting go and forgetting the self in direct engagement with one's experience, and bringing forth, maintaining, and affirming a sense of self, of personal agency, and of self-continuity. In one mode or dimension, self is multiple, relational, discontinuous, and ultimately nonexistent; in the other, self appears as singular, private, and continuous.

Letting Go and Coming Forth

Letting go and coming forth constitute a fundamental rhythm of life and may be useful metaphors for organizing our inquiry. As we shall see, they are neither entirely discrete nor simply sequentially related; rather, they are intrinsically synchronous.

I use the term *letting go* in a rather broad way, attempting to bring together various psychical activities. I relate it to the falling away of outmoded understandings and the opening to new experience and understandings. It originates as the encounter with difference, discrepancy, and dissatisfaction; with illness, death, loss, and mourning; and with aging and impermanence. Things don't go our way. Who among us, patient or analyst, has not been touched by suffering, *duhkha*, the first of the Four Noble Truths of Buddhism? Who has not been exposed to sickness, old age, and death, to helplessness and loss in some form? Sickness, old age, and death are three of the four "signs" (the fourth was seeing a monk, a seeker for the way) that led the historical Buddha Shakyamuni to search for resolution to the question of why there was such suffering. Ultimately, after many struggles, seated with firm resolve beneath the bodhi tree, he came to his understanding of suffering, his experience of liberation, and a long career of teaching others. The awareness of our mortality and of not living as fully as we might impels us. Each evening during Zen retreats, at the end of a long day of meditation and before retiring, the participants hear the following message:

> I beg to urge you everyone. Life and death is a grave matter. All things pass quickly away. Each of you must be completely alert, never neglectful, never indulgent.

Letting go is facilitated by what in Zen is metaphorically called "the sword that kills," an aspect of wise action that cuts away delusive understanding and protective conceptual structures that prevent us from encountering our circumstances directly. Life itself functions in exactly this way if we can learn from it. None of us has escaped unscathed over the course of our experience. This experiential current relates to unpacking, destruction, to unintegration, and finally to the encounter with that which cannot be measured—and then letting go of the idea of the immeasurable and simply being awake, in direct, moment-to-moment experience.

Bodhidharma, a Zen master who helped bring Zen from India to China, was asked upon his arrival by the emperor: "What is the first principle of Buddhism?" Bodhidharma replied: "Vast emptiness, nothing holy." The emperor was unsettled, to say the least. Dogen, the teacher primarily responsible for Zen taking root in Japan, sheds light on the path to self-knowledge in Zen:

> To study the Way is to study the self.
> To study the self is to forget the self.
> To forget the self is to be enlightened by
>   all things of the universe.

Compare this with the view of a contemporary psychoanalyst (Mitchell):

The basic mode within the object relations approach to the analytic process is the facilitation of a kind of unraveling. The protection and timelessness of the analytic situation, the permission to free associate, to disorganize, allows the sometimes smooth but thin casting around the self to dissolve and the individual strands that make up experience to separate themselves from each other and become defined and articulated.

One can see here both the parallels in approach and the differences in intention of the two paths. Traditionally, in Zen it has not been of particular importance that "the individual strands of our inner experience become defined and articulated." Rather, the approach has encouraged getting to the bottom of things, directly experiencing our essential nature. We do become aware of thoughts, feelings, images, and bodily sensations as they arise, although we do not necessarily examine in detail their patterning or personal meanings, conscious or unconscious, but instead focus our attention at a more fundamental level.

As with "letting go," I use the idea of "coming forth" to refer to a group of activities related to both emergence and gathering together. This is the aspect of cohering and coalescing, of creating personal agency, structure, stability, survival, and continuity. It is the realm of things appearing, of new schemata taking shape, and of symbol formation and self-formation. This coming forth and its significance in a life is captured in the *Gnostic Gospels*:

If you bring forth what is within you, what is within you will save you. If you do not bring forth what is within you, what you do not bring forth will destroy you.

This can be seen as what in Zen is metaphorically called "the sword that gives life," a bringing to life that makes us truly human. Desire, intentionality, meaning, even subjectivity itself—these relate to form, to coherence, to agency, to actualization, to the personal subject, and to time. In this mode, we are and are becoming something, somebody. We have a point of view, perceptions, desires. This relates to knowing. It may not always be clear or pleasant, it may involve ambiguity or conflict, but there is a sense of some self-structure, someone knowing that which is known. Mitchell writes:

> People often experience themselves at any given moment, as containing or being a self that is complete in the present; a sense of self often comes with a feeling of substantiality, presence, integrity, and fullness.

In letting go, letting be, there is nothing to become or attain and nothing left undone, nowhere to rush. This relates to the timeless, to not knowing and to unknowing, a negating of sorts. The field is open, spacious, and clear.

Emptiness

Shunyata, the shining void, often translated as "emptiness," sounds barren, but it is neither anomie nor vacuum, but rather the absence of self as absolute and continuous in time and space. Charged with potential, boundless and without measure, this emptiness is the fundamental ground of Zen. In psychotherapy, we can see its action in generative, non-defensive silence, sometimes called the fertile void—a deep, cooperative mutuality into which pieces can gather and out of which surprises, discoveries, new movement unfolds. Some think this is the goal of therapy; some think it underlies its method of free association. Perhaps both are true. If we are empty in this way, we are open to realizing our fundamental kinship not only with patients or our therapist but also with intimates, enemies, and the widening circle of life. We can allow and bear being constituted by, as well as co-constituting, all beings and phenomena. We may even appreciate and be enhanced by it. Joanna Macy, a Buddhist scholar and teacher, says:

> You are not a thing. You are not a substance or an essence separate from your experience of life. The juiciness of this, the wealth of the flowing river, is often left unsung, unappreciated. So the teachings can seem rather unappetizing. Selflessness can easily be misunderstood to mean that we are being erased. In truth, we don't erase the

self. We see through it. Throughout our lives, we have been trying so hard to fix that "I" we have each been lugging around. So when we drop the endless struggle to improve it or punish it, to make it noble, to mortify it, or to sacrifice it, the relief is tremendous.

Psychotherapists also appreciate this; Mitchell writes:

The rushing fluidity of human experience through time makes authenticity essentially and necessarily ambiguous. The fascination with and pursuit of that ambiguity lies at the heart of the analytic process.

In a spirit not unlike Mitchell described, meditative inquiry into this ambiguity, this field of not-knowing, underlies Zen practice in general and *koan* study, an insight practice of disciplined curiosity, in particular.

Koans

Koans are meditative, metaphorical themes usually drawn from spontaneous, everyday encounters between students and teachers, the folk stories of Zen. A *koan* is literally a "matter to be made clear." *Koan* practice allows one to discover the sacred in the particulars of one's daily experience. Here is an example from a collection titled *The Gateless Barrier*:

A monk asked Feng-hsueh, "Speech and silence are concerned with equality and differentiation. How can I transcend equality and differentiation?"
    Feng-hsueh said, "I always think of Chiang-nan in March; Partridges chirp among the many fragrant flowers."

Feng-hsueh was not trying to be "in the present" or avoiding remembering the past. He could not have been farther from that familiar conflict. Rather, he was coming forth unfettered and showing simply and personally just how speech and silence, equality and differentiation are actually transcended.

First steps in Zen practice involve cultivating the ability to attend, usually to the breath, and to settle into our experience. Eventually, inquiry deepens, and there is a qualitative shift as observer, observed, and observation are no longer separate entities. Yamada Koun Rōshi used to say that Zen is the practice of "forgetting the self in the process of uniting with something." Through wholehearted attention to each moment as it is, we come to rest in the question itself.

Another koan is "Who hears?" (Who is the master of hearing that sound?) *Kuan-Yin*, the archetypal embodiment of compassion in Buddhism, means "the one who perceives the sounds of the world," the sounds of suffering. Yet, there is also the laughter of children, and the crow of the rooster. The sensory apparatus in zazen is not in a state of deprivation, sounds are not shut out; to the contrary, we open ourselves and let them enter. But, the question is, "Who is the one who hears?" The Buddha's question was why there was suffering in the world. Our own deepest questions and those of our patients are not all that different. "Who am I?" "Why am I here?" "Why is life so hard?"—these are perennial human dilemmas.

Curiosity about origins is at work here. The question "Where did I come from?" refers, of course, to the intercourse of one's parents, the womb of the mother, the penis of the father, and the minds of both. However, in Zen, the koan, "Show me your original face before your parents were born," speaks to another dimension of human curiosity. Children's questions—"Where do I come from?" or "I know I came from mommy and daddy, but where did you, mommy and daddy, come from?"—although in part deflective, contain more than a kernel of real inquiry. Our response as parents, "From each of our mommies and daddies," leads us back to the mysteries of the beginnings of time and creation, which are animate in the present.

Practically speaking, the ability to split the ego and self-observe, although a crucial developmental achievement in psychotherapy and meditation, may be a necessary, but not sufficient, condition for emancipation. Whereas zazen includes non-judgmental observation of the arising and passing of thoughts, images, affects, and bodily sensations, inquiry begins in earnest when the subject—its object of attention and the attending itself (in Buddhism, the Three Wheels)—are no longer

sharply distinguished. In fact, when these distinctions are not operative at all—when the question itself is held in awareness, pregnant with
curiosity, and attempts to figure it out intellectually fade away—mental
turmoil gradually dies down. We are less under the sway of constrain-
ing conflictual perceptual structures. Concentrated but not narrowly
so, we become open and receptively absorbed.

Through continued, mindful practice, we may come to experience
the emptiness of all concepts, including the self. However, to be *stuck* in
emptiness is not the object of Zen. "Take another step," Zen master
Shih-shuang says:

> You who sit on the top of a hundred foot pole,
> although you have entered the way, it is not yet genuine.
> Take a step from the top of the pole
> and worlds of the Ten Directions are your total body.

Awakening

There are many stories of Zen students coming to awakening (*kensho*,
satori, realization, seeing into essential nature) through hearing a sound
or seeing an object as if for the first time. The ground has usually been
prepared by years of meditation and moment-to-moment attentiveness,
perhaps working with a koan. The mind is focused yet free from preoccupation, open, un-self-conscious in the usual ways. We gradually
become able to attend, to settle body and mind, to sustain focused
inquiry. We are surprised when we find that we are no longer thinking of
attaining anything at all; no longer trying to breathe, but rather simply
breathing; no longer speculating about an answer to a question, but
somehow having become the question itself. Do we breathe, or are we
breathed? We begin to allow ourselves to become absorbed in what we
do. We gradually stop "chasing out through the five senses" (as Meister
Eckhart says). The mind is settled, empty, alert, and receptive, having
come naturally to rest through self-awareness (not mind deadening). At
such a moment, anything can serve to awaken. Sometimes, it is the sound
of a bell, one's own sneeze, the act of standing up, or in the Buddha's case,
looking up at the morning star. All categorization—self–other, inside–
outside, subject–object, enlightened–deluded—gives way, and there is

an experience of coming alive that is not bound by such dualistic constructs. Bashō wrote a haiku that presents this:

> The old pond;
> A frog jumps in—
> The sound of the water.

This is not simply a matter of aesthetics; Bashō got *completely* wet. Nothing was missing, nothing left over. Sengai expresses this in his version:

> The old pond!
> Basho jumps in,
> The sound of the water!

Over the course of practice, this insight or enlightenment is clarified, refined, deepened, and personalized in our ordinary daily life, and then let go, so it does not become a stale artifact impeding further learning.

Yamada Rōshi would speak, for purposes of explanation, of each moment, each frame of experience as being like a fraction; the numerator is the particular phenomenon, and the denominator is empty infinity. Each lived moment—laughing or crying, throwing a ball, sharing an ice cream with my child—is like this. This is the radical understanding of Zen, immanent, but needing to be personally realized in real life, through practice. What obscures this realization are narrow, mistaken views of self, other, and mind based on an illusion of self as solid, substantial, and continuous in time and space. These mistaken views are rooted in subject–object duality.

Clinical Vignette

What follows is a highly selective, anecdotal account of a four-year, twice-a-week psychotherapy with Ellen, a thirty-five-year-old married woman, a graduate student in psychology, and a mother of three children. I focus on the unfolding of a specific, shared experience.

Ellen wanted more from her relationship with her husband, more enjoyment from being a mother, more from life. Over time, we explored various aspects of her dissatisfaction, multiple and occasionally conflictual meanings of her sense of not getting what she wanted. This dynamic emerged in the transference, and we examined it over many months, from different angles, in several configurations. After a turbulent period, Ellen began to wrestle in a qualitatively different way with her distress: its roots in her growing up and her relations with her parents, especially an anxious mother. It began to occur to Ellen that she herself had become an obstacle to "getting it," that somehow the urgency itself was part of the difficulty; the more she wanted, the further away it got. Her entire life, it seemed to her, had been shaped, even distorted, by this search. She began to have a sense of the hollowness, the falseness of it. This observation came with surprise and sadness and did not have a sense of self-blame. Periods of grieving followed; sometimes, it was clear as to what was being mourned, sometimes not.

About two years into the therapy, halfway into a session, she drifted into silence and began to talk slowly about how hard it was for her to just let herself be. There was a fleeting image of her mother, then a long silence. Her eyes filled with tears, but there was no struggling. Rather, there was a slow, meditative pace and quality to her reflections. I do not teach or speak about meditation to patients; this experience unfolded out of the work together. Silences lengthened and seemed to deepen. I felt a powerful shift in the affective climate. A cardinal was singing. It was bright and sunny that day, and light filtered into the office. After several minutes, she began to speak again in a very different way: "There is the tree," she said, gazing out the window at the avocados, "the bird is chirping, the light is shining through the leaves, it feels warm on my skin." This was not detachment as defense or escape; rather, she was unanxious, deeply settled, alive in the present moment. Each statement seemed to arise from silence itself and not to be an observation at all. As I experienced this sense of peace that was simultaneously alive, I had the image of a child feeling held so that she could completely let go, completely come to rest, "fall into" each moment, and, utterly unconcerned about moorings, simply be. But that was my image, a relational one, and while I felt affected and drawn into the experience, I also felt oddly in the presence of an absence, as if I were witnessing a transformation of sorts, albeit temporary, something bigger than the two of us. Each thing was just as it is. Just as it was, it filled the screen. What was absent was the sense of a separate experiencer, an observer separate from what she was observing. There was no trace of hollowness or pretense.

In the weeks that followed, as she reflected on what had happened, material about dependence and control emerged that could be worked through and integrated. Ellen looked back and felt that although it was but one experience among many, it had been a turning point. A knot had loosened from within, which she felt had to do with being alive—quite in contrast to being nice, compliant, and seductive or frustrated, demanding, unsatisfied, and hopeless. She could begin to let in—and to be more fully absorbed in—what she had been clamoring for but had realized she was afraid of and conflicted about. The experience occurred nearly thirty years ago, when I was several years post-licensure, and although I did not know quite what to make of it, I was intrigued because it was so moving, so helpful to Ellen, and because it seemed akin to the type of experience that in Zen often precedes realization.

Whether or not there was a relational frame to this experience, such as the "being alone in the presence of the other" I had imagined, I want instead to highlight a different aspect. The experience itself involved a relinquishment—a limiting self-organization dropped away, making possible what Buddhists might call a "glimmer of Suchness." In shedding her encrusted, familiar, but unsatisfying way of experiencing herself in the world, she came alive and curiously began, slowly, over time, to feel more herself. Mitchell quotes Graham Bass, who notes the great irony of the psychoanalytic experience; that in some respects, the patient is actually less known at the end of an analysis than at the beginning.

Mitchell writes that

one of the great benefits of the analytic process is that the more the analysand can tolerate experiencing multiple versions of himself, the stronger, more resilient, and durable he experiences himself to be.

I think this, in turn, facilitates a deepening exploration or "unraveling."

Meaning

Meaning—explicit, implied, conscious, unconscious, manifest, latent, conflicted, non-conflictual, constructed, discovered, intrapsychic, relational—is the bread and butter of analytic work. The vignette, however, described what seemed to be a nondual (although shared) experience. There was no meaning proper to it; rather, it was its own meaning. Inside and outside, subject and object, authentic and inauthentic, continuous and discontinuous: such polarities, such dialectical tensions themselves did not seem to be active. What could we say about the value of such an experience? Usually, value is a relative notion, defined in operational terms according to a particular frame of reference: What can I do with it? or, in Fromm's critique of contemporary life, What can I get from it or buy with it? Although valuation and utility were perhaps implicit, they were not experientially central to the experience. Yet, it was not an esoteric exchange, something otherworldly. It disrupted, catalyzed, and enriched her set of personal meanings and values.

Such experiences not only *represent*; they also present something fundamental. They not only symbolize; they also just *are*. Fromm writes:

If one follows the original aim of Freud, that of making the unconscious conscious, to its last consequences, one must free it from the limitations imposed on it by Freud's own instinctual orientation, and by the immediate task of curing symptoms. Then the aim becomes that of overcoming alienation, and the subject-object split in perceiving the world; then the uncovering of the unconscious means giving up the illusion of an indestructible separate ego which is to be enlarged and preserved as the Egyptian pharaohs hoped to preserve themselves as mummies for eternity. To be conscious of the unconscious means to be open, responding, to have nothing and to be.

There was not a separate experiencer standing outside the experience, commenting, narrating, as is usually the case, imbuing it with particular meaning. The experience was not the object, and we were not the subjects. This shared coming alive was in a way not bound or justified by traditional meaning criteria at all. Such experiences of touching down in a dimension of no-meaning-proper enrich one's sense of authenticity, aliveness, connection, and paradoxically, the sense of meaning in one's life. They illuminate what is truly of value and enrich and deepen our value system. Our ability to see, understand, and relate compassionately, not only to ourselves but to others as they are, is deepened. This reflects—in Zen as in analysis—a receptive emptying, a sloughing off of familiar me–you perceptual meaning-making grids. Mitchell writes:

> Self refers to the subjective organization of meanings one creates as one moves through time. An experience of self takes place necessarily in a moment of time; it fills one's psychic space, and other, alternative versions of self fade into the background.

One can call what Ellen and I shared an experience of self in time, facilitated by alternate versions of self having faded into the background. But the question, "What does this mean?" never crossed our minds. And while this was not a trance—either of us could have responded adequately to a mental status test if we had to—the coordinates of space and time that ordinarily anchor us were absent. Meaning-making per se or self-construction was not going on. Even calling it a variety of self-experience, as some self-psychologists do, introduces something whose very absence facilitates this kind of experience. *In time,* association, symbolization, remembering, integration began apace. But, they were not intrinsic to the experience itself.

Making meaning presupposes, literally arises out of, tolerable and generative moments of no-meaning. An analytic teacher of mine suggested that Ellen's experience might be understood as a kind of "going on being," such as Winnicott wrote about, which necessarily takes place over time. However, it was not shaped or constrained by time coordinates at all; there was precisely no yesterday, tomorrow, or today, for that matter. It was not the stuff of thinking, planning, or re-experiencing. And yet, it was not vacuous. While this experience took place over time, it was not time-bound; there was no past, present, or future to it. I am reminded again of Blake's verse:

> To see a World in a Grain of Sand
> And a Heaven in a Wildflower,
> Hold Infinity in the palm of your hand,
> And Eternity in an hour.

The loosening, even the temporary absence of such temporal and meaning-as-symbol criteria, in fact, facilitates such experiences. Fogel writes:

> Concepts, metaphors, symbols—all of these may function at varying degrees of distance from the realities they organize. The perfect, ideal symbol seems to, may express reality directly. Rather than standing for something true, it may function as a vehicle for the direct realization of truth.

Fogel is pointing not only to symbolic meaning, rich and important as it is, but also to a kind of presentational meaning, not unlike koan work in Zen.

Relinquishment, Emergence, and Identity

Although Zen practice has a long history of facilitating the realization of coming alive in falling away, it is not the exclusive domain of Zen but a perennial human experience. Over fifty years ago, when meditation was of less interest culturally, a college student, during a period of alien-

ation and turmoil when she was searching for resolution to deep self-
doubts and existential questions, was sitting in her room:

> There, alone in my room, sitting quietly on the edge of my bed and
> gazing at a small desk, not thinking of anything at all, in a moment
> too short to measure, the universe changed on its axis. The small,
> pale green desk at which I'd been so thoughtlessly gazing appeared
> now with a clarity, a depth of three-dimensionality, a freshness I
> had never imagined possible. At the same time, in a way that is
> utterly indescribable, my questions and doubts were gone as effort-
> lessly as chaff in the wind. I knew everything and all at once. Yet
> not in the sense that I had ever known anything before. A lumi-
> nous openness obliterated all fixed distinctions including "within"
> and "without." I found myself running along the street in joyous
> abandon. Sometimes when I was alone I simply danced as freely as
> I did as a child. The whole world seemed to have reversed itself, to
> have turned outside in. Activity flowed simply and effortlessly and
> to my amazement, seemingly without thought; nothing seemed to
> go out of bounds; there was no alternation between "self-control"
> and "letting go," but rather a rightness and spontaneity to all this
> flowing activity. This new kind of knowing was so pure and
> unadorned, so delicate, that nothing in the language of my past
> could express it. Neither sense nor feeling nor imagination con-
> tained it yet all were contained in it. In some indefinable way I
> knew with absolute certainty the changeless unity and harmony in
> change of the universe and the inseparability of all seeming oppo-
> sites. A paradoxical quality seemed to permeate all existence. Feel-
> ing myself centered as never before, at the same time I knew the
> whole universe to be centered at every point. All was meaningful,
> complete as it was, each bird, bud, midge, mole, atom, crystal, of
> total importance in itself. As in the notes of a great symphony,
> nothing was large or small, nothing of more or less importance to
> the whole.

Flora Courtois came to describe what happened as "open vision." She
was not using mind-altering substances, had no previous meditation

instruction, was not a member of a cult or active in any organized religion, and was not psychotic. While knowing more about this young
woman would place this account in the context of a particular human
life, and perhaps reveal multiple functions of such an experience, that is
a task for another time. Such information would not, however, detract
from what she described so vividly (and, because discursive thought
cannot capture it, inadequately).

Many years later, she had occasion to speak about what happened
that day to a respected senior Zen teacher. He acknowledged her experience and asked her to write about it. "You lost your way," he wrote in a
poem to her, "and now the way has extended in all directions." While it
is a direct, immediate, non-abstract, "knowing" that one can usually
present to the teacher, to talk *about* it misses the mark.

In a culture and a context quite different from Bashō's Japan, it
seemed that there was something about the work Ellen and I were doing
that resulted in a gradual but deep reappraisal of her self-representation.
It is significant, I think, that such experiences seem to occur over the
course of considerable and painful contact with areas of experience not
usually identified as "self." In Zen practice, as in psychotherapy and in
our later self-therapy, there are rude awakenings to our familiar, yet constricting, incomplete, and perhaps illusory, self-images. In Ellen's case,
slowly and with difficulty she became able to experience herself not only
as deprived, entitled, and seeking desperately, but also as obstructing.
This enabled her to become aware of the pain, the "consequences" (as
Grotstein puts it) of her constricting and protective self/other representational structure and strategy for dealing with anxiety and suffering.
Although her experience did not yield the kind of fundamental existential understanding as in Flora Courtois's case, it seemed nonetheless
that Ellen was drawing from the same wellspring and putting it to use
in the service of untying personal knots. Reification of one such experience is not my aim—after all it was part and parcel of a complex therapeutic process—but perhaps Ellen and I, unaware, had been tilling and
turning over the ground, enriching the soil, sharing and relinquishing
ourselves and our understandings, enabling a liberating, enlivening
experience such as this.

Mitchell writes of an incident from his own life that has some of the
qualities discussed:

When my daughter was about two or so, I remember my excitement at the prospect of taking walks with her, given her new ambulatory skills and her intense interest in being outdoors. However I soon found these walks agonizingly slow. My idea of a walk entailed brisk movement along a road or path. Her idea was quite different. The implications of this difference hit me one day when we encountered a fallen tree on the side of the road, about twenty yards from our house. The rest of the "walk" was spent exploring the fungal and insect life on, under, and around the tree. I remember my sudden realization that these walks would be no fun for me, merely a parental duty, if I held onto my idea of walks. As I was able to give that up and surrender to my daughter's rhythm and focus, a different type of experience opened up to me. I was able to find in that another way for me to be that took on great personal meaning for me.

Again, while not identical to realization in Zen practice, Mitchell's experience did *make real* for him something that had not been so before, due to his constricted viewpoint. The tree, the fungi, the insects, his daughter, their relationship, and Mitchell himself came to life in ways previously inaccessible to him. Were he a Zen student, his teacher would ask him to *present*, not explain, how this relates to his practice and his essential nature. I could imagine a very direct, vivid, and humorous presentation.

We might say that new experiential possibilities (or structures) emerged from an experience of dissonance and letting go (no-structure). They became integrated through unintegration, and Mitchell's identificatory repertoire was broadened through a disidentificatory experience, although "non-identificatory" might be a better word. Identity is an interesting notion. Something fell away, and out of that, something came forth, not quite in sequence, but with direct immediacy. We might say that what emerged identified Mitchell as much if not more than his identifying with it. His self was enriched by a non-self-experience.

Another analytic teacher of mine described a patient with whom, very slowly and with great difficulty, the analyst came to uncover, face, and give up the very thing that defined and anchored him most as an analyst: his hope and conviction that his patient could be helped and, further, would be helped by him. This internal shift, this radical relinquishment in the analyst, had a palpable impact on the emotional field between them. Paradoxically, only then did the impasse they were in untangle and new movement begin.

While the settings, aims, and methods are different in meditation and psychotherapy, the qualitative nature of these experiences overlap. I am not alone in having encountered such moments with patients. In psychotherapy or meditation practice (as in daily life), there are experiences that occur in the non-dual dimension. These involve a falling away and a coming to life, not only sequentially but also simultaneously, in a dimension where time is not bound and where even "falling away" and "coming forth" are absent. One might say that Ellen touched the farther reaches of her subjectivity, were it not for the fact that subject and object were not present as such. I think that at the outer edge of one's subjectivity, even that falls away. What remains? If I say "nothing," that is still positing something. The philosopher Masao Abe, responding to a question about emptiness, said: "Nothing is not something called nothing." Ellen's experience was not wish fulfillment or simple imagination. In fact, it is the very *absence* of wishing and related conflicts that enables such an experience to occur.

Imagine a solid block of cheese. Slowly, it becomes porous like Swiss cheese. Lying on the grass in the park gazing up at the clouds one perceives this. Our experience becomes less opaque, there is a "break in the clouds." During a retreat, a Zen practitioner had a dream in which she was playfully exploring a large house that had no exterior walls. She enjoyed the sun, the smells, and the sounds of the critters gleefully, as her own home, her own body. As the chatter in the mind quiets of its own, as constricting and conflictual identifications slowly come to light and loosen, as the hard-packed dirt is turned over and aerated, as T. S. Eliot's "certain certainties" are questioned, things can grow, differently. In the course of this loosening up, there are moments when the continuously hard-working narrator, the commentator, the control-central, conceptual meaning-making grid through which experiences are taken in, classified, and understood—through which we literally construct our self—falls away. This falling away can be distinguished from falling apart. These are ineffable moments, when we are not "making something," when what is immanent—closer to us than our own nose—can shine forth.

The epistemophilic instinct—the desire to know—is embodied in the wish to enter the mother's body and apprehend its contents and mysteries from the inside. This instinct may be broadened to include the thirst for direct human knowledge of our own birth and death, our existence itself and that of all beings. Getting to the heart of the matter, the body of knowledge, is fundamentally not a matter of inside or outside.

Relational and other analytic thinkers write of reviving collapsed symbolic capacity, expanding restricted narratives and experiential repertoires, and reconciling and balancing dialectical tensions. In the Zen view, however, it is the narrator, *himself or herself*, who must be understood to the bottom. We experience ourselves through our narrations of and reactions to direct experience. We create running commentaries on our lives and then take them as real, as "me." This happens automatically; we forget it occurred, and we then mistakenly take the commentary for the play. This comedy (or perhaps tragedy) of errors continues and gets quite complicated as we then react in varied and conflicted ways to our identificatory constructions, taking them in turn—our reactions—as "me." In so doing, we come to lead secondhand lives. This is truly a case of mistaken identity! And, what of our relationships with other beings, human and otherwise? We see others as in a dream, as if we were sleepwalking, through our socially conditioned and self-referencing perceptual filters. We do not see them at all, really, and so cannot relate with genuine compassion toward them.

Meaning, structure, integration, subjectivity, aliveness are enriched by direct experience in a domain of no-meaning, no-structure, unintegration, and the absence of sharply defined subject and object. A sense of self-identity was deepened as Ellen became less identified. She became more herself through an experience we might usually think of as not-much-like-self. Sartre wrote: "I am nearer to myself when I am far away." Wallace Stevens captures this quintessential human mystery in his poem, "Tea at the Palace of Hoon":

> I was the world in which I walked, and what I saw
> Or heard or felt came not but from myself;
> And there I found myself more truly and more strange.

In both psychoanalysis and Zen practice—and the paths have important differences—the personal self develops out of, is transformed by, and finds its most authentic and satisfying expression and structure through encountering and exploring generative emptiness. This coming to life is a spiritual experience and represents touching down into what has been known through the ages as the dimension of the sacred. It is facilitated, or to use Erikson's term, "activated" by—although not limited to—a transformative relationship between analysand and analyst or meditator and spiritual teacher, in which they encounter each other, share and relinquish themselves and their understandings, and are transformed by transforming the other. There is no creation, no encounter with the new, no "spontaneous gesture" (as D. W. Winnicott calls it) without a falling away, and usually not without significant anxiety and grief implicit in relinquishing versions of self-experience that are familiar.

There is a transformation, in a crucible as it were. In psychotherapy, the crucible is the therapeutic relationship in all its complexity—"real" and transferential, the process of free association, therapeutic listening, containing and metabolizing, and the intimate, unhurried sharing of two subjectivities. The framework in Zen study is the practice of zazen on the cushion, mindfulness of daily life experience, and the student's relationship with his sangha and teacher. One's daily life interactions and experiences also provide, in both endeavors, a field of intensified experience and interaction. The container provided by the analyst allows the analysand to deepen and extend his or her realm of experience. Zen teacher Charlotte Joko Beck calls this process as it unfolds, albeit with a different intention, the "ABC's of Zen, a Bigger Container." We suffer more, perhaps, in the sense of allowing and bearing more deeply felt and varied experience. As the container expands, it (along with the "sufferer") disappears and reconfigures—differently. Although we clearly do not become someone else, something new *is* created. Here are the words of Ogden on the experience of reading:

> This book will not be "understood" by you; you will not simply receive it, incorporate it, digest it, or the like. To the degree that you will have anything to do with it, you will transform it. (The word transform is too tepid a word to describe what you will do to it.) You will destroy it, and out of that destruction (in that destruction) will come a sound you will not fully recognize.

A vital, mature human life, with a psychological and spiritual dimension, involves the capacity to both fall away and to cohere, to let go and to come forth, to destroy and to create, to be something, somebody, and to be nothing at all. It involves the ability to move between the two, realizing moments where the two are identical, and moments when each appears as what it is, an organizing construct, and then falls away completely. I think genuine transcendence, truly being *alive*, is in their differentiation, harmonizing, and ultimately in their falling away in fresh, unmediated experience.

Theory

The interaction between psychoanalysis and meditation is not fundamentally a developmental, sequential, or what Ogden calls "a diachronic matter." He posited three modes of generating experience: the autistic-contiguous, the paranoid-schizoid, and the depressive. These dimensions are not experienced in absolute, pure form. Rather, in health, they are synchronically related, each fluidly creating (making possible), maintaining, and dialectically negating the other.

Mitchell also writes about analysis in a way that helps develop a framework for thinking about the interaction of psychotherapy and Zen:

Psychoanalysis at its best makes possible a more variegated experience of self. Past, present, fantasy, actuality interpenetrate each other. Not only are the intrapsychic and the interpersonal not incompatible, they are natural extensions of each other. In my view, the intrapsychic and the interpersonal are perpetually interpenetrating realms that continually fold back into one another.

Engler, in a seminal work, suggests that we need to have and be a self *before* we can forget the self. However, while spiritual experience *does* occur in the context of qualitatively different levels of self-object relations and ego development, I do not think that spiritual development is simply an end product of good-enough ego and self-object representational development. The notion of separate lines of development also does not capture it. Rather, these two dimensions—letting go and coming forth—which are common to both psychoanalytic and meditative experience and practice (although each privileged differently by the particular discipline), are fundamental capacities, potentialities, facets of our moment-to-moment lives; they are there from the beginning and create and give shape to our particular humanity. From the earliest moments, elements of each are present, and so it is throughout life. In developmental research, we are learning more about how infant and parent navigate optimally in a reciprocal fashion through conjunctures and disjunctures. Both are needed, and both parties to the interaction are capable of initiating either movement. Victoria Hamilton captured one important aspect of this interplay

> The experience of negation, or "the negative realization," and the formulation of the simple negative are linked to separation, differentiation, to the perception of contrast and differences, to the making of distinctions, to the command, "Don't," etc. However in my view these communications are tolerated in a context of togetherness, reciprocity, play, secure attachment and, above all, predictable presence or reunion.

Individuation and what is called "healthy psychic structure" develop through repeated good-enough navigation of such experiences. The process has its analogues in psychotherapy and in Zen practice as well. The teacher–student relationship, the sangha, the forms, structure, schedule—zazen itself—"hold" the student as the student attends deeply, as the falling away and emerging unfold.

Zen practice, like human development and psychotherapy, is a journey with sequential steps and watersheds; at the same time, each step is precious, ineffable, complete in itself, sacred. A Zen teaching conveys this: "You may practice Zen upwards, but each step is of equal substance." The (in)famous Zen stick, the *kotsu*, says another teacher picking it up, is golden through and through. "If I cut it here [at one end], golden. If I cut it here [in the middle], golden. Here [at the other end], golden." We can enter the sacred dimension at any "point," any "position," any "stage"—in any moment. As in analysis, the sudden and immediate coexists with the gradual, the painstaking, and at times, the imperceptible accretion of understanding.

The "mechanism" of this interaction, such as it is, functions quietly. When things are working, there is no permanent disjuncture, paradoxes are no longer intractable hindrances, there is a free and playful to and fro. "Authenticity for the analyst, as well as for the patient," Mitchell wrote, "is essentially ambiguous, more discernable in its absence than in its presence." It often strikes me that when we feel most alive we are least self-preoccupied. As with the notion of gravity, ego, object, self, even integration are simply explanatory concepts of aliveness—fingers pointing to the moon—that are more useful in helping describe and understand its absence—how it is compromised—than its presence. The simultaneity of letting go and coming alive becomes troublesomely paradoxical only when we attempt to catch its meaning in the net of either-or thinking.

It is when things are *not* working—when the gears are grinding, when experience is calcifying—that there has been a collapse of sorts into one of the modes. A meditator felt for some years that he had to extrude his sense of self as agent: "I sort of took myself out of the equation. There was no room for it in my Zen practice and with the group. We were to 'forget the self' and I took it literally. If I did this, then maybe there'd be the big payoff at the end." What a sense of betrayal and grief! In his case, self-denial did not translate into psychic collapse, although there have been such cases. Rather, collapse reflected an exclusive identification with experiences from the empty side of the spectrum, where affectively charged experiences of aggression, sadness, loss, competition, and conflict were excluded, resulting in an impoverishment of self-experience, fulfillment, enjoyment, and a sense of competence and meaning.

Psychotherapy has traditionally tended to privilege the side of structure, stability, adaptation, the development of personal agency, insight into the unconscious, and integration. Zen practice has tended to privilege the side of empty infinity, seeing into the nature of the self-structure and the identity of the experiencer himself or herself. "Forgetting the self" can be taken to mean a devaluation or extrusion of self as agent, but it does not necessarily imply that at all. Without good enough ego capacities, it is not easy to navigate our daily life. Permanent elimination of the ego is not the goal of Zen practice.

Integration

Looking comparatively at the paths of psychotherapy and Zen practice reveals these two dimensions—letting go and coming forth—as central to life. Navigating and experientially integrating them, inexorable and impossible as it is, is the play, the joy, and the travail of a lifetime for each of us.

Loewald, in a book review of the Freud–Jung letters, speaks down to earth of just such an integrative effort:

> Psychoanalysis, I believe, shares with modern existentialism the tenet that suprapersonal and transcendental aspects of human existence and of the unconscious and instinctual life (so much stressed by Jung) can be experienced and integrated convincingly—without escapist embellishments, otherworldly consolations and going off into the clouds—only in the concreteness of one's own personal life, including the ugliness, trivialities, and sham that go with it.

Loewald's words surprisingly echo the hard-won insights of many meditation practitioners and teachers and a growing ideal in the field: the importance of exploring the relation between spiritual insight and character development. Although Loewald took the Jungians to task for what he saw as their tendency to take refuge in escapist constructions, Jung and analytic psychology by no means have a monopoly on the tendency to jump from the ambiguity, complexity, unpredictability, conflict, and pain of our daily affective experience into other-worldly states. As Freud noted, this tendency is endemic to humankind and represents a significant motivation for religion and spiritual practice. It is a not uncommon and mostly unconscious fantasy that, through diligent efforts, one will be rewarded with an exemption from the vicissitudes of life, one will magically leap from the groans and travails and will "arrive," fully enlightened and purified. "Build it and they will come," becomes the meditator's *Field of Dreams*; do it, and *it* will come (and rescue you). Many meditators thus practice with one part of themselves and watch, expectantly awaiting, with another part. In this fantasy, it is assumed that a direct osmotic transfer of benefit from the spiritual to the characterological, practical-life experience level occurs. But, alas, this is not the case. Experience tells us that one can have insight into one's essential nature and still be a sociopath or an inveterate self-deceiving alcoholic, exploitative of others in cruel ways. Robert Jay Lifton's concept of the human capacity for "doubling," which arose out of his study of torturers in Nazi Germany and elsewhere, is troubling but instructive. One can be an apparently loving parent, a cultured human being and simultaneously a practicing sadist.

The two dimensions, therefore, do not, of necessity, overlap. Progress in one domain does not automatically yield equivalent progress in the other. Integration is necessary. A respected Zen teacher, commenting on the shocking suicide of a respected leader of the Rinzai school in Japan (one of the two primary approaches to Zen, now less polarized than they once were), explained it—and explained away, I am sure, his own despair and confusion as well—by saying that the person in question "must not have been fully enlightened." Another Zen teacher took a similar tack years ago when asked why those students who were progressing in their meditation practice, and were assuming leadership positions in the zendo, seemed outside of the zendo to behave in the same narrow, thoughtless, and arrogant ways they had at the outset of their practice. "They must not be truly doing *zazen* [Zen meditation]," he replied. The implication is that it could not be in the nature of the particular path itself; it must be the particular student's application of the method. While this might be true in some cases, this kind of response simply props up the system status quo and delays its inevitable self-examination. (In psychoanalysis, a parallel myth might be the "fully analyzed" person.) But, as Zen takes root in the West, the examination is in full swing, and there is keen interest currently in the relationship between meditation practice and the clarity of spiritual insight on the one hand and the thick mix of our complex and often conflicted subjective and relational experience on the other. The teachings are there in Zen, as this verse by Keizan Zenji conveys.

Though clear waters range to the vast blue autumn sky
How can they compare with the hazy moon on a spring night?
Most people want to have it pure white,

But sweep as you will, you cannot empty the mind.
   (frontispiece)

However, their implications are only now being fully explored as Zen practice encounters modern Western culture with its more developed psychological awareness.

There is a story in Bobrow that conveys the interplay of the affective, relational dimension with the sacred:

> The congregation is gathered in an orthodox synagogue for the High Holy Days, and they are fervently davening [praying], rocking side to side. The religious climate is thick, alive with the devotional spirit. The rabbi is facing the Torah, chanting, praising the Almighty, "Lord, I am not worthy! In my heart I know that I am nothing." The cantor listens to the rabbi's words and joins him at the ark. He declares, "Lord, even though I have led your children today in fervent prayer, in beautiful sacred melody, I know that I am really nothing." Then a simple Jew who has been praying devotedly all day stands up in the middle of the synagogue and cries out, "Lord, I just want you to know I am nothing!" The cantor leans over to the rabbi and whispers, "Look who thinks he's nothing!"

Transcendence can be used as self-inflation or escape. Some meditators mistake it for—or use it to avoid—transference. Others find unconscious affinity in ego-syntonic experiences of emptiness. For example, for someone with a personal history and unconscious self-representations significantly shaped by repeated loss, "transcendence to emptiness" can be a temporary way to protect oneself and keep from awareness residues of traumatic experience. Transcendence is not something one adds or patches on. It is not something one achieves, attains, or gains. Rather, it is a qualitatively different lived perspective on being human, arising out of an ongoing sloughing off. It involves a fundamental shift in one's relationship to the perceived obstacle, a new way of being with one's experience.

Dealing only with the content of the psyche has been compared to redecorating one's jail cell or rearranging the deck chairs on the *Titanic*. The *structure* of how we relate to and construct the problem, how the obstacle's very existence is sustained by a dualistic subject–object split—there is me, and there is my problem—is often ignored, assumed as part of the furniture of cultural and philosophical assumptions we inherited from Descartes and others. Psychotherapy and Zen share a commitment to making direct contact with one's experience and working with it. Whereas in contemporary psychoanalysis, in which our self-structures are explored and become more differentiated, pliable, integrated, and less unconscious, brittle, and split off, in Zen one inquires into the very nature of the structure in which the problem is embedded and through which it is maintained.

Erikson, in his study of Gandhi, demonstrates a subtle understanding of the spiritual dimension in a human life:

> Each of us exists with a unique consciousness and a responsibility of his own which makes him at the same time zero and everything, a center of absolute silence, and the vortex of apocalyptic participation. Gandhi's actualism, then, first of all consisted in his knowledge of, and ability to gain strength from, the fact that nothing is more powerful in this world than conscious nothingness if it is paired with the gift of giving and accepting actuality. [He was able] to give meaning to what others must deny at all times but cannot really forget for a moment. Freud, in one of his "economic" moods, might well have said that, psychologically speaking, such men save others not so much from their sins (this Freud would not have claimed to know) but from the fantastic effort *not* [emphasis mine] to see the most obvious of facts: that life is bounded by not-life.

Not only is life bounded by not-life, but also it is made up of not-life elements. The mind in Zen is not enclosed by or defined solely as "the brain." In the next chapter, "Fertile Mind," we explore models of the mind and its activity in psychotherapy and Zen.

CHAPTER 2

Fertile Mind

So . . . there was nothing left for me but to remember the wise saying that there are more things in heaven and earth than are dreamed of in our philosophy. Anyone who could succeed in eliminating his pre-existing convictions even more thoroughly could no doubt discover even more such things.

—FREUD

To study the Way is to study the self
To study the self is to forget the self
To forget the self is to be enlightened by all things of the universe.

—DOGEN

The nature, knowledge, use, and enjoyment of the mind are areas of growing importance in psychotherapy. In exploring models of mind and their influence in psychotherapy and Zen, I examine the blind spots and anxieties that plague practitioners of both paths, the interplay of knowing and illusion and of illumination-transcendence and ordinary moment-to-moment experience.

The epistemophilic impulse—the desire to know—is reflected in the infant's unconscious wish to enter the mother's body and apprehend its contents and treasures from within. The mother's body—nipple, breast, skin, arms, vagina, womb, organs, blood vessels, the blood itself—is one metaphor. The mother's mind, however, is another. We want to know our own mind *and* the other's mind, to keep the other "in mind," and to be kept in mind by him or her. A "meeting of minds," however transient, can have particular depth and poignancy. I suggest that the desire to know the mind of self and other may be broadened to include the desire for direct knowledge of the essential nature of our own life and death, our existence itself, and that of all beings. In Buddhism, this desire is called *bodhicitta*, or aspiration for awakening. In Zen, getting to the heart of the matter, realizing our mind—the body of knowledge—is fundamentally not a matter of inside or outside.

The notion of mind is evolving dramatically within psychotherapy. Freud's early formulations, based on the thermodynamic model of the times, that there were determinate and determinable causes and quantifiable relations between discrete elements that could be measured in quantifiable terms, have given way to several revisions. The impact of ego psychology, object relations, self-psychological theory, and infant developmental research has led to new models of the mind. More recent intersubjective models do not view the mind as residing solely in the brain or the psyche of the patient or, for that matter, the therapist. The therapist does not simply stand outside the situation, objectively observe the productions of the subject, and make uncontaminated clinical interventions that result in a change to the subject's mental condition. New developments in how the mind and the analytic situation are construed reflect a fundamental paradigm shift in fields as diverse as biology, cognition, physics, and cosmology. The Zen view of mind, ancient as it is, overlaps with and may help bring into focus some of these changes in the psychological view.

The word *sesshin*, a Zen meditation retreat, literally means "to touch the mind." How do we do this? This mind, like the self, is empty. It contains nothing absolute, proprietary, or permanent; it is essentially insubstantial. We might say, "I am walking, I am loving, I am eating, I am imagining." But, is there really a mind *separate from* the activities? Enclosed by the skin? Perhaps pulling the strings is a core motivational nexus driving the machine. Wise teachers are everywhere, would we but recognize them. In *The Gateless Barrier*, Robert Aitken Rōshi relates a surprising encounter in ancient China:

> Te-shan was a well-established scholar who lectured frequently on the Diamond Sutra, an important Mahayana Buddhist text, in

Western Szechuan province. He apparently felt threatened by the Zen teaching of realization that is not established on words and was wary of transmission outside tradition. So he traveled several hundred miles south to Hunan province with the avowed purpose of stamping out such heresy.

On the road to Li-chou with its many Zen monasteries, he stopped at a wayside refreshment stand. Here he met a great teacher of Zen who, like others of her sex, the Chinese recorders sadly fail to identify by name. Te-shan didn't pay any particular attention to her, but she discerned the potential of her new customer as he asked for tien-hsin. This Buddhist term means "refreshment," but the old woman played with its etymology: "punctuate the mind."

"Your reverence," this wise old woman politely asked, "what sort of literature do you have there in your cart?"

. . . "Notes and commentaries on the Diamond Sutra," he replied shortly. The old woman [said] . . . "I hear the Diamond Sutra says, 'Past mind cannot be grasped, present mind cannot be grasped, future mind cannot be grasped.' Which mind does Your Reverence intend to . . . refresh?"

Duh! For all his wisdom, Te-shan was confounded by the old woman. He recognized in a moment that he had been mistaken— not only in overlooking the virtue of the tea seller, but also in his "knowledge" of the sutra. He was ready to practice.

It is surprising and mysterious that although empty of permanent identity, this mind laughs, weeps, takes the children to school, goes to the bathroom, cooks dinner, makes love, gets lost, and finds its way.

The very insubstantiality of the mind implies and makes possible its complementary feature: interdependence. The image is the Jewel Net of Indra. Each of us is a point in a net in which there are mirrors at each knot of a vast web, and each point reflects and contains every other point of the web, not unlike the hologram. It is precisely because the self and the mind have no absolute substance that we literally make up each other, we are composed by one another. We are all intimately connected, multicentered selves. Thich Nhat Hanh, a Vietnamese Zen teacher, says we "inter-are" with all beings. This is in the same spirit as that of British psychoanalyst D. W. Winnicott: We cannot say "infant" without saying "mother;" we cannot say "mother–baby unit" without saying "father" (because father is part of mother's unconscious). We cannot say "paper" without saying "tree, leaves, rain, sun, earth, lumberjack, storekeeper." They are all inherent in the piece of paper. *This* is because *that* is. Buddhists call this *paticca samuppada*, mutual causality, or dependent co-arising.

To come alive is to realize this interpenetration. Neville Symington uses the felicitous phrase "fertile mutuality" and unpacks the ways in which—through our unconscious response to trauma, in our deepest emotional response to ourselves and others—we either self-centeredly repudiate this fertility and encapsulate ourselves or we embrace it, giving rise to what he calls "the lifegiver."

The Buddha sat in meditation under the bodhi tree until he saw into the nature of human suffering (and, of course, his own). Legend has it that at dawn one day, he looked up and glimpsed the morning star. Everything fell away, and he exclaimed, "I and all beings have at this moment attained the way." Enlightenment in Zen is simultaneously the enlightenment of bushes and grasses, tadpoles and quasars, ancestors and infants. In realizing our own essential nature, we realize the nature of all things.

Charles Spezzano quotes Adam Phillips, who refers to the psychological dimension of unconscious affective communication as a "hidden black market," the obscured exchange and mutual composition of our emotional lives. I think the Internet is *already* palpably and dynamically active, but we are unaware of its activity. In a lecture, Robert Stoller once related a story Ralph Greenson told him about how Greenson "knew" a relative had been in an accident although the two of them were thousands of miles apart. "The subject was quickly dropped," Stoller said. How do patients know when our silence is retributive or when our attention has wandered and we are no longer with them in the same receptive way? We know that they know, even if they do not let themselves perceive it. Each of us also knows, each of us communicates affectively in such a way, yet we do not know that we are doing it or how. It is *as if* there *were* an actual web: touch here and the message gets across there, instantaneously. Although we often cannot decode it, we experience its effects.

In *Emotion and Spirit*, Neville Symington writes of the "unseen emotional action" within and between people. Awareness and transformation in this field *are* the spiritual work of psychoanalysis for him. Although such unconscious activity may not be apparent, it is there, active, and we can and must become aware of it. It is not secret; in fact, it takes shape and operates in our daily interactions. What is meant, after all, by the oft-heard statement about parenting, "It's not what you say but who you are"? If we are unaware of its activity, as we commonly are, no matter how "enlightened," mature, helpful, and insightful we may be, we remain out of touch and fundamentally encapsulated. We may value our freedom of thought, but unless we become privy to this web, our freedom itself can function as a prison.

This intimately interdependent field, the fundamental ground of Hua-Yen Buddhism, is described in lyrical detail in the *Avatamsaka Sutra*, written about two thousand years ago. It bears an uncanny resemblance to the "intersubjective field" of contemporary psychoanalysis. Neither tradition, of course, holds a patent on it. Walt Whitman was familiar with this web: "I am large, I contain multitudes" he wrote in *Song of Myself.* So, in her own way, is a seriously troubled patient of a colleague, who said to her analyst: "If I don't have the experience of people in me, and me in them, my life and my death have no meaning. My life is counting on being in you and you in me."

Autonomy and separateness were terrifying and unintegrated for this woman. While we are insubstantial and interconnected creatures, there is still something mysteriously unique and distinctive about our actions, about each point in the net, the mark we leave in our wake, the way distinctive tendencies coalesce as our person. This absolute uniqueness, represented in infinitely rich variety (the *Nirmanakaya*) is, in Buddhist philosophy, one of the three "Bodies of the Buddha," or aspects of awakening, that are embodied in our moment-to-moment daily life experience. The other two are clarity-emptiness (the *Dharmakaya*) and interdependence-oneness (the *Sambhogakaya*). For purposes of discussion, these aspects are distinguished; in deepest experience, they do not oppose each other at all.

Blind Spots

It is a common misconception of meditative practitioners that spiritual practice and insight bring, ipso facto, an exemption from life's emotional vicissitudes and imperfections—ultimate salvation. How-ever, the fruits of either path—psychoanalytic or contemplative—can be hijacked at any point along the way, exploited for motives outside our awareness, and turned into something else. We must ask, "In the service of what?" Even insights themselves can obstruct our true emotional activity. Our understanding can become like a frozen, stale intellectual object. Zen practice, while emancipatory, can itself be used to obscure awareness of what is happening internally and interpersonally, just as therapist and patient too can collude, ignoring or unconsciously encour-aging an obfuscating or deadening process.

A seasoned Buddhist teacher with deep insight into essential nature and a well-developed psychological sensibility makes the point at a sem-inar that there is fundamentally "nothing to know." As he says so, how-ever, he conveys precisely the opposite: that he *does* know and the others do not. He is not aware that this is happening, but others are. A thera-pist has insight into corruption as being a key element in the dynamics of perversion, yet the therapist is totally unaware that her own activities set in motion conditions that undermine the integrity of a clinic where he or she is a key staff member. A parent complains that his or her child eats too many sweets; within minutes, completely unaware of any con-nection to what he or she just said, the parent fills up on candies. A group of seasoned psychotherapists meet for a week, with expert facili-tation, to iron out interpersonal tensions. The meeting ends with unan-imous agreement regarding its efficacy. Within days, things explode, and schisms are rampant.

Symington describes how this process develops in the analytic situa-tion. For him, understanding—spiritual or psychological—is not an abstract event, detached from the emotional field between two people. Rather, the analyst's experience in the analytic field and his interpretive activity become vehicles for bringing into consciousness such split-off psychic activity, much of which he sees as destructive, and for liberating integrity. Enlightenment and truth here begin with the awareness of this unconscious emotional activity. Insight, conscience, freedom, and compassion develop in concert.

None of us is exempt. Each new self-representational structure is both a discovery and possibly the next blind spot that obstructs further learn-ing. Language helps us to symbolize effectively and creatively as we live through a mode in which "things in themselves" can be concrete and frightening. Language too can also serve to avoid a deeper encounter with ourselves and our fellows, as we actually are, and with a sacred, yet surprisingly ordinary, "things in themselves."

Anxiety

Anxiety usually arises in the face of a turning on its head of basic assumptions of who I am, what I do, and what my relationship with other beings is. Batchelor describes how Ernest Hemingway spoke of sitting at his desk each morning to face "the horror of a blank sheet of paper":

> He found himself (as any writer can confirm) having to produce by the end of the day a series of words arranged in a way that has never before been imagined. You sit there, alone, hovering on the cusp between nothing and something. This is not a blank, stale nothing; it is an awesome nothing charged with unrealized potential. And the hovering is the kind that can fill you with dread. Rearrangement of the items on your desk assumes an irresistible attraction.

Not only in meditation and artistic creation does such anxiety arise, but also at the very outset of a psychotherapy and then intermittingly during it. Letting go and coming forth, discussed in Chapter 1, are each accompanied by anxiety. I recall telling Aitken Rōshi how frightened I was during an intense period of practice. He replied that there was nothing to be afraid of. "Easy for you to say," I replied since he had, in my view, "crossed over to the other shore," that is, experienced awakening. I had heard but did not directly know that Samsara and Nirvana were indistinguishable. And, the "nothing" he referenced was exactly what I was afraid of. Forging a person and developing a voice of one's own in psychotherapy, or personalizing essential nature in Zen practice, brings with it anxiety. A patient described feeling adrift in a deep blue sea that was simultaneously inviting and frightening. Various specific and personal meanings of this sea emerged over time, but the patient was also referring to her growing experience of enjoying and yet being terrified by the freedom to explore and not be constrained by who she thought she was, by her limiting conceptualizations of self, other, and world.

The dread of which Erikson and Batchelor speak is similar, but not reducible to, castration anxiety, separation anxiety, or even annihilation anxiety. It is the dread implicit in the struggle to be really alive, to awaken—the dread of dying to what is known, of letting go of reassuring but limiting identifications and assuming one's place, coming to rest, in the mystery of each moment. It is knowing, as Kierkegaard wrote, that the dreadful has already happened, that it has already fallen away, and we are quite porous indeed. That we cannot *possibly* get *there* from *here*, that *this* is *it*. We are not invulnerable; things are not predictable, there is no ultimate control, we do not and cannot know everything; there is no permanent abode, no absolute meaning, or fantasized resting place. It is as we uncover and relinquish these notions and the matrix in which they are embedded that we can experience freedom and joy. This process can inspire not only anxiety but also a powerful sense of betrayal and grief. Mourning is a passageway through which we can come to life.

Death, Knowing, and Illusion

For many, fear of death seems related not only to physical deterioration, the loss of capacities we have taken for granted, and their psychological impact, but also to the sheer unpredictability and the seeming randomness of life—the limits of our ability to know. Waiting for the results of medical tests can evoke this kind of feeling. Helplessness indeed: Magical thinking can return in the most "mature" among us; belief in a powerful, protective—or at least a knowing—deity can appear in the most hardened of atheists. Buddhism is known as the "Middle Way," originally a path distinct from both asceticism and blind sensual indulgence. Here, the Middle Way might be the cultivation of a way to be with oneself (and others) that mitigates the rush either to all-knowing authority worship on the one hand or mind-numbing hopelessness and its consequences on the other.

But, death is not simply the passing of this body; we know the body wears out. Death is there in each lived moment, a gateway. In notes that were to become an autobiography, D. W. Winnicott wrote: "Oh God!

May I be alive when I die." Perhaps accepting and even learning to rest in the not-knowing, in the mystery, is a springboard to wisdom and to the "peace which passeth understanding." I am reminded of how Bion responded to Grotstein, when the latter, in analysis with Bion, said, "I understand," in response to an interpretation. With a jaundiced eye toward understanding, Bion replied in annoyance: "Why didn't you say, 'overstand' or 'circumstand'?" Another time, in response to an interpretation, Grotstein said to Bion, "I follow you." Bion replied, "I was afraid of that."

It is not simply that spiritual experience (and particularly its cultivation or avoidance, as it were, in much organized religion) is intrinsically obsessive, as Freud thinks, although it may be put by an individual or group at the service of obsessional defenses. Rather, obsessiveness and other "defenses"—manic and otherwise—can arise in the wake of burgeoning awareness of the immediacy, the vividness, and the empty, spacious playground of existence. A colleague was describing the experience of absorbed delight in the presence of the work of Manet. She worried that there might be some omnipotence attached to it. Omnipotence, however, could not be further from the experience itself; omnipotence would be the attempt to reproduce at will such an experience, to bring it under one's control.

The nature of the mind and the self in psychoanalysis is explored in the debate about discontinuous versus continuous experience. Mitchell examines this issue cogently in an essay, "On the Illusion of the Experience of a Separate Self," a revised version of which is now called "Multiple Selves, Singular Self." The original title captured a useful tension in the contrasting meanings of *illusion*. Illusion, in the Winnicottian sense, is at the heart of play and freedom of mind. Yet, the word is also used to describe self-deception. One must have a discrete sense of self to function effectively and to live a fulfilling life, just as one must have, for example, a relatively differentiated body image and developed ego structure. To have a sense of self with threads of continuity to organizing storylines, a sense of historicity is critical. However, on examination—psychoanalytic or meditative—the structures of the mind, the constellations of me–you patterns through which we construct our experience of the world and ourselves, are far more fluid than we thought; in fact, one might say they are illusory.

San Francisco psychoanalyst Charles Fisher examines the experience of the troubled adolescent and young adult. He suggests that:

A sense of identity, defined as inner sameness and continuity, is like a snapshot of a system which is in constant motion. It captures features which are characteristic and familiar, but creates the illusion that we are organized in a more static way than we really are.

It is this very perception, and the experience that comes from it, that can be the springboard for change. And yet, says Mitchell, too much discontinuity may result in dread of fragmentation—"the discontinuities are too discontinuous"—while too much continuity leads to paralysis and stagnation. The fundamental purpose of Zen practice lies not in the balancing of this dialectic tension but in facilitating direct experience of a realm in which the distinctions themselves fall away and no longer constrain perception. During the course of Zen practice, as in daily life itself, one can get caught up in, even collapse into, either the world of emptiness or the world of form.

Illumination and the Ordinary

Self-knowledge or "touching the mind," is, in Zen, the *experience* that dualistic notions—such as continuity and discontinuity, self and other, form and emptiness—are not fundamentally separate: not two, not even "one." In the Heart Sutra, we come to the heart of the matter: Emptiness *is* form, form *is* emptiness.

The particular is itself the universal. The sacred—the fertile void itself—is reflected in the particular, in each being, as it comes forth anew in each moment. Deep realization of this in the moments of one's daily life brings a change of heart. Hakuin Zenji, in the *Song of Zazen*, writes, "All beings by nature are Buddha as ice by nature is water. Apart from water, there is no ice, apart from beings, no Buddha."

However, like unseen emotional action, this knowledge is obscured from ordinary consciousness. (Bandying the concepts without integration through practice can lead to self-justificatory mischief: "It's all one, we're all empty, I am Buddha," and so on, can be used to rationalize all manner of narcissistic, ignorant, and cruel behavior.) Our most cherished views of self and other, of our very existence, must give way, literally fall away. This relinquishment—for Symington the result of an "act of freedom," an unconscious choice at the deepest strata of our being in the context of a fertilizing analytic relationship, in Zen the natural fruit of sustained practice of nonjudgmental, nondualistic attentiveness and deep meditative inquiry—is the core action at the heart of transformational or transcendent experience, a much-used but perhaps somewhat trivialized notion these days.

The apparent paradox is that only by "forgetting the self" can we truly come to ourselves, can we come to *experience* the stuff of the self as the sacred. Self and object fall away. Yamada Rōshi, or old teacher, at the time a middle-aged businessman and Zen student, was returning from work in Tokyo one day. While reading a book on the train, he came upon the phrase: "Mind is none other than the mountains and rivers and the great wide earth, the sun, the moon and the stars" (Dogen). He had read the words many times before, but they had not come alive for him. Everything fell away, and there was only great laughter. What was so funny? Through an experience of empty infinity, we can know *directly* (in contrast to *knowing about*) the personal and the sacred as identical. While habitual and narrow views, including the dualism of deluded and enlightened beings, did fall away for Yamada Rōshi, it was less the kind of falling apart that we associate with fragmentation and dread than it was a *falling into fertility*. Meister Eckhart says, "The eye with which I see God is the very same eye with which he sees me." Soen Sa Nim, a Korean Zen teacher, used to say: "God is always calling but the phone is busy." I might add that she does not leave a name when she calls. You can try to pick up the message later, but it is like reheating cold coffee.

Our personal experience is not extinguished but rather is enriched in the realm of time and space, meaning, purpose, intention, choice, responsibility. We reinhabit the world of coming and going, shopping, getting to work, and feeding the baby. And, we are the same but not the same. "Singing and dancing are the voice of the *Tao*" (the awakened Way), writes Hakuin, and not only singing and dancing, but also weeping and feeling angry. Suffering does not disappear forever. It is rather that our relation to suffering is subverted. No cessation of suffering or unending Nirvana takes its place, as some think is implied in the Buddha's teaching in the Four Noble Truths on suffering and the ending of suffering. Rather, just as I see, just as I hear, just as I feel, that's it. The fog has cleared, the internal mediatory dialogue has sloughed off, and the vividness can shine through, born of neither subject nor object, yet right in the midst of, and *as*, the very "obstruction" itself. Obstructions do not permanently vanish; it is simply that when they arise, they no longer obstruct. Thought, imagery, affective and sensory experience, memory, personal history, and meaning do not disappear forever. As Hakuin writes, "This very place is the Lotus land, this very body, the Buddha." Rather than being buffeted around, we are "coming and going, never astray."

With understanding of the emptiness, oneness, and uniqueness of the mind comes a sense of freedom and, simultaneously, compassion for all beings. Things have been turned on their axes, and each moment, each being—including the one right here, with this particular birth date, birthplace; these particular parents; this particular gender, skin color, height, and weight—each just as it is, in its very ordinariness, its good, bad, and ugliness, is infinitely precious. The other is none other than myself and yet, simultaneously, is completely other: distinct, unique, sacred. All beings, animate and inanimate, are none other than the multicentered mind itself. We can see how this contrasts with the collapsed, concrete, "things in themselves" of Melanie Klein's paranoid–schizoid position.

Liberation on Two Tracks

Human experience cannot be captured by a theoretical formulation; by its nature it eludes final, definitive elaboration. Like a good response to a koan, a truly alive moment is beyond conceptual description. It must be embodied, lived. Discursive language cannot fundamentally convey it, although some language, like poetry, comes close. I fall prey to this most human of foibles, the attempt to capture in an image or a structure that inevitably slips through such a net. I do so because I think there is value in expanding our view of what it means to grow as a human being, to cultivate and deepen the best of the perennial qualities that make us human, bearing in mind that the map is *not* the territory, and walking the land is not the same as reading the blueprint.

Both paths, psychotherapy and Zen, involve the activities of letting go and coming forth, although the two disciplines have tended traditionally to privilege one aspect more than the other. For purposes of comparison, the two approaches may be thought of as containing different "proportions" of each activity. The image of a double helix captures something of their dynamic relationship. Each strand is discrete, yet each intersects the other and, in so doing, changes the other and is itself changed. Working in concert, the whole evolves in the direction of deeper aliveness, truth, integrated self-knowledge, and compassion for others.

Psychoanalysis affords the opportunity to develop experiential knowledge of self and other in (and out of) intimate relationship and deepened, integrated awareness of personal and interpersonal activity in the realm of the unconscious emotional field. The analytic relationship and the heart-mind (the Japanese *kokoro*) of the analyst provides the experiential container, the ground in which the analysand brings the self to life as a separate and interdependent person. Zen practice offers the opportunity to see into the essential identity of the self-structure, of the experiencer, himself.

The particular "wisdoms" of the psychoanalytic and meditative traditions can work hand in hand, enriching one another. For example, contrary to expectations of unending bliss, as meditators access deeper dimensions of unconflicted attentiveness—out of the unfolding spacious and nonjudgmental quality of attention—previously unintegrated, dissociated, or conflictual affective material may gradually emerge, occasionally as psychophysical experiences. McDonald, a seasoned meditation teacher with a personal history of serious trauma, vividly describes her own confounding, harrowing, yet finally illuminating path toward integrity that took her through both meditation practice and intensive personal psychotherapy.

Regular meditation practice can help certain analytic or psychotherapy patients contain and metabolize ambiguous, conflicted, or overwhelming experience and become more able to observe closely the interplay of mental, emotional, and somatic factors in the creation and maintenance of certain painful psychic realities. Meditation practitioners often find that psychotherapy or psychoanalysis can, in turn, free them up to continue to deepen their inquiry into existential matters, and to embody and enjoy the fruits of their practice and discoveries in their daily lives and activity.

During an initial session, a prospective analyst asked whether my meditative experience might make it difficult to benefit from analysis. This concern, while understandable, not only proved unfounded but also was in contrast to what other analysts and analytic therapists have discovered about how meditation can broaden and deepen their ability to practice their craft, listen, connect, touch and be touched, and understand their patients, themselves, and the process of change.

As I began to realize that these two paths of inquiry, understanding, and healing spoke to separate yet cross-fertilizing capacities and activities of the psyche, integration became an interest. My sense, however, is that we cannot really "get it together"; it is together. Articulating how this is so, and not altogether so, is the enjoyable and perhaps impossible challenge.

Early on, a dream helped. I was preparing to return to Hawaii (where I had studied Zen and founded a nursery school) after some years on the East Coast where I was finishing my graduate studies. I awoke one morning with a dream: "East, West, Center." My associations were first to the East-West Center, a facility at the University of Hawaii that my Zen teacher had helped direct earlier in his career. Then, there was a temporal association: I had first been in the Far West, then in the East, and now I was going to stop off in San Francisco for my orals. Next, there was a spatial one: East (Cambridge and New York), West (Hawaii), Center (San Francisco). Then, it occurred to me that I had just finished my studies in Western psychology and was returning to complete studies in Eastern meditative practice. These associations were interesting but incomplete. My attention drifted, and after a minute or so, it hit me: East, West (two streams), and center! But in this moment, the "center," such as it was, was no longer a theoretical integration of a dialectic but an experience curiously unidentified with, yet not strictly separate from, myself. Further, the "East" and the "West" (as separate entities) seemed to have long since gone!

Nearly twenty years after this dream, I realized something of which I had not been aware. During a class on dreams, it dawned on me all of a sudden, yet as if I had always known it, that the dream also represented my reworking of conception, birth, and differentiation from parents who had spent time separately on opposite coasts of the country. This may illustrate what I referred to previously as the multidirectional continuum of curiosity about origins, in both its personal-historical and more broadly existential aspects.

The clarifying and ongoing integration of the sacred with the personal, the ineffable with the affectively human, is a lifelong task, as is, in its own way, the integration of insight and new experience into the human character in an analysis and in our (often unaddressed but inevitable) post-therapy lives. "The challenge of course," writes Mitchell, "is to find a way to integrate the depths of self experience discovered in the 'unreal' analytic situation into the 'realities' of ordinary life." The parallel in Zen training is: How is insight into life and death, *gnosis*, the fruit of meditative practice on and off the cushion lived in the hurly-burly of everyday life? Life ensures there is no shortage of opportunities.

Although the key unconscious decision may involve, as Bion writes, whether or not to evade frustration, and although this inner work is painful, unpredictable, and never how we imagined, neither is it just grim. Suffering is not enough. Both paths can be joyful, as implied in Freud's notion of the "playground," Vamik Volkan's "pleasure of knowing," and Hakuin's "singing and dancing." When afflictions are no other than enlightenment, psychic suffering, although not eliminated, is like the ebb and flow of the tides, illusion and reality like the play of shadows on the ocean, and the waves themselves present the "incredible lightness of being," alive and awake.

The ability to experience ourselves in novel ways is at the heart of successful negotiation, not only of adolescence and young adulthood, as Fisher writes, but also of psychoanalysis and life itself, at every point along the developmental spectrum. In Zen, suffering is said to be caused by attachment, not attachment to each other or the attachment of a baby to its parents. Zen scholar and teacher Katsuki Sekida once said, "Non-attachment, all I hear is non-attachment! If you weren't attached you'd be dead!"

Rather, it is our unconscious predilection for protective—sometimes destructive and always narrow, limiting, and fundamentally illusory—views of self and other that lies at the source of our anguish. Becoming aware of how such views permeate our mind, our bodies, our affective and relational experience, our very lives—how they literally constitute and constrain our "identity"—is the beginning of Zen practice.

Jack Engler describes the apparent conflict inherent in the fact that what in psychoanalysis is a developmental achievement—differentiating a separate self (or, we might say, a mind)—is in Buddhism the very source of suffering. As Yasutani Rōshi, one of the first Zen teachers to come to teach in America, said: "The core delusion is that I am here and you are there." But this, despite being axiomatic in most contemplative traditions, is not quite accurate. I do not think it is the *separate* self (or the autonomous mind), illusory as it is, that is the problem. To the contrary, a differentiated self is crucial. Rather, what generates suffering is the habitual, automatic, and tenacious attachment to constricting versions of such a self and its relations to others that informs and shapes and drives our experience and behavior.

Engler concludes with the notion that "one must have a self before one loses it," a notion that has gained much popular currency. That is, from an expanded developmental perspective, both are achievements but having a self precedes letting go of the self. I suggest, however, that the two are neither mutually exclusive nor simply sequentially related. Rather, we must *both* have (create) *and* not have (lose, destroy, see into) a self. Further, we must struggle with, ultimately accept, and hopefully come to enjoy their differentiation, their interpenetration, their necessary although incomplete integration, and their falling away in each moment of fresh, lived experience.

Rather than having to construct a self *before* we can discover no-self, as Engler suggests, I think it *takes* a (distinctive, personal) self to fully *embody* our essential (no-self) nature. And as one unravels, experiences, and realizes the empty, multicentered nature of all beings and of consciousness itself, the (particular, personal) self and its unique qualities are potentiated, brought to life and fruition. This process seems closer to the experience of contemporary psychoanalysis, to the edge of current meditative practice, and to life itself.

In the next two chapters, I examine the respective modes of attention, or *dhyana*, in Zen and psychotherapy. I begin, in Chapter 3, "Harvesting the Ordinary," by exploring reverie, a subset of attentiveness, how it is conceived and managed in each path, and what it can tell us about liberation. In Chapter 4, "Presence of Mind," I explore how models of the mind affect the ways is which attention is used in psychotherapy and Zen.

CHAPTER 3

Harvesting the Ordinary

A painting is a series of marks joined together to form an object over which our eyes may freely roam.

—PIERRE BONNARD

When we are suffering, we sometimes look for help. In Zen and psychotherapy, it begins by stopping, looking, and listening—attending closely to what is happening, how we are living, and finding a new way to be with ourselves and our experience, in the presence of another, be it a psychotherapist or Zen teacher, a meditation, a supervision, or a study group. In this chapter, I examine how ordinary experience is often neglected and how it can be reclaimed and harvested—transformed and transformational. One aspect of ordinary experience is reverie—an important subset of attention, or *dhyana*, and one of the tools we use to do the work and play of psychotherapy. I look at reverie's function, activity, and aims in Zen, the psychotherapeutic process, and everyday life and explore overlapping and diverging elements of this attentional process as it operates in each practice. Reveries—mental, emotional, and somatic—gleaned from just beneath the threshold of consciousness, can serve as pointers to subtle shifts in developmental processes, while being transformational in their own right.

Reverie and Psychotherapy

In the psychotherapy setting, reverie is a meditation à deux. Reverie means "dream" (from the French *revere*). Another meaning comes from the Latin *radix*, meaning "root." In his poem "Sleep," the psychoanalyst D. W. Winnicott writes passionately:

> Let down your tap root
> to the center of your soul,
> suck up the sap
> from the infinite source
> of your unconscious
> and
> Be evergreen.

Is Winnicott too dramatic? Not according to Bion, who wrote with similar conviction about truth being as necessary for survival as food, being the nutriment most necessary for psychic growth. Winnicott was referring to his dream life, to a creative vision of the unconscious that animated his work and his life. The "root" in Winnicott's poem also describes a place or root source we are aiming for—the unconscious.

In Bion's view, the mother takes in the infant's overwhelming anxiety and, in her attuned and idiosyncratic way, works it over, transforms it unconsciously, and then responsively returns it to the infant in a usable form. For Ogden, reverie is part of the process of dreaming: "In the tradition of Bion, I use the term dreaming to refer to unconscious psychological work that one does with one's emotional experience." He continues: "When an individual's emotional experience is so disturbing that he is unable to dream it (i.e., to do unconscious psychological work with it), he requires the help of another person to dream his formerly undreamable experience." Ogden also describes reverie as occurring at the "frontiers of dreaming," between unconscious and preconscious experience: "The unconscious conversation that in sleep we experience as dreaming, in the analytic setting we experience as reverie. The analyst's reveries are his waking dreams." Not limited to the individual, and not adequately described as content, reveries also take shape in the therapeutic field. Ogden says:

Reverie is a process in which metaphors are created that give shape to the analyst's experience of the unconscious dimensions of the analytic relationship . . . Reverie is a principal form of representation of the unconscious (largely intersubjective) experience of analyst and analysand.

Grotstein calls this the activity of the "dreaming ensemble," and it is a developmental achievement. The capacity for reverie is a signal of evolving psychological freedom and health. Ferro says that when the therapeutic pair can work in concert, the field itself dreams and wants to express itself. It becomes a field of "transformation in dreaming."

Clinical Examples

Sandra is grappling with letting go of a relationship. "Cutting him loose," she says, recognizing his freedom as she takes possession of her own, "would be hard." She would grieve and be tempted to drink. There is quite a long silence. In the silence, I have a daydream about a TV commercial in which a teenage boy doing his homework is drawn to an image on TV: A woman is undressing. The boy looks to see if anyone is around and then hones in. The accompanying music has an erotic beat, singing that "the heat is rising." As the woman is about to take off her slip, the boy's mother appears, switches the channel, and says, "What are you doing?" "Uhh . . . nothing," he says, caught and flustered.

As I slowly realize that my attention has wandered, I see Sandra smiling a nervous smile. (I actually was not aware that I had been daydreaming and had not registered the sexual nature of the daydream.) I ask about her smile, and she says she "doesn't know." We discuss things rather gingerly, and after some time, I suggest that sexual feelings may have been present. She thinks she was "just feeling caring." If the feelings were sexual, they were "out the door," she says. This resonates anew, re-sounds, in a timed-release manner, and then I really access the daydream I had. This is similar to Freud's notion of nachtraglichkeit, the retroactive attribution of new meaning: I wake up to something I thought I already knew. I suggest that if sexual feelings were there, she might throw them out the door. She laughs and begins to talk about a new excitement she felt about leaving her current boyfriend, with whom she had not had sex and control and power conflicts seemed to dominate, and maybe finding a new love. She said that yesterday she was looking at old pictures of herself taken with a former boyfriend with whom she did have a sexual relationship. She was amazed to see that, once upon a time, she was able to feel that way. She looks at me and says, "I thought to myself, 'I've got to get me one . . . tomorrow'" (the day of our present session).

I wonder to myself: "Is she urgently warding off fragmenting or depressive feelings by eroticizing? Are real sexual feelings emerging in the transference? If so, how are they being used?" I don't know exactly yet, although I have hunches. I do not want to quickly interpret it as defensive erotization because Sandra seems dead sexually, and we had never really been able to talk about it. Emotion and thinking, containment and insight are contained within this movement of unfolding truth. It is not simply a matter of "coming from the gut."

Sandra becomes more able, during the ensuing hours, to talk about the shame and disgust associated with sexual feelings; her teenage years; her work, where she saw couples hugging, which stirred strong feelings in her, and the ways she coped with the resulting conflicts and intense desires, like craving and eating lots of chocolate. We are able to speak about what is coming to life in the emotional field between us. It is embarrassing and painful for her. Extra-transference material folds in. She describes coming home late from work and finding her dog depressed because Sandra has been so busy, irritable, tired, and drained that she did not play enough with her. I say, "You respond with the part of you that wants someone to play with you, listen to and pay attention to you, and give you a hug." Tears well up in Sandra's eyes, and her hard expression softens remarkably. It is a powerful moment. Desire and pain come alive in the room.

In the next hour, she relates a dream that leads to a memory of seeing her parents nude. As a matter of course, each paraded around naked, and Sandra would pretend she felt nothing, that it was normal. She would freeze over and numb out. In subsequent hours, she continues to rework teenage conflicts and examine relationships with women, and with her mother in particular, in more depth. Past and present are contained within this movement. She realizes profoundly and poignantly that there is "something missing" in her, which makes her feel exquisitely vulnerable and ashamed around others.

I cite this example to illustrate several points. First, silence can be generative—not simply depriving or frustrating—of reverie from both of us. Living through this experience, from which she urgently wanted relief, led to a useful unfolding for Sandra. By both of us letting what would resonate within the silence on multiple sensory channels—reverie—a way emerged to bring it into our dialogue, which in turn rippled out into and condensed aspects of her personality, including loving desires of all kinds and the conflicts and terrors associated with them. "Dwelling nowhere, let the mind come forth," is a Zen koan. When two can dwell in fertile silence, useful and usable truths emerge.

Second, a profoundly accepting, nonjudgmental, inclusive attitude toward all our internal experience, which includes reverie, is a hallmark of both the analyst's free-floating attention and the way to and expression of Buddhist mindfulness. What is overlooked as ordinary or discarded as obstructive, if borne and allowed to develop, can prove to be a fruitful way into difficult dimensions of the patient's internal experience and complex tangles in the unconscious relational field.

Third, the case example of Sandra illustrates what we actually do in our everyday work as psychotherapists. There is *already* a meditative element in contemporary psychoanalysis. While a meditatively attentive analyst (e.g., Ogden) need not practice Zen to make use of his or her reveries, an interest in and capacity for using this pathway to constructing or discovering usable analytic truths is helpful. Meditation practice may help us manage the powerful anxieties inherent in bearing and working with seemingly impossible states of mind, not overlook the most ordinary ones, and plumb them with care and creativity—all of which enhances our analytic attentiveness.

Reverie is an omnidirectional process that does not stop at the consulting room door. Katrina was a patient who would anesthetize her own and my mind in a fantasy that we were in a cocoon together. It was safe, but came with a price: It could become suffocating. Neither of us could think, and, for her, moving outward boded danger. At the end of an hour, our exchanges and her train of associations brought her to witches and *The Wizard of Oz*. The hour continued in my own reveries. Later that day, as I was swimming, a scene from *The Wizard of Oz* arose in my mind; I saw Dorothy throw water on the wicked witch, who screamed, "I'm drowning, I'm drowning!" It seemed to me that this was a fear my patient had about her intrusive mother, who could overwhelm her and could also desert her if she was not compliant or tried to differentiate herself. I also noted that this image came to me in the water, where one could drown if one did not know how to swim by oneself and did not risk doing so. As I mused on this later, I recalled what the witch, if memory serves, actually screamed. It was: "I'm melting, I'm melting!" This seemed different from being inundated by her mother (or mother-analyst) in the encapsulated cocoon or endangered if she tried to break free. Rather, it brought to mind letting herself melt into the experience of being together sexually, something that she had struggled with in her marriage and occasionally in feelings toward me.

In psychotherapy, reverie can help the therapist (and patient) orient to what is happening unconsciously in the relational field, independent of the content at play. The reveries were also a pointer to dynamic content themes taking shape in our work. Minds inter-are, and they extend in space and through time. These extratherapeutic elaborations of our joint reverie floated up during what is for me a rather meditative activity, swimming. They helped me speak more cogently in subsequent hours, and the work deepened as a result.

Sometimes, the fruit of reverie is not solely a pointer but transformational in its own right. In Chapter 1, "Coming to Life," I elaborated a reverie-like experience in psychotherapy with a patient I call Ellen. In the middle of a session, Ellen had drifted into silence and then slowly began describing how hard it was for her to just let herself be. Then:

There was a fleeting image of her mother, then a long silence. Her eyes filled with tears, but there was no struggling. Rather, there was a slow, meditative pace and quality to her reflections. Silences lengthened and seemed to deepen. I felt a powerful shift in the affective climate. A cardinal was singing. It was bright and sunny that day, and light filtered into the office. After several minutes, she began to speak again in a very different way: "There is the tree," she said, gazing out the window at the avocados, "the bird is chirping, the light is shining through the leaves, it feels warm on my skin."

In ensuing sessions, Ellen reflected on what happened and felt that this had been a turning point: A knot had loosened from within, which she felt had to do with being alive.

There is a word in Hebrew, *teshuvah*, that literally means "repentance" but more accurately refers to an inward *turning toward the truth* of the moment. As we muster up the energy and resolve, and choose, moment by moment, to attend to what is going on, as we turn toward the truth of what is actually happening, in and around us, our mind, feelings, and bodily sensations gradually settle. Symington calls this "choosing the lifegiver," an unconscious turning toward inner truth and away from narcissistic self-encapsulation. While this turning toward is a hopeful gesture, it also presupposes faith and both requires and develops the element Bion felt was so central in psychic growth: the capacity to tolerate rather than evade frustration. Freud was speaking of a similar process when he wrote about the analyst's evenly hovering attention. He advised us to surrender ourselves to our "own unconscious mental activity . . . so as to 'try to catch the drift of the patient's unconscious'" with our own. Elsewhere, he wrote of turning our unconscious like a receptor organ toward the unconscious of the patient. And, of course, the patient's attention is likewise turned toward the analyst's. This theme is developed further in Chapter 6, "Knowing the Truth."

Reverie and Zen

In Zen, as we practice mindful and nonjudgmental awareness of our body and breathing (described in Chapter 1, "Coming to Life"), we find that usually we can only do it imperfectly. Our attention wanders. We try to recognize when this has happened, take note of what is going on—planning, feeling angry, pain in the back followed by commentary, followed by more pain, and so on—and let our focus return to our practice, let ourselves again become receptively absorbed with the aim of penetrating the veils of delusive thinking and realizing our essential nature. In "just-sitting," or *shikantaza*, there is awareness without an object, difficult to wrap our discursive minds around and a challenging practice. Because we are human, turbulent mental, emotional, and somatic states do not evaporate once and for all, but they have less of a grip on us as we become aware of how reactive we are to our direct experience and how this amplifies our distress. In some contemporary Buddhist approaches, practitioners continue to take note of what arises and focus on what arises in the attention wandering in a welcoming way. Some Buddhist practitioners even use the meditative frame to see "what comes up" and attend retreats with a curiosity not unlike going into a psychotherapy session.

Although the relationship between Zen teacher and student is not exempt from transference/countertransference feelings, they are not cultivated as a primary focus for growth and learning. Rather, they form the background context that facilitates the meditative process. This context receives explicit attention by the Zen learning pair mostly when it becomes an impediment or a snag in the process. The unobjectionable positive transference is not questioned or usually examined together unless the level of idealization or devaluation interferes with the student and teacher working effectively together when both members can face this fact (which sadly is not always the case). The same holds for varieties of anxiety, and the defensive and protective measures mobilized to manage the anxiety, that are at play in the relational field. But, the quality and function of reverie in both disciplines are similar.

One way to put our taproot down in Zen is to work with a *koan*, a concentration practice of inquiry. *Koan* study, described more fully in Chapter 1, presumes a certain capacity for focused attention. Perhaps in this way koan study is unlike reverie, in which we give ourselves over to tuning in to the drift of the unconscious. A common misunderstanding is that koans are designed to frustrate the discursive mind. Koans are not frustrating mind twisters; they can be playful. When the old teacher Yanguan asks his attendant to bring him the rhinoceros fan, the attendant replies that it is broken. Yanguan says, "Then bring me the rhinoceros." Young children can do this, but very smart grown-ups might have some difficulty. Where is that rhinoceros? The question, held patiently, like a confusing set of emotional or bodily experiences, asks itself, works on itself. In a moment that takes no time at all, we may break free from the capsule and know things without intermediary, as if from the inside out. The rhinoceros frolics joyfully, and our ordinary mind is a vivid reality we live and can present in simple, even humorous, ways.

In Wallace Stevens's "Tea at the Palace of Hoon," he describes the flavor of this kind of waking up: "I was the world in which I walked/ and what I saw Or heard or felt came not but from myself/And there I found myself more truly and more strange." Here, there is intrinsic connection—the jewel is no longer hidden, no longer external, or for that matter internal. It is so. Each thing shines in its own distinctiveness—completely unique, yet, at once, void of reified permanence and containing each and every other being. The realm of play opens wide.

Affective experience and our capacity for creative transsubjective experience may work more in concert than we imagine. Although I do not interpret Zen students' dreams, I naturally listen as both a Zen teacher and a psychoanalyst. The following vignettes illustrate the relation of Zen experience and insight with psychodynamics that are illuminated through attunement to reverie.

> Our Zen group was on a wilderness meditation retreat. A student of mine saw clearly that things were beyond description and had no permanent substance. He was in touch with his surroundings and was not enclosed in his skin or his mind capsule. However, for some time in dokusan, he insisted on the ungraspability of things—that essential nature, if you will, was beyond words and could not be spoken. He could not yet bring forth a personalized expression of his koan, "Let Mt. Tamalpais take three steps." He was stuck on ungraspability. As we met under an oak tree, the phrase, "Don't speak unless you're spoken to," floated into my mind. At a moment when he seemed particularly insistent about the truth's unspeakability, I shared this with him. It had no small impact and brought to mind the atmosphere in his family of origin,

which we had only spoken of in passing. He was the son of two ministers who inspired him spiritually but whose teachings about politeness and selflessness had been reactively internalized. He was snagged and could not let himself have an experience of alive, differentiated unity with all things, and enjoy and embody it. Somehow, it represented being irreverent, unspiritual, and not selfless enough. Paradox of paradoxes! An internal attachment to the notion of selflessness and an internal conflict about selfishness were obstructing the flowering of what in a way he had already realized about the nature of life flowing through him and his relationship to it. Later, something fell away and broke free, his koan came clear, and there was a palpable sense of freedom and aliveness.

Do experiences such as my student's, Flora Courtois's, and even Ellen's change us once and forever? Do we stay "evergreen" as Winnicott wrote? From my experience and observations, we do not. Like bread, it needs to be baked each day, each moment. Such experiences—big and small— end, and we return to the world of coming and going, thinking, feeling, worrying, loving, and hating. Changed perhaps, but we return nonetheless. Psychotherapy does not end with deep, affectively charged internal and relational insight or with termination. Zen practice does not end with an experience of awakening or even with koan study. I have observed some cases where such experiences put nary a dent in someone's internal life and how they relate to other people. In rare cases, the experience can shake and shape a life, as it did with Flora Courtois. Experience can be put at the service of different aspects of the personality and made use of in different ways. What is liberating in one moment can become like stale bread in another or be hijacked and become the source of arrogance and conceit. Seeing this in action is no small awakening. It is the stuff not solely of getting *enlightened* but of *enlightening* the moments of life. Yasutani Rōshi told a practitioner, after she completed her study of over five hundred koans, that her practice had now begun.

The first line of D. W. Winnicott's poem, "Let down your tap root" is something that I have heard Aitken Rōshi say in the dojo during *sesshin*: "Let it down right where you are." This "letting down" implies an attentional activity: focused meditation on the cushion and moment-to-moment mindfulness practice in Zen—in psychotherapy, the patient's free associations, the therapist's evenly hovering attention, and their joint capacity for an engagement in reverie. For Winnicott, the taproot is let down into the depths of the unconscious. In Zen, an analogue might be that it is let down into our fundamental or essential nature. Not a static thing, it is like the great sea whose essence is water but which takes the form of many kinds of waves and contains all kinds of life. Are these two processes and root sources the same? They are similar but not identical.

Overlap and Divergence

The therapist and patient, and Zen student and teacher, till the fields of the ordinary. They root around, as it were, in the stuff of mental, emotional, and somatic life: thoughts, feelings, perceptions, sensory experience, musings, reveries, bodily experience, memories, preoccupations, and the like. It is in this simultaneously ordinary and complex soil of daily experience—including the surround—that both learning couples are grounded. Through persistent, welcoming—we might say "reverent"—attentiveness to our experience, we can settle deeply. In meditation practice, we often begin by focusing on our breathing, but after a time we enter into the experience and become the breathing itself. The varieties of reverie that emerge during meditation practice can be powerful experiences in their own right, not unlike dreams in psychotherapy, contributing as they can to the growing capacities, over the course of a therapy, to dream and make use of our dreaming.

Standing and Understanding

A Buddhist teacher who used to practice psychotherapy was talking with her husband, a psychoanalyst. He had just returned from the office and was telling her how much he enjoyed working and understanding things. She replied, "Me, too, but sometimes I like it when I can just *stand* things." Standing and understanding—each is part and parcel of psychoanalysis and Zen. Standing is an element of dhyana, understanding of *prajna*. The capacity to hold and be with our immediate experience develops during—and is paradoxically necessary for—both practices. Containment and insight develop in concert and build on one another. We begin where we are and develop the tools to do the work and play as we go. There is a lively interplay between "standing" and understanding. Can we bear what Meltzer and Harris calls the "full thought" or what John Kabat-Zinn, drawing from *Zorba the Greek*, calls "the full catastrophe"? Can we live our immediate experience fully and come through alive, even enlivened? Poet Galway Kinnell expresses the shift in our experience of the ordinary in his poem, "Flower Herding on Mount Monandock": "The song of the whippoorwill stops and the dimension of depth seizes everything"—a common event, a sound we might never notice. Poetry can come close to expressing an experience of the immeasurable. This aim in some Zen traditions is different from the aim of reverie in psychotherapy, although both can be liberating.

Both paths are concerned with the reclamation, cultivation, and harvesting of the ordinary, and through skillful-enough attentiveness, its transformation. The plants we tend, rooted in this stuff of ordinary living, include not only what we have repressed, split off, or not yet represented symbolically but also what we pass over, take for granted, and do not perceive, properly attend to, or even register. It might be through oversight, neglect, or ignorance that we miss it and so cannot make use of it. Although the unconscious is the central focus of psychoanalysis— as Anne Alvarez pointed out in her work on the link between unconscious fantasy and physical movement in space, and infant researchers have written about in terms of procedural memory—rich experience, even treasure, can lie right beside our awareness, not only under it. It is how we contact and encounter these neglected or passed-over contents and processes of daily experience, standing, and understanding, that determines whether they become useful, perhaps even transformative.

In both psychotherapy and Zen, reverie is a path to ordinary experience, and ordinary experience is a doorway to a deeper quality of direct knowledge of self and world and to greater freedom. Attending to what is outside awareness, in this sense, and researching through free association for access to unconscious sources are not mutually exclusive but mutually potentiating activities.

As the Buddha was dying, he told his followers, "Make of yourselves a lamp." To wake to what the Hasidic masters called the divine sparks in *all* things, we need to be in attendance at the moments of our life— open, without limiting preconceptions, particularly in the affectively powerful moments: painful, exciting, or even ecstatic ones. By attending without judgment to the flow of life rushing through us, by devoted attention to our immediate experience, not simply on the meditation cushion but as we go about our daily tasks, we create space in which to observe more and more freely. Finding ourselves holding our breath, we create breathing room, being room. Gradually, as this background space and focus develop, our capacity for steady observation grows and sharpens. In the midst of this, we may become immersed and forget ourselves in the act of doing something—a creative forgetting, which brings us to life in a new way.

Our internal experience is sometimes a knotted jumble. Slowly, it becomes more porous, like Swiss cheese. It is like lying on the grass in the park gazing up at the clouds. Things becomes less opaque, there is a break in the clouds. In Chapter 1, I write about a woman, meditating during a retreat, who dreamt that she was playfully exploring a large house that had no exterior walls. She enjoyed the sun, the smells, and the sounds of the critters gleefully, as her own home, her own body. We therapists might respond with alarm, thinking this represented the absence of containment or a fragmented self or body experience. But, the dreamer found it expansive and encouraging. Although it occurred in a Zen setting, it is similar to Ellen's experience in psychotherapy. The chatter in the mind gradually quiets on its own, creating clearance for things to grow, differently. In the course of this loosening up, there are moments when the hardworking internal commentator, the meaning-making grid through which experiences are taken in, classified, and understood—through which we literally construct our self—drops away. This falling away can be distinguished from falling apart. These are ineffable moments, when we are not "making something," where what is immanent—closer to us than our own nose—can begin to shine forth. It can be as simple as laughing, weeping, or diapering our baby. There is only that laugh; nothing is missing, nothing is left over.

Like Ellen, the dreamer was close to what in Zen is called an experience of realization. It was percolating in her. While too much can be made of enlightenment experiences, the process and the genuine experience—minus the hype and idealization—remain of interest. Along the way, there can be *makyo*, Japanese for "strange thought," a reverie actually, which is not uncommon after one has been doing intensive meditation for some time. Years ago, while on retreat, Aitken Rōshi saw himself deep in chanting with his compatriots in the sanctum of a medieval monastery. The experience echoed of the ancient; it just floated up. I saw myself on an unfathomably long beach, looking out at a vast sea. Once, while lying on the grass looking up at a shower tree, not thinking of anything in particular, I became absorbed. There was a gust of wind, and as a blossom came twirling down to the ground, its path was crystal clear, everything else was "dark." Boundaries blurred, and I thought for a moment that the blossom was twirling for me. This thought had a touch of omnipotence, but it was also a guidepost to the Zen process, an encouraging sign of increasing intimacy with my experience. In Ellen, the dreamer, Aitken Rōshi, and myself, these reveries were indicators of a deepening in the process, a harbinger of a greater freedom of mind, the growing capacity to be alive in the moments of life we live, to engage completely and find fulfillment there.

Without the capacity for liberated attention, which the capacity for reverie indicates, we are imprisoned by the inability to find true contentment. Our cage is a kind of self-encapsulation where brain equals mind; the internal world is a closed system; self-preoccupation is high; and the self is experienced as enclosed by the skin, locked in spirals of ruminating thought, spawning anxiety, doubt, grasping, and aversion. Here, we are isolated and cut off from our roots, out of touch with our unconscious life and our immediate sensory, bodily, and emotional experience.

Liberation and Attention

Freedom, then, is the liberty to be in touch with, bear with, and enjoy the ordinary—and, just maybe, grasp its extraordinary nature. Many centuries ago, a man entered the practice hall where the old master was giving a talk. He brashly challenged the teacher: "I can walk over coals with bare feet without a mark, and I can teleport myself anywhere in the cosmos at will. What is your miracle?" The teacher replied, "I don't know, I don't have such powers as you. My miracle is, when I'm hungry I eat, when I'm tired I go to sleep." We could add walking on the green earth, responding to our child's question, sipping a cup of tea, awakening with a dream and letting it sift through and reveal its meanings—

simple miracles, simple pleasures. In psychotherapy, Ellen also tasted from this well.

It is not simply in the privileged settings of the consulting room and the dojo where such emancipatory experience can occur. Can we experience liberation and peace in the relative world, even under great duress? Thich Nhat Hanh tells the story of a friend who was in prison and having an awful time during solitary confinement. Nhat Hanh wrote his friend a letter and said that right where his friend was, he could find a breath of fresh air, a sense of freedom, in the degree of awareness with which he did everyday activities. He suggested a simple tangerine meditation: slowing down and immersing himself in eating a tangerine, attentively, with full-hearted awareness. It made all the difference in the world to his friend.

As the preceding and following examples show, one does not have to practice Zen to experience life in this way. It is what Huxley calls a "perennial experience," available to all. College student Flora Courtois (see Chapter 1) inquired intensively and privately into what reality really was and had a naturally occurring experience of awakening. Her account of realization is similar to a kind of reverie the French philosopher Bachelard, in his book *The Poetics of Space*, calls "poetic or cosmic reverie." It is a dreaming of self and world into being. The word reverie also means "wild" and "delight." The wild and delightful aspects are clear. And for Courtois, it certainly up*rooted* her ordinary ways of seeing self, other, and world; shook her to her roots; and took her to her roots. This was not reverie in the sense of being lost in self-referential ruminations. It represented profound experiential understanding, born of long-"standing" inquiry. Like the analytic patient's reverie, in a way it had no use at all.

What roots does it take us to? Roots quite similar to those we make use of and discover in psychoanalysis. Henry James writes,

> Experience is never limited, and it is never complete; it is an immense sensibility, a kind of huge spider-web of the finest silken threads suspended in the chamber of consciousness.

Notice the echo of a parallel image, the Jeweled Net of Indra, where connectedness and distinctiveness co-arise. Each of us is a point in a net in which there are mirrors at each knot of a vast web, and each point reflects and contains every other point of the web. Reverie reflects this mutuality, helps create it, and takes us there. Spezzano quotes Adam Phillips, who referred to unconscious affective communication as a "hidden black market," the unseen exchange and mutual composition of our emotional lives. Our affective life shapes the web of interconnectedness and defines our humanity. Through affects, we organize our experience, derive meaning, know ourselves and others, and are known by them. Regulating our emotional life is a core human activity—on the couch, on the meditation cushion, and in our daily lives.

Courtois was freely looking, and her world turned upside down. I suggest that in this kind of emancipatory experience, affect—as defining of our humanity as it is—may be a contextual accompaniment to a deeper current rather than being at the source. Courtois's experience required an uprooting, a momentary dropping away of body, mind, and feeling constellations. Then, the simple immanence burst forth with full affective accompaniment. Being human, affect is the shaping context, but is it the essence, if there is one, of this kind of freeing shift? I'm not so sure.

Flora was gazing at a green desk. Recently, I was gazing at the cover of a book that had a famous *Life* magazine photo of a G.I., with a shell-shocked, glazed-over look on his face. Suddenly, I "remembered" that my father loved this photo, and that he had served in the infantry in World War II, lost two brothers, one during and one just after the war. "Broken," I imagined, and maybe looking to become whole and lose and heal himself at the same time, he became involved with my mother. I was the result of their passionate union. The impact of this moment of psychic intensity provided months of emotional learning. Flora and I were each exercising our freedom of attention, a reverie of sorts, each incorporating the universal and the personal (emotional) but in different proportions. Flora's was more on the universal and mine more on the personal, or emotional, register. Our experiences were both expressive of the activity of freedom as well as generative of experiences that were liberating, but in different ways. Our eyes, as Bonnard writes, were free to roam. In the silence, connections were made that helped free us, differently.

I think it is the palpable presence of the analyst and Zen teacher that is a key to standing and understanding and to developing the capacities to do so freely. Not the concept "presence," glibly spoken of these days in spiritual circles, or a vegetative and self-conscious attempt at meditating, but an actual receptive and responsive being alive in the company of an other—"live company," as Alvarez says. Speaking or silent, it is at work. It does not just contain; it evokes and helps things grow.

There is a refrain from an old pop song that goes, "How deep is your love?" We might retranslate this: How spacious is the heart-mind of the analyst or the Zen teacher? How spacious and *therefore* connected is the field between those in each learning couple? Reverie, reverence, and freedom of mind go together. When all the particular dynamic content themes have been seen into and played out (they never are, of course), when all the enlightenment experiences have been had, it is this activity itself—wide, embracing, reverent, ever-deepening awareness of what is so—that sustains and nourishes us. With Shakespeare, I say that "the readiness is all." We simultaneously need and must create a free mind for such a capacity to grow. The doing is the creating. This may be the most important capacity our patients and Zen students and we ourselves learn, in concert, and take into our daily lives. It may be our truest treasure.

In Chapter 4, "Presence of Mind," I extend this exploration of reverie, reverence, and freedom of mind into presence and how it unfolds in Zen, psychotherapy, and daily living.

CHAPTER 4

Presence of Mind

*I do not think that the mind really exists as an entity—possibly
a startling thing for a psychologist to say.*
— ERNEST JONES

Dwelling nowhere, bring forth that mind.
— THE DIAMOND SUTRA

How we formulate the mind and how it operates shape the way we work
as psychotherapists and the way we practice as meditators. Our conscious theoretical and technical predilections are the tip of the iceberg,
undergirded by a dynamic network of preconscious guiding assumptions, beliefs, personal theories, and implicit guiding values. In the
"Introduction," I wrote about a moment when I wondered what would
happen when our thoughts stopped shaping the world; there was a brief
glimmer of the universal dimension. Some time later I also took to heart
a Buddhist teaching from the Dhammapada on cause and effect, the
relative or karmic perspective. Here, the Buddha speaks not only about
the influence of our working theories but also more deeply writes, "We
are what we think, having become what we thought." Content and
form, structure and process, contained and container—the "what" and
the "how"—although useful for purposes of discussion, can obscure a
nondualistic dimension of who we are and how we impact one another.

We have examined how psychotherapy and Buddhism are distinct
and different disciplines; in one sense, therapy is concerned with

personal and emotional integration, while Buddhism involves a quest for direct knowledge of the fundamental meaning, the essential nature, of living and dying. In this chapter, I explore how models of mind affect the ways in which attention is deployed in psychotherapy and Zen. I discuss the meditative elements of each and, in particular, the experience of presence. I shape my discussion using the concepts of mentalization, the practice of mindfulness, and the teaching of no-mind. And, I describe how elements of psychotherapy and Buddhism are already in dialogue concerning these concepts and how, by extending, deepening, and refining this conversation, it is mutually enriching by facilitating cross-fertilization.

Mentalization or *reflective function* refers to the capacity to reflect on mental states and to understand and interpret human conduct in terms of the states of mind—thought, emotion, and bodily sensation—that underlie it. *Mindfulness* refers in part to Buddhist mindfulness meditation, a core practice in the Theravada school of Buddhism (sometimes called the Hinayana or "lesser vehicle" but here more accurately meaning the "teachings of the elders"). The classical Theravada approach emphasizes the importance of bare awareness of mental, emotional, and somatic states as the path to see into, unhitch, and decondition from desires and attachments, and liberate ourselves from the delusive self-structures and suffering they engender. This school originated in India with the historical Buddha Gautama, also called Shakyamuni, and reached prominence in Sri Lanka, Thailand, Vietnam, and Burma. *No-mind* refers in part to a teaching of the Mahayana school ("great vehicle"), which developed in India and tended to emphasize practices that facilitate direct experience of our essential nature beyond dualistic concepts, such as self and no-self and self and other, and the embodiment of this realization in daily living. Here, personal liberation arises in concert with, and for the benefit of, all beings. Mahayana Buddhism spread throughout China, Korea, Vietnam, Japan, and Tibet, reaching particular form in Zen. Over the past century and particularly in the last thirty years, teachings and practices from both the Theravada and Mahayana schools have taken root in the West, where they are comingling, creating a pluralism analogous to the current psychoanalytic scene.

Each of these terms—mentalization, mindfulness, and no-mind—presumes a process (attentional activity) and a bedrock structure (view or experience of mind). Each also involves or implies a dialogic dimension that, with regard to Buddhism, is surprisingly at odds with conventional wisdom.

Mentalization

The convergence between Buddhist meditation and psychoanalytic research can be expressed as follows: It is not primarily *what* we experience—painful or pleasurable as it may be—that determines our sense of well-being or security. Rather, the key factor is the extent to which we are able to attend to (reflect on) that experience and find or make it meaningful. As Fonagy points out, the capacity to reflect fruitfully—or mentalize—on experience is correlated with the quality of primary attachment relationships. The more secure the attachment, the more possible it is to reflect on, bear, and learn from even the most painful experience. This capacity is shaped in turn by the caregiver's ability to mentalize or reflect on states of mind. A key ingredient in this intergenerational process is the caregiver's ability to hold the baby *in mind* as someone *with a mind* of his or her own, someone with intentions, mental states (coalescing bundles of emotions, thoughts, and bodily sensations), beliefs, and desires. This capacity appears to be at the heart of the caregiver's ability to recognize, attune, and respond in a transformational way to the infant's mental, emotional, and somatic states. Schore details how neurobiological development, attachment, and human emotional and attentional capacities evolve in concert. Bion's notions of containment, reverie, and alpha function, which lead to the capacity to "think," Winnicott's "holding environment," and Sandler's "concept of safety" are analogous although not identical to Fonagy's reflective function.

When we think of presence, we tend to think of the "relationship" side of what the analyst provides, generally empathy, concern, and interest, in contrast to his interpretive activity. When we think of the phrase "presence of mind," we might imagine someone who is cool under pressure, not driven by blind impulse, able to tolerate complexity and uncertainty without jumping to conclusions, able to assess a situation, weigh the alternatives, and act in a thoughtful way—a good person to have around in a crisis. Or, perhaps, we think of a state of mind that is receptive yet durable, reflecting a certain equanimity and patience, a state from which one responds in accord with circumstances. Its functioning and exercise need not be limited to problem-solving and can have, in and of itself, salutary effects. It implies a container—presence—and a substance or contained—mind. However, it is less a thing than the absence of reactivity and suggests at once equanimity, strength, and responsiveness. Does presence derive its benefits, even its very meaning, from a certain absence? What about the homonym *presents*? Is presence something that bestows a growthful influence on those who come into contact with it? Is it a gift or implicit somehow in the process of giving? Although we may talk *about* something, say ultimate reality in Zen or a troubling affect in psychotherapy, each process places value on the muffin fresh out of the oven, embodied, "presented" in living form, not simply talked about abstractly. Suzanne Langer, an inspiration for Independent analysts in England and contemporary Zen masters alike, writes about such a presentational dimension of symbolization, as does Fogel in his book on Loewald.

The capacity for attentiveness that is at once enduring and relatively serene—while also pliable and able to recognize and respond flexibly in accord with changing (even traumatic) internal and external circumstances—is a quality that cuts across child development, the attentional activity of patient and analyst, and not surprisingly, meditator and spiritual teacher. It is an aim of psychotherapy as well as the means to the aim. Presence of mind reflects not only a way of being and communicating with others but also a way of regarding the processes and contents of one's mind. It is not just instrumental but *in and of itself* has healing, enlivening, or in Buddhist parlance, awakening properties. It conveys love and insight, compassion and wisdom. It represents not only the content of consciousness but also the quality of consciousness at play. Perhaps, it cannot be "given," after all, because that would make the receiver quite self-conscious, but it can be lived together and retrospectively feels like a gift.

Let us look at some implications of this convergence between Zen and psychotherapy concerning presence of mind. Dissatisfaction, pain, loss, and trauma are inherent in living. However, whether these result in anguish, torment, or disability, or are integrated into a life of growth and creativity depends on particular attentional capacities and their deployment.

We are what we make of the cards we are dealt, but what we make is contingent upon a particular aspect of what we are dealt, namely, provision of conditions for developing the ability to attend. To grow this capacity, to develop a mind of our own, we paradoxically need access to the mind of an "other." In Fonagy's view, the infant finds itself in the mind of the other, as Winnicott sees the infant finding itself in the eyes and expression of the other. A self (or we might say a mind) is "born of illusion because mother and father believe that a self is there and call it into being by their own responsiveness," as Sanville says. The ingredients necessary for the growth of mind privileged by these thinkers are provided in a safe, protective, and responsive environment in which the play of illusion and metaphor can develop. Another, privileged more in Bion's and Freud's accounts, is the capacity to tolerate frustration and endure emotional pain. "Standing" (affect regulation) and understanding painful mental states and the self that experiences and suffers them (liberating insight) develop hand in hand.

A few years ago, Thich Nhat Hanh spoke at a large public gathering. Ninety percent of the forty questioners asked about managing emotions they found troublesome and seemed more concerned about becoming better able to stand than deeply understand their emotional experience. One might have imagined that people with such concerns would more likely find their way into the consulting room than the meditation hall. Likewise, the universal and existential question "Who am I?" and the desire for deeper insight that brought people to Zen practice is ironically being addressed almost just as often these days in the consulting room.

Mindfulness

The equivalent among Western Buddhist meditators of the psychotherapeutic idea of "thinking about" disturbing mental-emotional-somatic states is learning to "sit with" them, with "sitting" also a synonym for "meditating." Whether one is motivated by *bodhicitta*—the aspiration for enlightenment or liberation—most contemporary Buddhist practitioners spend significant periods of time sitting with painful, confusing, conflictual, or not-as-yet-represented affective experience.

In classical mindfulness meditation, we cultivate bare attention to the moment-to-moment flux of our thoughts, feelings, and bodily sensations, how these interact to produce all variety of states, and how we pursue some states and are aversive to others. We take note of our reactions to the texture and rhythms of bare experience—as it is or as it arises and passes—how it bundles together into repetitive versions of "I," versions that usually include representations of other as well. Practitioners cultivate welcoming, nonjudgmental awareness of how they constellate and maintain repetitive, affectively charged narratives featuring "me" and "mine" front and center, in mixtures of positive and negative versions, and how they selectively crave and "attach to"—indeed construct—these narratives, generating dissatisfaction and suffering. The "I" that is constellated is gradually seen into and through and is shed as a more fluid, less-ensnared way of being in the world grows.

If reflective function implies the capacity to understand human behavior in terms of states of mind, then mindfulness practice is quite in accord. This practice, and the growing freedom to observe that is implicit in it, is also in ways congenial with Bion's idea of the analyst's being without memory, desire, and understanding; the poet John Keats's concept of "negative capability"; Ogden's development of Bion's notion of reverie; and Freud's concepts of evenly hovering attention and free association. In her seminal 1960 work, British psychoanalyst Marion Milner described what she called the "concentration of the body," a way of attending deeply to her bodily sensations while also listening to the content of the patient's narrative, which was more helpful in generating capacities for symbolization than clever interpretations. From a neuropsychoanalytic perspective, Schore wrote that "the therapist's ability to . . . self-regulate . . . the stressful alterations in his/her bodily state evoked by the patient's transferential communication" is key. Citing Freedman and Lavendar, Schore describes the analyst's "'reparative withdrawal,' a self-regulating maneuver that allows continued access to a state in which a symbolizing process can take place." He adds that it is the therapist's awareness of his/her "bodily signals and his/her capacity to auto-regulate the disruption in state . . . that literally determines whether the countertransference is destructive or constructive, 'symbolizing' or 'desymbolizing.'" In the most troubling moments, willful attempts to change our state of mind by wriggling free from "what is" only seem to make things worse and even tighten the vise.

The capacity to explore and engage with experience is sometimes taken for granted by meditation teachers and not seen as a developmental achievement. "Just notice what's happening" is easier said than done, especially when what emerges on the cushion is painful. The dialogic element can also be overlooked. There is inevitably a certain faith or trust in the teacher, practice, tradition or lineage, the group we practice with, the location—all these create a kind of holding environment or container for the growth of this capacity and its exercise. We do not "sit with it" in a vacuum. The ability grows in the doing and helps us self-regulate as we explore more deeply. It is simultaneously instrumental—a way to reach an aim, liberation from suffering, and an aid in resolving disturbance—beneficial in and of itself irrespective of aim or content, and presentational, which is expressive of core meaning and intrinsic value.

It is not only the technique of attention that is at play but also how and to what ends it is used. "Noting" feelings in mindfulness meditation can be done in a mechanical, detached, even obsessional manner without engaging them at all. To reap the harvest of experience, we have to suffer "properly," not masochistically but by the activity of *allowing* (a meaning of "suffering") in a wholehearted and attentive way. This letting go reflects an unconscious choice in Symington; an unconscious decision in Rangell; *zich zu ubergebin*, or surrendering to the drift, in Freud; and a turning toward truth or *teshuvah* in mystical Judaism.

Suffering

From process, let us now move to bedrock. In classical Buddhism, life is examined through the lenses of *dukkha*, *annica*, and *annata*—suffering, impermanence, and no-self, respectively. "There is suffering" is the first of the Buddha's Four Noble Truths. Suffering is caused by attachment or clinging to misguided views of who one is and the way things are. Contemporary students of Buddhism frequently confound the term *attachment*, meaning clinging to formulations (constructions) of "me" and "mine," with *attachment* that means the lifegiving process of connection necessary for the growth of the very reflective capacities necessary for meditation practice and inquiry. One way to understand the different uses of the term is to think of the classical Buddhist use as referring to breakdown products and processes of not-good-enough attachment and development (we might say that emotional experience becomes unprocessable trauma in the absence of good-enough "othering"). In reaction to these, we construct and maintain, often to our detriment, protective and obstructive structures. It is these reactively generated structures of mind—entrenched and usually unconscious, often in conflict with one another, and sometimes malevolent (and therefore the cause of real anguish and guilt)—that are the object of Buddhist meditative practice, not the human need for living attachments, which lasts throughout life in evolving forms.

Likewise, some Buddhist teachers see therapists as maintaining and shoring up the "ego," which is considered the key factor of delusion and suffering. A confusion of tongues is probably at play here. I think they are referring to reactively constructed or precociously developed and cathected mental structures, what Buddhists might call "ego attachments," rather than securely developed ego capacities or functions that have no need for a self-conscious and rigid "I" in order to function with vigor and creativity.

In the classical Buddhist view, too, we cannot escape suffering. Rather, it is how we meet and engage with suffering, the attentional quality of the encounter, that is key. What contemporary developmental psychology calls "rupture" is inevitable—so the capacity for repair or transformation is essential. Whether we unwittingly create anguish for ourselves and others or find value and meaning, even transformation and insight, is contingent on how we approach suffering. "Suffering is inevitable, anguish is optional" may seem to trivialize the agonies humans are subject to, but the idea is analogous to the understandings emerging from infant and neurobiological research. The capacity to bear affective experience, pleasurable and painful, is a prerequisite for, and a by-product of, transformative understanding, and is front and center in contemporary Buddhism and psychoanalysis.

No-Mind

There is a paradox at the heart of human experience. We must develop a "feeler" to feel, a "thinker" to think, a "dreamer" to dream—in short, a mind with which to bear and attend fruitfully to the states of mind we encounter and learn from them. Yet, when this process is moving along well, there is no thinker, feeler, or dreamer—no mind—apart from the living experience. The subject of mind, a mind of one's own, is critical, yet we only become aware of it when it does not work well. We could say that it is a background function whose concretization is a breakdown product. This is reflected in the quote by Ernest Jones: "I do not think that the mind really exists as an entity." Winnicott writes of the tendency to localize the mind in the head or elsewhere and describes how the mental apparatus can become an end in itself, a mind object, when the reciprocal caregiver–infant mutuality goes awry and the mental capacities of the infant have to take over prematurely to ensure survival.

> The mind does not exist as an entity in the individual's scheme of things provided the individual psyche-soma has come satisfactorily through the very early developmental stages; mind is then no more than a special case of the functioning of the psyche-soma. In the study of the developing individual, the mind will often be found to be developing a false entity and a false localization.

Where *is* the Mind? The mind that "cannot be grasped" is, in Winnicott's words, not "localized" in time or space. As we have seen, the meaning of the word *sesshin* (an intensive Zen meditation retreat) is to touch the mind, perceive the mind, convey the mind. In Zen, mind is *empty*, not vacuous but void of absolute or permanent material—a field of potentiality. Our conceptions about reality form a discursive veil that obscures it. Although the mind has no thing in it, it breathes, sits down, stands up, goes to sleep, shops, gets sick, laughs, and weeps. When we look closely, we cannot find a static entity, we cannot find an agent. If such is found, there has been a derailment, or in Zen terms, we have fallen into ignorance or delusion.

Bodhidharma is a legendary Zen figure who brought Zen from India to China. In this story, he is doing zazen in a cave:

> Standing outside, shivering in the snow, a monk says, "Your disciple's mind has no peace as yet. I beg you, Master, please put it to rest." Bodhidharma says, "Bring me your mind and I will put it to

rest." The monk says, "I have searched for my mind but I cannot find it." Bodhidarma replies, "I have completely put it to rest for you."

Bodhidarma did not mean that he had magically transformed the monk's reality. He was simply presenting fundamental reality that the monk had come into contact with but had not yet realized or personalized.

A mind that is empty is, by virtue of this very quality, *interconnected*. Minds "inter-are." This is in accord with Fonagy's model and Bion's reformulation of Klein's ideas on projective identification to reflect an unconscious communicational field, function, and motive. The Buddhist image we have explored is the Jewel Net of Indra. Each being, sentient or not, is a point in a vast net in which there are mirrors at each knot. Each point reflects and contains every other point of the web, not unlike the hologram. It is precisely *because* the self and the mind have no absolute substance that we are interconnected and multicentered selves. We cannot say "wrapping paper" without saying "tree, branches, rain, sun, earth, lumberjack, storekeeper." *This is* because *that is*. In realizing our own essential nature, we realize the nature of all things.

In Zen, emptiness and interdependence co-arise with *intimacy*. This is at once the mind essence, the aim of practice, and the way to its realization. Yet, none of these distinctions is required for its presence. It characterizes the spontaneous and illuminating dialogues between Zen teacher and student:

Jizo asked Hogen, "Where are you going?" Hogen replied, "I am wandering at random." Jizo asked, "What do you think of wandering?" "I don't know," Hogen replied. Jizo said, "Not-knowing is most intimate." At this Hogen awakened suddenly.

Freud's distinction between psychical and material reality sets the stage for psychoanalysis and remains central. But, what intimacy did Hogen become suddenly aware? Was it inner or outer? Sacred or profane? Empty or full? Self or other? Fantasy or reality? From a Zen perspective, we can say that it arose as a fertile field of empty interconnection where he found himself unsnared by any of these dualities.

For purposes of discussion, we call it nondualistic. Hogen's realization was not conceptual, however, or mystical. Yet, he could have presented it simply and with vivid particularity. Another Zen teacher said, "Morning to evening, I am always intimate with it." Preoccupation with clinging and "attachment" or with their resolution, the classical factors of suffering, are absent here.

We have also read about Yamada Rōshi, who, while reading a book on the train, came upon the phrase, "Mind is none other than the mountains and rivers and the great wide earth, the sun, the moon and the stars" (Dogen). Everything fell away, and he roared with laughter. What was so funny? In Zen, it is through an experience of empty infinity that we can know *directly* (in contrast to *knowing about*) the intersection of personal and the sacred. No longer a container for our anxieties, a projection screen for unbearable aspects of self-experience, or even a facilitating environment, the "other" is none other than the self, yet confusion does not result, and particularity is vivid and not collapsed. The search for something outside, even meaning, ceases; the "aim" is closer than our own nose. The apparent paradox is that, only with "forgetting the self" (the reactive structures of mind whose narratives we identify with and mistake for who we are) can we come to ourselves and find intimacy with others. Observation, the bread and butter of classical mindfulness meditation and psychoanalytic exploration, gives way to nondualistic immersion. Are we breathing, or are we being breathed? When the actor, the action, and that which is acted upon fall away, we may come alive to a reality referred to as "suchness" that is not conveyed adequately by the terms dualism, nonduality, or any category.

Differences and Complementarity

In this section, I highlight some differences between Zen and psychotherapy and suggest how they may be a source of mutual enrichment in illuminating presence of mind. In Zen, when self and other fall away and we awaken to the intimate co-arising of self and world, or in Theravada practice when we see through and disidentify from ignorant perceptions and reality constructions of a fixed selfhood, there can develop an unconscious tendency to consider oneself immunized against disturbances in the relational realm. Even practitioners with long personal psychotherapy experience, even those who are themselves therapists, can fall prey to unconscious spiritual arrogance, sometimes described as being "fully analyzed." Freedom of mind becomes tethered by a sense of invincibility or superiority. In its wake, the vivid, interpenetrating awareness of the "other"—"I" resonating intimately with the trees, moon, and stars—becomes mechanical and compartmentalized, characterized by a collapsed "external" reality. The living experience of finding oneself affirmed and alive in the most ordinary activities of living, like standing up or sitting down, can take on a cookbook, stilted, behavioristic quality. There may be scant awareness of the "other" in one's own intrapsychic and interpersonal unconscious emotional experience.

For example, a highly esteemed and experienced Buddhist teacher saw nonattachment to self and dismantling of the ego as the core of his teachings and practice. Ironically, he could be quite preoccupied with how he appeared when he taught, whether he would be perceived as cruel or unresponsive to a coteacher, for example, and wondered why, in an ad for a workshop, his name appeared in larger type than the other presenter. I think he was worried that he wasn't "empty" enough and would appear to be self-aggrandizing.

Off the cushion, outside the meditation hall, or beyond the temple compound, in interpersonal relations—particularly those that reflect a certain mutual investment or attachment—the hard-won attentional capacities and insights can seem to evaporate. Psychotherapy can be a way to bring the very values inherent in Buddhism itself— self-knowledge, wisdom, compassion for self and others—into play in daily living, a way to develop insight-in-action. But, one must allow that there are things one is not aware of, that one "has" an unconscious with which one is well advised to make friends. There is a privileging in meditative circles of the capacity to become conscious of conflicts and obstacles and overcome them through personal conscious attentiveness. The "other" needed for insight both in the intrapsychic and in the interpersonal realm can be overlooked.

Narcissistic strivings, competition, aggression, sexuality, unprocessed trauma—these are some of the specific issues that perplex and stymie meditators. They are "others" that are not particularly welcomed or easily borne and learned from. Some traditional Zen and classical Theravada teachers have themselves been going through psychotherapy and exploring ways to integrate what they learn into classical teachings. While desirable, this can sometimes bring problems of its own—"a confusion of tongues"—like when Buddhist teachers who are also therapists do therapy with their students and teach meditation to their patients. There is also a naiveté about the power of transference and countertransference feelings in intensive teacher–student relations, even among renowned Buddhist teachers with long experience as psychotherapists. This has helped create conditions for boundary violations and ethical misconduct, usually by male teachers. While teachers generally benefit from psychological knowledge and therapy, naiveté remains, and female students still become romantically involved with their male teachers, some continuing their intensive study with lovers and husbands all the way through to their own Dharma transmission (certification as independent teachers). In this regard, I have been struck not only by naiveté but also by a hubristic streak that may conceal unconscious motives the teacher, student, and the organization may not wish to examine.

What has psychotherapy to learn from the epistemology and attentional practices of Zen and Theravada Buddhism? Mindfulness practice, while it can overprivilege conscious attentional capacities, can also complement the psychoanalytic perspective in ways similar to how the idea of procedural memory is complementing the dynamic unconscious. Certain material and certain modes of awareness are not exactly unconscious or preconscious. As we noted, Alvarez has written about what is just outside, alongside, or underneath our awareness. If a patient or analyst is practicing mindfulness alongside psychotherapy—for example, is cultivating a wide, welcoming, nonjudgmental awareness of bodily states and how these interact with emotional experience—this can deepen, extend, and energize what might otherwise be a dry intellectual treatment. In the service of self-knowledge, this can also complement, even deepen and flesh out the associational capacities traditionally fostered in psychoanalysis. It is not only what this *makes me think of*—the associational chain—that is important, but also the sound, look, smell, and feel of what it is that I am actually thinking, feeling, and sensing. We become curious about the meaning of certain thoughts, feelings, or bodily sensations that arise and how they connect with our troubles in living, but even so, certain experiences have intrinsic meaning and

transformational power outside realms of meaning making, symbolization, and insight: the unconscious made conscious. Mindfulness practice extends our capacity for and the range and depth of experience
while expanding the palette of what makes analytic experience valuable.
For many people who have difficulty recognizing affective states, mindfulness practice helps them develop this capacity.

Simple experiences entered into fully, such as breathing, can have
remarkable impact. D. W. Winnicott describes a woman of forty-seven
with false self-character traits, who regressed, in his developmental
scheme, to a very early experience in which living is equivalent to breathing. Twenty-five years ago, before I read his work, "Mind and Its Relation to the Psyche-Soma," I had a similar experience with a patient,
Ellen (see Chapter 1, "Coming to Life," and Chapter 3, "Harvesting the
Ordinary") involving what we might think of as "being alone in the
presence of the other" or sharing a kind of early "quiet alert" state. But,
why think of these as simply regressive, even if by this we mean a regression to dependence in the service of independence, a regression in the
service of the ego, or in Bateson's terms, a falling back to leap? There is
both benign and malignant regression, and our ability to tolerate the
benign version may, as Sanville points out, relate to having a progressive
view of human development. However, we might also think of these
experiences as novel forms of being alive that carry great weight and
power, despite not being formally in the realm of time at all. The consol-
idation of distinctions between past and present, inner and outer, self
and other is a critical developmental achievement, yet it can also trip us
up and constrain us. D. W. Winnicott's ideas on the intermediate area
of experience help, but they do not quite capture the nondual nature of
experience that Zen practice facilitates and I believe psychoanalysis also
potentially makes available.

I was working with a patient who was also a meditator who struggled
with seeing that she wanted me to recognize her distinctiveness as a person and a woman in ways her alternately indulging and bullying father
had not. I pointed out how she seemed to speak animatedly and develop
a head of steam and then stop and switch modes, saying she was "getting
off track" and there was "another way" (a more meditative way to deal, it
seemed, with the strong conflicting emotions arising out of intense
attachments). She could not make use of it and eventually bristled. We

were able to see that she was responding to me, and in some ways I to her, as she had felt her father do—father knew best. This struggle peaked in a trying session before a weekend break. We returned to find that we each had thought about the encounter. She felt she had not been able to hear what I was saying, wondered why, and wanted me to run my ideas by her again. I said that in thinking things over, I realized that she not only was wriggling anxiously out of an emotionally charged account but was animated by a desire to heal her father-therapist, to show him "another way" that is more compassionate and less intolerant and domineering than his own. It turned out that she had tried to get him to go with her to visit her spiritual teacher with just this in mind. Somehow, we had created more space to think together. She said there was something she wanted to tell me about her meditation experience but was not sure I could get it. We waited in silence; I felt receptive and sensed the same between us. She began, slowly and in a completely different mode, to speak about having resumed sitting again. She described in moving, simple language how she experienced the weight of her body on the floor, the feeling of the air exiting her nostrils and floating by her lips, the muscles around the chest relaxing, "just breathing in and out." This was "presentational" in a non-self-conscious way, not an abstract reportage. After a while, she paused, and I suggested that she felt alive. It had not occurred to her, she said, but that was how she felt, simply alive. Then she added, in the same affective mode, that she also felt like she had the right to be alive. Later, she added that she wanted to protect that right. This folded into and enhanced various dynamic themes.

There is something primordial about the experiencing of breathing and inhabiting one's body in an open and alive way. But, why stop at breathing? We often pass over simple realities of living such as walking, cooking, eating, talking, touching, digging in the ground, and feeling, thinking, and dreaming themselves—perhaps in our desire to understand deeper meanings. Can we harvest the ordinary activities of living—inner and outer, pleasant and painful—engaging them, *in and of themselves*, as expressive shapes of living mind itself? What if transformational capacities based on deep, internalized understanding of mind and self develop such that the inevitable ruptures and the negative affect states they engender are no longer perceived as obstacles to be resisted and no longer generate surplus suffering? Would there be a reduced need for repair? What if affect regulation were no longer such a primary preoccupation but rather an integrated background function? Could we open to deeper knowledge and appreciation of what our lives and death are?

A line from a pop song, "The secret of life is enjoying the passage of time," brings us toward the question of aim. If suffering, or *dukkha*, is inherent in life, life is also short, and impermanence, or *annica*, is our lot. This is a growing realization and catalyst for growth or despair in both analysis and meditation practice. What obstructs our ability to allow the moments of living themselves, without added or associated "meaning," to *present* life itself to us, through and as us, and for us to have the *presence of mind* to be in attendance and encounter it, if not as a gift, then with curiosity?

Psychotherapeutic explanations run the gamut; a partial list includes excessive envy, developmental deficits, a psychoneurological makeup unable to contain our capacity and appetite for experience, superego harshness, irrational guilt, unbearable anxiety, and masochism. The obstructions are as diverse as the individual character. But from the Buddhist point of view, these explanations, valid as they may be given the theoretical vantage points from which they emerge, are incomplete. The problem lies in our attentional approach to reality. From the Theravada perspective, we do not observe closely enough. From the Zen point of view, we have not entered into the experience wholeheartedly. There is still an observer observing something external to it. We are like a cat running after our own tail and so cannot benefit from the awakening power of the moment, whatever its content. If each being, each moment, contains the whole universe, then it is a doorway to and a manifestation of ultimate reality. Let's not mystify it: Zen experience is immanent and nonconceptual. We miss it because our phone line is busy.

A senior colleague described a therapist in supervision with her who was speaking about her father, who was also a therapist. The man was nearing the end of life, beloved friends were dying, the world was in a shambles, and all his considerable efforts at helping make it a better place were for naught. Although he had reached many people in his work—something his daughter pointed out to him—this was depressing. He understood intersubjectivity and liked the idea his daughter suggested of concentric circles of beneficent influence spreading out like a mandala from each of the persons whose life he had touched. But it seemed to her that this was not the way it actually felt to him. Could we say that this therapist, like each of us, has an epistemological blind spot that coexisted, metaphorically speaking, with an "attention deficit?" Blake writes, and Buddhist intersubjectivity teaches, about seeing the world in a grain of sand and eternity in an hour. Would such understanding, personalized, make his pain at seeing his time on earth end without achieving the "external" standards of his dream easier to bear? Might he be more available to enjoy not only the "smaller"-scale achievements but the ordinary moments that remain?

In Zen, essential nature is unfathomable and, like in the work of Bion, must be "been." But how? Neither inside nor outside, private nor public, sensual nor nonsensual, essential nature is vividly expressed through all channels when constricting dualistic views are not obscuring. Beyond categories, mind operates as our senses, emotions, thoughts, pains and pleasures, the sun, the moon, and the earth. Is this inner? Is this outer? How can that which cannot be described come forth, without translation or transduction? This is difficult for our minds to fathom. Why? It is our mind.

I suggest that the attentional approach that characterizes presence of mind is a receptive, nonjudgmental equanimity that does not simply contain; it fathoms, or *knows*, and recognizes while retaining the potential to respond spontaneously and flexibly in accord with circumstances. Mind comes forth in multitudinous and surprising ways when our feelers and sensors—our eyes, ears, nose, tongue, body, and mind—are open and alert multidirectionally and nonvigilantly, acknowledging inner and outer, emotion and thought, past and present, reality and fantasy, without becoming snagged on or privileging either pole—when such categories (and the theories of mind that underlie them) do not constrain perception.

Perhaps it is our presence, born of freedom of mind, that we as analysts give our patients. This implies an absence, but I do not see it as depriving. It is a provision of something that cannot be given. Our patients' responses, likewise, may be how they give of themselves, as we embody and bring the mind to life together, moment by moment. We could say that the capacity for mentalization is an important element of the *dhyana* or attentiveness of psychotherapy; the realization and internalization of no-mind is *prajna* or wisdom; and its embodiment in daily life through mindful awareness a living out of awakened action, or *sila*.

In Chapter 5, "Singularity, Intersubjectivity, and the Immeasurable," I examine how views of our basic nature shape how we think about health and disturbance as well as the spiritual dimension in psychotherapy and in life.

CHAPTER 5

Singularity, Intersubjectivity, and the Immeasurable

In this chapter, I explore the dimensions of relationality in the psychotherapeutic process and in Zen. The guiding working theories of psychotherapy derive from views of our basic nature, in particular fundamental singularity on the one hand and bedrock intersubjectivity on the other. They also are informed by views about suffering—seen as a derailment of development—and therapeutic action. To challenge the view of the self as an isolate, I use the contrasting prism of Zen Buddhism, which offers perspectives that may be enriching.

These ideas coalesced over the course of several stimulating exchanges in a class I taught on Winnicott at the Psychoanalytic Institute of Northern California (PINC). D. W. Winnicott's paper, "Communicating and Not Communicating Leading to a Study of Certain Opposites," inspired a spectrum of viewpoints on human experience. One person saw Winnicott's notion of the "incommunicado self" as a wellspring out of which all things emerge (and perhaps to which they return). Another felt a phenomenological resonance with the idea and linked it to the experience of listening to Ravel. The former is a metaphorical understanding, the latter a phenomenological experience—both are important. I want to explore two questions. First, does Winnicott's "hard fact" that, in our heart of hearts, we are an "isolate, permanently noncommunicating, permanently unknown, unfound" adequately describe and illuminate such metaphors and experiences? Second, does associating mysticism (or spirituality) with an incommunicado isolate do justice to mysticism and psychotherapy?

As one student described it, D. W. Winnicott seems to refer to difference, the encounter with otherness, the "hard fact" of how solitary and how alone we are. I think this puts us in touch with our own difference and separateness as well. This realization can lead to depressive, existential, and other anxieties as well as to greater autonomy, intimacy, and freedom. Winnicott writes of a development in which the infant communicates that he is not communicating. The healthy use of non-communication helps us feel real. It is important that the therapist recognize this moment and distinguish it from other kinds of silences. Winnicott writes:

> There is something we must allow for in our work, the patient's non-communication as a positive contribution. We must ask ourselves, does our technique allow for the patient to communicate that he or she is not communicating? For this to happen, we as analysts must be ready for the signal: "I am not communicating," and be able to distinguish it from the distress signal associated with a failure of communication. There is a link here with the idea of being alone in the presence of someone.

This lived, attuned respect for the sanctity and the communicated privacy of the patient's inner life is similar in form if not in content to the mother's refraining from asking the toddler whether the teddy bear was found or made up, real or imaginary. Moments such as D. W. Winnicott describes, linked together over time between mother and baby, contribute to the baby's capacity to experience self and (m)other as separate yet together. Such moment-chains facilitate the baby's coming to experience "the object as objectively perceived," in contrast to being generated in the area of omnipotence through an act of creative illusion (the subjective object). In Fonagy's view, the child comes to have and be able to use a mind of its own through being experienced and responded to by a facilitating other as someone with such a mind.

However, in making the leap to an incommunicado core, D. W. Winnicott begins to lose me. Although he writes of the coexistence of two trends—the urgent need to communicate and the more urgent need not to be found—he equates being found with being cannibalized and infinitely exploited. I think he mistakes a reactively constructed survival-driven entity constellated out of trauma with the freely functioning psychesoma-self activity that he writes about earlier. This activity, we might say, is neither self nor not-self, neither hidden nor apparent, neither lost nor found. It cannot be captured by either polar opposite but appears freely now as one, now as the other, each in paradoxical relation, or each composing varying "proportions" of the moment-to-moment flux. This phenomenon is like Matte Blanco's notion of symmetrical (feeling) and asymmetrical (thinking) logic that operate simultaneously in the unconscious. Winnicott writes that his argument needs an environmental failure but then posits the incommunicado core (and, by implication, the dread of being found) as a *normative* structure or state of affairs.

In a lucid discussion of de Bianchedi, Dithrich brings together Winnicott and Bion and links the mystical in psychoanalysis with intuition and the true self, which he sees as infinite. I find these bridges useful. What is the true self, and how is it infinite? Dithrich describes it as ultimately unknowable and isolated and, because (intrinsically) dreading exposure, needing to be "fiercely protected" and "vigilantly guarded." "The fact of essential isolation" then leads him to embrace, like Bion, the necessity for an atmosphere of deprivation and detachment in the therapist–patient encounter. The view of human bedrock leads to a prescription for therapeutic activity. What are we deprived of? Although Dithrich suggests a dialectical approach in which formality and "essential separateness" help create the possibility of freedom and passion, his view of therapeutic activity seems to suggest elements of a classical theory that places a premium on frustrating instinctual desires. It seems not to acknowledge the importance of a safe and secure setting whose importance Bowlby, Fonagy, and contemporary infant researchers have demonstrated.

This may relate to Bion's view of the relation between sensory experience and the mystical dimension. Bion sees "O" (ultimate reality and the psychoanalytic object alike) as nonsensual. The sensory pathways must be transcended by a willful suspension of memory and desire. This links with the notion of an incommunicado, unknowable, isolate. I think it is not so much the sensory data pathways themselves that obscure. But rather, to the contrary, it is the *use* to which we put them. All the senses, including the sixth one, can be allies in the joint search for and creation of analytic truth, especially when we are not *"chasing out through the five senses,"* as Meister Eckhart calls it. Likewise, I think it is not memory and desire themselves that the analyst needs to willfully suspend. Rather, in cultivating a wide, inclusive, and nonjudgmental awareness—presence of mind, body, and emotions—the analyst's unconscious attachments to narrow, constricting, and repetitive versions of memory, desire, and understanding, and his identification with and need to defend them, recede. Direct, intuitive knowing can occur. (Dithrich reminds us that Bion also encourages making use of the senses in formulating an interpretation. Oelsner and Eigen stressed that Bion knew that it was not simply the existence of psychic capacities—for example, alpha function—that was important but the use to which they are put. So, where is it written that good thinkers need to be consistent?)

What is the patient deprived *of*? Ideally, it is of intrusive and presumptive therapeutic arrogance, of the premature collapse of the analyst's capacities to think, feel, dream, be, and respond. What does the therapist detach *from*? We cannot excise memory, desire, and understanding even if we wanted to. Rather, to my mind, we practice detachment (or better, using a term from Buddhism, "nonattachment")—via conscious and unconscious acts of attentive expansion—from being *snagged on and unconsciously driven by* narrowly constellated versions of memory, desire, and understanding as we cultivate, occasionally under great duress, our freedom of mind. I like to think that a therapeutic setting that is receptive *and* responsive—fully embodied and sensorially alive—is an important provision, rather than the object of deprivation. It does not ignore difference, but instead embraces it. Victoria Hamilton's thinking is relevant here:

> The experience of negation, or "the negative realization," and the formulation of the simple negative are linked to separation, differentiation, to the perception of contrast and differences, to the making of distinctions, to the command "Don't," etc. However in my view these communications are *tolerated* in a context of togeth-

erness, reciprocity, play, secure attachment and above all, predict-able presence or reunion. (italics in original)

This description fleshes out *how* we want to be found, how our uniqueness and difference and our awareness of others' differences are recognized and handled, how this encounter can be usable and growth-ful rather than overly traumatic. D. Winnicott describes a "simple non-communicating" where there is a free to and fro between commu-nicating and not communicating. Later, he makes a similar point regarding the opposites: emptiness and form. We might think of such a fluid movement between unintegration and integration, emptiness and form, the conundrum—is this one or the other?—does not arise; the question is neither posed nor answered. Myriad forms emerge from (generative) emptiness and return again to the wellspring.

Bion's seminal contributions to psychoanalysis include bringing into focus its interplay with perennial existential and spiritual dimensions of human life. He writes that O cannot be known but must be embodied or "been." This can be mystifying. Blake's verse again is relevant as he presents this elusive "been":

> To see a World in a Grain of Sand
> And a Heaven in a Wildflower,
> Hold Infinity in the palm of your hand
> And Eternity in an hour.

We might say that as our capacity for truth deepens, as self-preoccupation, constricted perception, and the need to defend any self recede, O—or Heaven—becomes *available* in the most ordinary phe-nomena: a wildflower, a weed, a laugh, a tear. Vast worlds and universes are contained in a grain of sand or an ice cream cone. Boundless time, eternity itself, is present in this very moment. What of infinity? In the palm of our hand, the tapping on the keyboard, the sound of the baby crying to be changed. Blake here expresses and embodies the living unity of emptiness and form. O and K—being and knowing, sacred and human, universal and particular—are neither rigidly apart nor col-lapsed. According to Zen Buddhism, this living unity escapes us because we are trapped in self-centered, dualistic thinking. D. W. Winnicott's ideas on the mind object, the forfeiture of the psyche-soma, and the development of the false self flesh out the development of this dualism.

Dithrich equates the Zen koan with experiencing and being in contrast to intellectual knowing, but this is not accurate. When such dualistic categories themselves drop away, what remains? The literal meaning of *koan* is a "matter to be made clear." Koans are metaphorical narratives, usually drawn from spontaneous, everyday encounters between student and teacher, the folk stories of Zen. In Zen practice, they provide a window that shows the whole truth but from a single vantage point, a way to experience the intersection of the sacred in the particulars of daily experience. *Koans* are not frustrating mind twisters—they can be playful. When the old teacher Yanguan asks his attendant to bring him the rhinoceros fan, the attendant replies that it is broken. Yanguan says, "Then bring me the rhinoceros." Young children can do this, but very smart grown-ups might have some difficulty. Where is that rhinoceros? We cannot bring it forth if we hold the idea of O or the true self as permanently noncommunicating, permanently unknown and isolated. Likewise, if we are snagged on detachment, "Detachment, detachment, all I hear is detachment!" said one Zen teacher. "If you weren't attached, you'd be dead."

The koan question held patiently, like a confusing set of emotional or bodily experiences, asks itself, works on itself. In a moment that takes no time at all, we may break free and know things without intermediary, as if from the inside out. The rhinoceros frolics joyfully, and our ordinary mind is a vivid reality we live and can express in simple, even humorous, ways. There is intrinsic connection that does not collapse difference. O is no longer hidden, no longer external (as an idea), or for that matter internal. Mental ping-pong—Is this inner? Is this outer?—does not constrain perception. It is simply so. This is called "Suchness" in Zen. Each thing shines in its own distinctiveness, completely unique, yet containing each and every other being. The realm of play opens wide.

O *is* unknown and unknowable; that is, it cannot be known as a subject knows an object. This duality is ego syntonic and trips us up quite a bit. One way we get around it is by conceiving of intuition as a two-step: at-one-ment followed by translation. Although this formulation is experience-near and reflects a process dimension common to psychoanalysis and Zen practice—we practice thus to encourage this—it is not the *only* way we know, in the consulting room or the *dokusan* room (where Zen teacher and student meet) or in life. Intuition means direct, unmediated knowing. O cannot be "been" by chasing out through the senses, yet it is embodied in birdsong, the flavor of dark chocolate, the smell and touch of a loved one, and the scowl of an adversary. This is difficult to "wrap our mind around." Why? It *is* our mind.

Let us look imaginatively at my colleague's experience of listening to music. In part, it may be reactive, a constructive detaching from the strain of the daily grind of relating, a turning away from people and the demands of "civilized" living. Yet, it also has a contemplative feel to it, a pause that refreshes, allowing the sounds of Ravel to be, to wash over the listener. Business as usual, the hurly-burly of social relations, does not press in. A certain privacy is taken and cherished; a claim is staked to the right to such experience. It is a creative retreat that reflects an immersion in sound and the interplay of the melodies, rhythms, and textures with the listener's responses. It is an aesthetic experience where there is no object per se, but rather something akin to what Balint called a "harmonious interpenetrating mix-up."

I do not think this is captured by the notion of a permanently noncommunicating core. It seems the obverse of permanence. I imagine a state where the listener is open and responsive to the nuances of the music, the affective shifts, the flow. Is this noncommunicating? Perhaps, in regard to an actual or internal intrusive or presuming other, but there seems the most intimate of communication with the music, with Ravel, with beauty, and potentially with elements of the person's own psyche. The music is not an object that needs things and makes demands, claims, and attributions. Rather, it offers itself as it is, and the listener is with it and of it. Where does the music begin and listener end? I'm reminded of Chuang-Tsu, the Taoist poet who wondered—such was the intimacy of an encounter with a butterfly—if he was Chuang-Tsu dreaming he was a butterfly or a butterfly dreaming he was Chuang-Tsu. Balint, Chuang-Tsu, and D. W. Winnicott's intermediate area of experience overlap here.

Words give shape to insights that in turn form the building blocks of theory. Theory, whether we are aware of it or not, perhaps especially when we are not, conditions our perceptions and actions in the consulting room. In his remarkable paper, "Communicating and Not Communicating Leading to a Study of Certain Opposites," D. W. Winnicott uses several terms that, to my mind, result in an unnecessarily static and uncharacteristically nonparadoxical formulation of human bedrock. I think they express a version of primary narcissism that seems ironically like the "cul-de-sac" he writes about, in that, by definition, they do not cross-fertilize with contributions such as mother–infant mutuality, psychoanalysis as the overlap between two play areas, and creative illusion. Unlike many of his other ideas, including most recently the fear of breakdown, it does not find confirmation in infant research studies.

I think D. W. Winnicott's notion of the incommunicado core refers to a constructed rather than a given structure that arises out of a reaction to, or fear of, trauma. While it may attempt to preserve an important mystery about human behavior, it may also have been developed in reaction to what he felt was the intrusive interpretational style of some of the Kleinians of that era and their privileging the analyst's knowing. It can serve, I imagine, as a corrective to hubris ("megalomania" in de Bianchedi's 2001 article) regarding the rectitude of our knowledge and our all-too-human tendency to foist such certitude on others. For Winnicott, interpretation reveals the limits of our knowledge rather than our omniscience. This may be in part the source of the fantasy of being infinitely exploited that in turn leads to the notion of an unreachable core where we are protectively shielded.

Do we need "wellspring 'time outs'"? Yes. Do we take them proactively as well as reactively? Yes. Does communicating our noncommunicating in such moments help us feel real (and discover expanded realities)? Yes. Is it important that we feel confident enough in our *capacity* to both feel integral and surrender whole-object relating? Yes. But, the terminology Winnicott uses here, the view of human bedrock it expresses, and the theory he forges seem reactive and at cross-purposes.

In such states of mind, there is no hindrance, no concern with self or other because they are absent as fixed, permanent entities. There is nothing to protect and defend, no core at all. It is only when this nondualistic activity is threatened (impinged upon, prematurely named or worse) do we instinctively and reactively defend, protect, and as a by-product, create fixed structures. These structures can become malevolent, take on a life of their own, and exact a heavy price for the survival they ensure. I think the constellation of a core, permanently incommunicado (true) self that needs fierce defending is *in reaction*. When we are operating freely, there are no fetters, there is aliveness that is its own meaning and needs no justification. It is unfortunate to associate mysticism with an incommunicado core or with any core at all, be it a personal one (D. W. Winnicott) or an Unknowable "O"-ne (Bion) needing transformation into the personal realm. The question—personal or mystical?—does not arise. In the Diamond Sutra, an old Buddhist text, enlightenment is described as follows: Because there is nothing (fixed, permanent, and absolute) such as Buddha, we *call it* Buddha. (Buddha here refers not to the historical figure but to the truth of awakening.) Perhaps the "true" self is like this: fundamentally ineffable and yet simultaneously coming forth—now laughing, now weeping, now learning, now getting muddled.

Do we need the other's mind (and heart and touch) to develop a (private, autonomous) mind of our own? Does the intersubjective field need differentiated minds to really communicate with one another? If these are both true, then we are *simultaneously* private, unique, and unknowable and intimately interdependent and coconstructed. The paradoxical interplay is preserved, and the mystery can be plumbed by each of us.

In Chapter 6, "Knowing the Truth," I focus on truth and its everyday, clinical, and existential iterations in Zen and psychotherapy. Truth is a motivational force with ethical implications, and we can turn toward or turn away from it, consciously and unconsciously.

CHAPTER 6

Knowing the Truth

And you shall know the truth and the truth shall set you free.
—JOHN, 8:32

Not the intense moment
Isolated, with no before and after,
But a lifetime burning in every moment
—T. S. ELIOT, "EAST COKER"

In a wildly popular song, Tina Turner belts out the lyrics: "What's love got to do, got to do with it? What's love but a secondhand emotion?" In our postmodern mindset, could we not say the same for the notion of truth in psychotherapy? Don't we know that it is constructed, not discovered, negotiated rather than interpreted? Why raise an old warhorse from the scrap heap?

The ideas in this chapter developed from working with several psychotherapy patients. They also emerged from an ongoing effort to integrate, within my own thinking and practice, 35 years of practicing psychotherapy and Zen Buddhism. I hope they can provide a lens for looking at the experience of doing psychotherapy, and I hope they will add an important element that, in addition to unconscious emotional communication in the relational field, contributes to the Zen ideal of *dhyana* (attentive practice), *prajna* (wisdom), and *sila* (awakened action) coming into alignment. I have discussed how any experience can be put at the service of aims other than the intended ones. "Turning toward truth," conscious and unconscious, can play a part.

In the film *Billy Elliot*, Billy's father is a stern, bitter, and hard man, a miner, from whom Billy hides his interest in ballet. Somehow, despite himself, the father softens and ends up taking Billy to class. On the way, he is confronted by his elder son, who is identified with the father and their shared struggles for economic justice. Sensing a powerful, betraying turnaround, this son implores and begs his father not to go. The father exclaims: "He's only just a kid!" The transformation reflected in his words astounds us. We know, of course, that Billy is a kid. It is obvious. But, father and the viewer together realize this ordinary truth for the first time. Michael Parsons captures this in the title of his paper, "Suddenly Finding It Really Matters." He describes an analysis with a woman who brought them both "rather sharply against the realization that distinguishing fantasy from reality really matters." This is a truth every therapist knows. But, their work together made him realize it for the first time. In Zen, too, it is the ordinary, not the extraordinarily mystical, that astounds, viewed from a new perspective, the scales fallen from the eyes. This is captured in a dialogue from the film. Billy and his father are riding in the bus on the way to London for the ballet competition. Billy asks: "So, how's London?" "Dunno," says his father. "Why?" continues Billy. "Never been," father replies, "no mines there." Billy says, "Is that all you think about?" Trapped in the tunnel vision that comes from the overdetermined habit of seeing only that which is "mine," not only did the father not know London, he could not recognize Billy's distinctive humanity.

Truth is an elusive but fundamental dimension of human life, and we discover it for ourselves. I believe it is an inner willingness to directly know our truth that determines how and to what ends experience is made use of. It is truth that nourishes and sets us free. I am not referring to positivist or ecclesiastical truth, received from on high—truth with a capital T—but truth with a small t, the truth of the moment, which by nature carries a sense of moment, of psychic gravitas. I do not attempt to define it because that would be like reheating good coffee. But, I explore, describe, and perhaps evoke it.

Truth involves authentic experience with two people in intimate attendance or one person in intimate relation to an "other": animal, vegetable, or mineral—sentient or not. It comes unbidden, without fanfare and whistles, but often with a start, and is simultaneously emotional, gnostic, and mutative, reflecting and giving shape to an inner shift that has already happened. We want such experience, yet struggle against it. Truth, as I am using the term, is less a fixed place we get to once and for all than a moment-by-moment, unpredictable emerging that is created as we discover it and that, by its nature, authenticates itself and carries a sense of conviction. The means are not separate from the ends—it develops in the doing. Thinking and feeling, knowing and doing, experiencing and being here do not oppose or exclude each other. Truth is also an underlying motivational force and core value inherent in, and given living form through, being human. This capacity grows during the course of a genuine psychotherapeutic process and authentic Zen practice, but it can also elude both paths.

Intrinsic to this truth, I suggest, is an inner, unconscious "turning toward," or surrendering, that is simultaneously an act of giving. It implies turning away, disidentifying, or detaching from narrow, protective, unconscious conceptual and perceptual self-structures. Therapist and patient give of themselves through a joint giving over to and the painful and joyful moments of realization and the widened horizons that emerge. This is liberating, and this freedom co-arises with an ethical turning.

I briefly review the philosophical debate relating to truth in psychotherapy in light of several epistemological questions. I then explore the experience of truth, what fosters and impedes it, and its activity. I revisit unconscious communication, the presence and quality of attentiveness of the analyst, and the ethical dimension of the analytic process, including the notion of psychic responsibility. I weave in ideas from Zen Buddhism and look at how psychotherapy and Zen speak in distinctive yet mutually potentiating voices about core human dilemmas, values, and potentials with which they share commmon ground, in particular truth and freedom.

Martin

Martin declares during an analytic hour, "This is my time, and I can do with it what I want." This can represent a discovery, a newfound sense of freedom. Or, as I experienced often with him, it can also mean that he is completely erasing all trace of emotional impact my previous statement might have had. Discriminating omnipotence from freedom is important here. The question is: To what use is experience being put? What is the capacity we use to discern this? Does it involve using our "lizard brain"—something neuroscience is articulating with increasing clearly?

Bion calls it "intuition"; D. W. Winnicott describes it as the mother's capacity to sense and adapt to the infant's needs, arising from primary maternal preoccupation; Freud calls it *zich zu ubergeben*, the analyst's giving himself over or surrendering to his own unconscious activity to "catch the drift" of the patient's unconscious; Rayner thinks it involves an "aesthetic judgment"; Klauber considers it an "unconscious assessment"; and Ogden says it is "listening for something human." The Hebrew word *teshuvah* means "repentance" but more fundamentally refers to a turning toward truth. The act of taking refuge, in Buddhism—"I take refuge in the Buddha" (and the Dharma and the Sangha)—may likewise be translated as "I turn toward" or "I find my home in." As parents, we use this instinctive capacity to tune in to our infant and distinguish the quality and meaning of the infant's cry, which informs our response.

Each of these ways of thinking about such activity implies, I believe, an unconscious or preconscious apperception and assessment of the authenticity of the patient's communicated experience. The word *human*, after all, can refer to a wide range of activities, including deception. Gilbert and Sullivan wrote, "Skim milk masquerades as cream." So, Ogden's "listening for something human" implies listening for something genuinely human. Likewise for the notion of "aliveness": The manic defense can appear to be aliveness; a thief might say he felt quite "alive" after a successful heist. It is through a discerning resonance in truth that something is perceived as truly human. Real aliveness must co-arise with truth.

The word *trieb* has been translated as "instinct," although many think "drive" better fits the original German. Freudian drive theory has fallen into disrepute these days, but the French translation of *trieb* as "pulsion" may reveal another dimension. While *pulsion* may be translated as "impulse," there is a live pulse in impulse. As analysts, we wonder "What is going on here? What is 'driving' the communication?" In ordinary speech, we say, "Where is he coming from?" From an energic point of view, we might ask, "What is the psychic fuel operating?" "What is pulsing through one's psychic veins, so to speak, through this moment together?" In the reverberations, the echo, we may put our finger on the pulse.

In working with a patient where dissociation predominated, play was more like a shell game, the obstructive barriers protective but also prickly, keeping life out and others off guard and unaware of the truly empty shell. When I felt overwhelmed, lost, or confused in an hour, I found myself quieting—internally attending to breath and body, sitting in the midst of the confusion, continuing to listen. I came to see that something else was also going on, but metaphors for this experience took months to emerge. It was as if I were activating a kind of global positioning system. When there were particularly big gaps between what this patient was saying, how he appeared to be feeling, and how I felt in his presence, I would imagine myself as a resonance chamber, receiving the verbal and nonverbal data from without and within and taking a sounding of the whole of it.

It felt like putting out tendrils, something metaphorically akin to affective sonar, beneath the threshold of words and noticing what came back and how it resonated. A chord was struck—what were the individual notes that comprised it? What were the overtones and the harmonics? It was like dropping a pebble into a pond; ripples spread out, which continued to spread well past the analytic hour. Strange as it sounds, I wondered if the metaphorical tendrils were something like truth sensors. With this type of patient, for whom multiplicity could be a mind-scrambling defense, this activity helped me survive, maintain the capacity to recognize and make use of my internal responses, and continue on in a somewhat useful fashion.

Martin Continued

For the first year or two of analysis, Martin would complain frequently that I gave him nothing and was only clinical with him. However, quite often, just as I began to speak, he would interrupt me. It took him some time to see this, despite my trying to bring it to his attention, inviting us to look at it together and interpreting along varied lines. I felt alternatively frustrated, erased, detached, and disconnected. After weeks of this, in one hour all of a sudden something occurred to me. The next time he interrupted, I said, "When I'm about to say something, it's like my idea is something creative of mine, a connection I've made between things, but it feels like I generated it without you, like when parents have a baby, and a brother feels left out. And you cut it, you cut me off." I was surprised when he responded "Yes . . . and I love cutting the links." I did not yet know about Bion's idea of "attacks on linking," but here it was. He continued speaking of cutting links, "like sausage links strung together out of the package."

In a sense, he was continuing his associations to my interpretation, a sign that the analytic process was working. But, in the overtones there was a manic quality. It seemed that he was not really letting in the impact of what had been said but spinning anxiously away from it. Later, we came to see that this was one way he would "deconstruct" things. This word, deconstruct, emerged out of a dream he had in which he took over the reins of the boss of a construction company and dismantled projects at will. He deconstructed anything I said, often gleefully. This activity also had various fantasy meanings and attendant anxieties, including those related to forging intimate attachments, which we explored as possible.

Seeing how Martin would associate richly to and develop an idea, while in the same breath distorting it beyond use and so missing the opportunity for learning, was eye opening. When I pointed out what I thought was happening, he would listen, sometimes recognize it and agree, then spin off again, saying with scorn, "I do it because I can." It slowly became clear that to accord me a place in the room, a place and a voice in his psyche, was terrifying. The club Martin wanted to belong to had to have only him as a member. How unfulfilling his deconstructions were, how hollow and false the "free-dom" he exercised in indulging in what he referred to as his "exultant vengefulness." He continued to tell me stories about how his behavior would alienate bosses, lovers, long-time friends, and family. Slowly, we became able to look at the truth of this. Since this was also how he knit himself together, the process was quite painful.

The capacity to turn toward and generate this kind of emotional truth is central. Patients differ in their willingness and capacity to actually do this, irrespective of the diagnostic picture. Some, despite profound cumulative trauma and severe deficits in ego capacities, are like psychoanalytic troopers, pilgrims even, who seem motivated by a thirst for truth and the willingness to go as deep as it takes. Analyst Adrienne Applegarth called this quality "having guts." I think of it as what we make, from one moment to the next, with the cards we are dealt.

Epistemology

The nineteenth century saw the rise of a reaction to what were viewed as the unsubstantiated and arbitrary claims of religious revelation. Positivism meant that you could be certain about something. Truth was decoupled from magic and became subject to being tested, submitted to objective criteria of proof, and replication. It did not come down from on high or derive its authority from papal or other decree. Freud developed his groundbreaking ideas in an age when the positivistic outlook dominated.

The search for objectivity in matters of the human mind and heart has gradually given way to an appreciation of the subjective elements in the psychotherapeutic process. One form of psychodynamic therapy, psychoanalysis, is presently in an identity crisis. It is variously described as a science, a natural religion, an art, a meaning-making hermeneutic endeavor, a form of poetry, and a meditation à deux. What is the nature of the beast? "What," asks Charles Spezzano, "is the ground on which psychoanalysis stands?" As Victoria Hamilton shows, such questions and the theories we develop to respond to them do not exist in a vacuum, independent of the preconscious clusters of beliefs, values, and

experiences of the psychoanalysts who pose them. So, the questions—
"What is our true nature?" and "What is the fundamental ground we
stand on?"—become quite relevant.

While Owen Renik writes of the "irreducible subjectivity" of the
analytic endeavor, completely jettisoning the idea of an objective
observer, others like Glenn Gabbard and philosopher Marcia Cavell are
reintroducing the idea of objectivity in ways different from the positivistic approach of 19th century science.

One of Cavell's main ideas is that there is a shared, public objective
reality "out there"—which is not the same as the individual's subjective
"sense of reality"—that is knowable, although not completely or for certain. Rather, this concept of an objective truth external to private reality
makes possible our subjectivity and our internal experience. The latter
needs the former; one cannot exist without the other. The concept of an
objective reality that is shared—external and public—is paradoxically
necessary for us to think and become subjects with a complex and
unique internal world that can intersubjectively interact with the private worlds of others.

Gabbard reminds us that there is an *object* in the word *objectivity*. The
person of the analyst, by virtue of his position as external to the patient's
subjectivity, gives him a crucial vantage point from which to convey
impressions different from the patient's own reality. Becoming a "subject," some feel, inevitably involves an encounter with "otherness"—
becoming the object lived, so to speak, by unconscious processes. Some
value the importance of developing the capacity to move and hold the
tension between subjective and objective experiences of self. Epistemology deals with how we know what we know. Those privileging subjectivity tend to think that the best knower is the one closest to the data.
Gabbard and others speak for the value of a stance external to the
patient's internal world.

As we have read, for Bion and Grotstein, who has creatively developed some of Bion's ideas, the ground of psychoanalysis is "O," an unsat-
urated sign he uses to refer to truth, ultimate reality. O encompasses,
but is not identical with, the unconscious, the ground of psychic reality
according to Freud and others. Also referred to as emotional truth, psychic truth, and the psychoanalytic object, O cannot be known or understood directly; it must be "been." Unless transduced for the infant

through a sacred covenant, says Grotstein, by an attuned and metabolizing other (the parent), O is equated with profound anxiety, nameless dread, and disorganizing chaos. It operates silently. We can make ourselves receptive to it by an attentiveness akin to a mother's reverie by which she tunes into and dreams her infant. Similarly, by abandoning memory, desire, understanding, and "the irritable searching after certainty," the analyst may dream his patient. Elizabeth T. de Bianchedi said that this "dreaming" (Bion's dream work alpha) implies

> mind to mind contact . . . really being able to feel in one's mind what the other is feeling . . . the activity of intuition. Not simply nighttime dream activity, it is a mental function that operates passionately, through which we transform raw perceptions into images to be stored.

The analyst, open to the patient, takes the patient in, creates the patient's emotional experience anew, and conveys it in a usable way. This activity builds the capacity to tolerate and represent heretofore inexpressible and unrepresentable experience.

Bion says that although we embody O, we cannot know it directly but only through its transformations or transductions, via a "K" or knowledge link. This is reflected in the "selected fact"—that which "floats up," for example, in the analytic hour. This fundamental and ineffable truth is not of a sensual nature, but we can put ourselves in attunement with it through intuition, which Bion also sees as nonsensual. "Minus K" ("–K") refers to actively not knowing, destroying the capacity to know, or lying.

When we genuinely practice Freud's advice to the analyst to maintain evenly suspended attention, we come to hear from the self in ways we had not anticipated, says Bollas. In such a state, we echo with the unconscious of the other. Although Freud, in certain ways, represented the Western intellectual tradition par excellence, in this instruction and in his discovery of free association he subverted our Western epistemological tradition that is founded on the pursuit of knowledge. Grotstein says "understanding is overrated; 'O' is transduced after the fact in a realization of something we already knew or were." Lest we think only Kleinians are interested in this dimension, none other than Karl

Menninger would speak about the "willpower of desirelessness," and Stephen Applebaum writes, in a beautiful unpublished paper on evocativeness, that "something uncontrolled is going on here."

Many of the debates in psychoanalysis today, however, still evidence a split between subject and object. Whether psychic truth and the analytic process itself are a construction or a discovery is one such example. Dialectical thinking helps, but even the most elegant contemporary formulations retain some measure of dualism, similar to what we might call the "commuting" model where we oscillate between the subjective and objective modes of experience.

Buddhism and the Moments of Living

What can Buddhism contribute to these discussions? Buddhist meditation practice and mindfulness in daily living help us enter intimately into the moments of living, no matter what their content, and maintain mindful, nonjudgmental awareness in their midst, even under great strain and anxiety. We develop the capacity to observe very closely our feelings, thoughts, breath, and bodily sensations, as they are, and as they interact, one with the other, to create all manner of pleasurable, unpleasurable, and "neutral" states of mind and being. We cultivate wholehearted or bare attention to the present moment, just as it is. When we drift off, we recognize where we are and return to our focus. In the beginning, this is usually our breathing. We "turn" and return, again and again, developing and strengthening the capacity to attend to our immediate experience. Self-knowledge usually implies a knower, a "something" that is known, and a process called knowing. We take these for granted—and they are at the heart of our intellectual tradition. In Zen practice, as we become able to settle body and mind and attend deeply, we find that we are no longer thinking of attaining any particular state, we are no longer a subject trying to achieve an objective, even mindful breathing. We are simply breathing. We allow ourselves to become receptively absorbed.

A capacity for nondualistic knowing develops, akin to intuition—knowing without intermediary. Conceptual structures rooted in subject–object duality drop away as we become intimate with our "object" of study. Truth, or true nature, is not something "out there," not a "position" that allows us to maintain a detached perspective. Insight comes about when the knower, the known, and the knowing fall away as discrete entities. We become able to touch life as it is, and be touched by it, as it pulses through us. Dogen, a seminal thirteenth-century Zen teacher, wrote of the paradox: "To study the self is to forget the self. To forget the self is to be awakened by all beings." It is surprising that the quality of awareness here is not a blurred amalgam but rather vivid and discerning.

Now, this is an unusual idea—observation without a discrete subject who observes and an object that is observed; action without an actor and something acted upon; and knowledge without a knower and a known. There is no juggler here doing a balancing act between his subjective and objective sides. Yet, differences are not collapsed.

In Zen, the fundamental ground of our lives, our true human nature, may be called *generative emptiness*, charged with potential. The many beings distinctively present it: The bird sings it, our child whines it, the wind blows it, our stomach growls it. The extraordinary is not apart from, but part and parcel of, ordinary moments of living and dying. Sleepwalking through life or leading secondhand lives, we miss it. Once, when the Buddha was teaching, he twirled a flower. One of his disciples, Mahakasyapa, smiled. He directly realized something simple, lucid, and precious, yet not esoteric at all. This story is often used to describe the process of transmission from master to student in Zen. What was "transmitted"?

It is not embodied, sensual experience itself that creates and perpetuates the cycle of unsatisfactoriness and anguish; rather, it is "chasing out through the five senses," as Meister Eckhart calls it—grasping after, attaching to, identifying with, manipulating, and thereby exploiting sensory experience. We cannot find serenity or encounter truth through such grasping and clinging or through its opposite pole, aversion. But when, neither grasping after nor pushing away, it takes us unawares and bursts forth in a living moment, what we see, hear, smell, taste, and touch is unfathomable reality itself—in contrast to Bion's formulation of O, which requires a transduction and is nonsensual. We are incarnate creatures after all. This direct knowing is a passionate affair, and we do well not to repeat the early tearing asunder of flesh and spirit that brought in its wake the body–mind split that we are only now revisioning.

Because the self has no absolute permanent identity, we find fundamental libidinal affinity with our fellow beings. *Because* we are empty,
we "inter-are" with one another. The situations, people, and inner phenomena I encounter, just as they are, are nothing but ultimate reality
itself. Standing up, sitting down, laughing, weeping—these are jewels
we do not recognize as our own treasure. This is not an abstraction, not
a credo to rally around or debate, but a perennial human experience,
arising from a falling away (distinguished from falling apart) that is
simultaneously a falling together.

So, truth is public and shared in a profound, experiential sense, not as
an abstract concept, as with Cavell. It is also unknowable and inaccessible through the senses, as Bion writes, but only if we mean dualistic
knowing, as a subject knows an object.

Margaret Arden says that postmodernists have seized on the uncertainty principle as a fetish. In Zen, the concept of not-knowing is not the
alpha and *omega*, but rather represents getting stuck in emptiness. The
psychotherapeutic counterpart would be a theoretical overvaluing of
the "deconstructive" aspects of the analytic process. We can make use of
not-knowing just as we do knowing—in growthful *and* in obstructive
ways. Not-knowing is in vogue in some circles these days, and we tend to
speak about it more than we actually do it. We can also get caught up in
not knowing what we already know, say the unthought known, without
knowing it.

Free association, for example, is a great leap. When we actually do it,
we really do not know what will emerge next. It subversively undermines
ordinary experience and certainty. But, we reify and privilege this aspect
at the peril of disowning our capacity for direct, transformative, nondualistic knowing. "Take a step from the top of a 100-foot pole," a Zen
koan urges us. A true word, please. A gesture of truth. Parading the
deconstructionist banner, we cannot do this. It is not esoteric at all. The
point is that tolerating ambiguity, complexity, and not-knowing, we
come to know things about ourselves we were unaware of. We realize
very ordinary truths, including the limits of our knowledge, nondualistically and quite intimately. This knowledge is not discursive. Lived
afresh in each moment, it is provisional and only slowly and partially
integrated, but it can have great weight, great "moment." Evocativeness,

the expression of profoundly resonant experience, arises when dualistic notions of subject-urgently-pursuing-object drop away.

In Zen, our true nature cannot be fathomed by thinking about it or figuring it out, but it is embodied in each moment of ordinary experience. We have only to let the scales fall from our eyes and wake up from our dualistic slumber. As Layman Pang, a revered and down-to-earth Zen practitioner in T'ang period China, wrote:

> My daily activities are not unusual,
> I'm just naturally in harmony with them
> Grasping nothing, discarding nothing
> In every place, there's no hindrance . . .
> [My] supernatural powers and marvelous activity—
> Drawing water and carrying firewood.

This miraculous and simultaneously ordinary "things as they are"—"Suchness" in Buddhism—is also referred to as the *Tathagata*. It literally means "thus come" or intimacy with what is and with that which arises and passes. The painter and psychoanalyst Marion Milner describes something similar when she speaks of encountering the "sheer thusness, the separate and unique identity of the thing." "Every point of thought is the center of an intellectual world," wrote Keats (Letters I, 242–243). We humans are at once empty, unique, and in intimate relation with the world. This echoes the Buddhist metaphor of Indra's Net, where every being is like a mirror at each point in a vast dynamic web, reflecting and containing all the other points. How can we be simultaneously a distinctive point and the center of a world? We do not know, but we are. It is so. Is this subjective? Is it objective? Both? Neither? Is it transitional experience? Probably closest to the last of these, it is not adequately captured by any category. As Bion wrote, it must be "been."

The Buddha was not a god but a man, and the truths he lived and taught were not esoteric and abstract. He told inquirers, "Don't take my word for it, don't take it on faith; go have a look for yourself." In this spirit, let us examine the conditions that facilitate the emergence of truth and the ethical dimension in psychotherapy and at the heart of our lives.

The Therapist's Presence

The attentional activity I am describing requires something akin to one's complete presence or, if you will, being. Paradoxically, this depends on what Keats (1817) calls "negative capability"—less is more. It draws on unconscious emotional communication and makes use of, but is not equivalent to, projective identification. It is less intrusive, destructive, and controlling than the variant so well described by Melanie Klein and more like the communicative version described by Bion. Yet, it cannot occur, I believe, between two discrete "containers" into and out of which various contents are passed. D. W. Winnicott's notion of intermediate or potential space, the overlapping of two play areas, is closer, but these terms can give a misleadingly abstract and "spacy" impression.

Rilke wrote:

> Someone who is ready for everything, who doesn't exclude any experience, even the most incomprehensible, will *sound the depths* [italics added] of his own being.

Taking a sounding—resonating with self, other, with life itself—is not simply empathy or containment. It has a discerning, fathoming quality that helps us *know* more profoundly and truly. It brings a breath of freedom. It involves two bodies, two brains. Reverie is a resonating process. The mother, using all channels, knows the infant's state within the matrix of her entire being. Her intuitive responses co-arise with, and are not separate from, this knowledge. A living, vibrating emotional field takes shape. Not unlike Indra's Net, this field of emotional interconnection stimulates the growth of neural connections in the brain essential for affective life and creative thinking. In Zen, we speak of something akin, a "formless field of benefaction."

Jeremy

Jeremy is a patient who was so fragmented and plagued by dread that he could not speak of what troubled him. It was palpable. Without conscious aim, I found myself settling

deeply, trying to find my breath, and focusing on this splin-
tering feeling of growing terror inhabiting my body. Very
slowly, it began to melt away, and I found a deep breath and
began to relax. I glanced over at Jeremy and, remarkably, he
looked at me as if he, too, knew that something unusual had
happened. His face, expression, and affect had shifted and the
dread and fragmentation had eased. Not a word had been
exchanged. In time he began to find words to describe his
experience.

I began to realize that things like this happen not infrequently. I am
reminded here again of Marion Milner's paper, "The Concentration of
the Body," and her book, *The Hands of the Living God*. Milner describes
how she experimented with attending meditatively to her bodily sensations while doing analysis with certain patients. She found that, with
these patients, classical interpretations sometimes were not useful.
Rather, an inner focus on her own breath and physiological states, while
simultaneously maintaining contact with the patient, seemed to help
these patients develop the capacity to fathom their internal realities and
eventually make use of symbols and words to represent and communicate them.

Such experiences are not tricks; they flesh out the meaning of the term
holding environment. Patients in analysis often come to the point where
they feel faced with the prospect of placing themselves in the analyst's
hands. "Am I in good hands?" they ask, with varying degrees of anxiety.
Fonagy and his coworkers identify a critical component of children's
capacity to "think." It has to do with developing an internal image of an
attentive "other" who holds the child in mind as someone with an internal world. But, development is not only mental, as Freud reminds us
when he writes that the first "I" feelings were of a bodily I. The first contact the infant has is with mother's unconscious via her internal chemis-
try, sounds, and smells and, later, after birth, the quality of her touch.

We may not physically touch our patients, but emotionally we do—in
the way we "hold" them, not only in our minds but also in our bodily
attentiveness. *Kokoro* is a Japanese word for "mind" that means "heart-
mind." I think we read, know, and hold our patients with an embodied

heart-mind. We do not provide emotionally and then know, contain, and interpret: It is one movement.

I think this activity promotes the emergence and the transformative potential of truth. We become like primal objects, the fundamental elements of life itself: earth, water, fire, and air. If one's heart-mind is an ocean, then sounds, words, and feelings will resound deeply and freely. If one's heart-mind is like fertile earth, then seeds take root and grow, differently. The patient recognizes and responds to such a climate, but often cannot accept or make use of it. While we work toward recognizing, symbolizing, and expressing in words our internal experience of the inter-subjective process that is psychoanalysis, silence itself can be a catalyst.

Attentiveness and Ethics

In Buddhism, dhyana and sila—attentive practice and awakened ethical activity, respectively—inter-are. In psychotherapy, receptive and responsive attentiveness to conscious, preconscious, and unconscious experience is not an isolated skill that exists in a vacuum. Intrinsic to it, I suggest, is an inner "turning toward" truth that is simultaneously an act of giving, a letting in of the other. This act implies becoming aware of and turning away or detaching from narrow, protective, unconscious self-structures. In our attempts to survive, to not know painful truths, our "solutions" create their own problems and, in some cases, can become malevolent. Freedom to know ourselves in action co-arises with an ethical turning. In this section, I examine the relationship of attentiveness and ethics.

Neville Symington posits that, in response to trauma, the infant either chooses or repudiates an internal object that the infant names "the lifegiver." In choosing the lifegiver, the infant creates it and, with it, a source of creative emotional life. In repudiating it, the infant unconsciously identifies with fragmented aspects of traumatizing situations and people and encloses him- or herself in a narcissistic envelope, much like an autistic encapsulate. This choice is akin, although not identical, to D. W. Winnicott's description of a precocious constellation of a false self and Bick's concept of a tough "second skin." Symington calls repudiation the narcissistic option and sees it as the crux of much psychological disturbance. He does not subscribe to the notion of good or healthy narcissism and bad or destructive narcissism, most eloquently put forth by Otto Kernberg. Rather the narcissistic option is set in contradistinction to the creative, life-giving, truth-affirming internal choice.

Repudiating the lifegiver is rooted, Symington says, in anxiety about the devastating potential of psychic pain. In describing this process, he is valuing the capacity to tolerate frustration. Attributing intentionality to the infant, Symington emphasizes the unconscious dimension of this choice and speaks of evading or turning away from. This formulation does not neglect the role of the emotional surround in the etiology of trauma; rather, it speaks to the infant's participation in his unfolding development. What we make with the cards we are dealt—psychic responsibility—begins, according to these thinkers, earlier than we might think. When we decide to turn away from pain, we may turn away from life as well. While this can be reactive and survival driven, the protective structures we develop take on a life of their own. They can become quite obstructive, even malevolent, forces to be reckoned with.

I have been impressed by the frequency and power of patients' reactions, not only to my mistakes—ineffective provision or inadequate interventions—but also to the good interpretation or the containing presence—for example, when something I say or the way I am strikes a deep chord and touches them. I do not subscribe to the Kleinian theory of constitutional destructiveness and envy, although I recognize their presence and power in part as by-products of the kind of repudiative unconscious choice I am speaking about. Neither do I think humans are innately good. Rather, we are intrinsically capable of good and evil, but neither is written in. The choice of the life-giving other creates a space inside for an other to exist. The obverse of narcissism is not an arbitrarily mandated "reality" to which we passively resign ourselves, but the creative source itself, with all its thrills and agonies. Let me give a few examples.

Trying to fathom what might be going on with a patient who I sense is dissembling, I make a comment that strikes a chord. He is moved to tears. Automatically, he changes the subject or "goes away." I point this out. Gradually, painstakingly, he becomes able to report some of his actual internal reactions. I notice the words he uses: "I can't give you that much"; "I can't give you credit."

We hear it in ordinary language. A host to a show invites the audience to "Give it up for" the performer the host is introducing, meaning "Let's recognize and welcome the performer." There are variations: "giving in" or submitting; "giving up" or relinquishing; and of course, "giving over to" or surrendering. In Buddhism, *Dana*, or giving, is one of the *Paramitas*, or perfections. The word *integrity* implies wholeness and, simultaneously, ethical fortitude. The French expression for becoming aware of something in a profound and immediate way—*prendre conscience*—literally means taking hold of conscience. I think there is an act of conscience implicit in understanding—"becoming 'conscious of'"—that relates to assuming responsibility for our psychic lives.

This process involves giving up and giving. In a sense, it is relinquishing omnipotent control of the object, according it autonomy, and therefore accepting that it has something to offer—a considerable developmental achievement, needing to be continually remade, like fresh bread. Grotstein says, "We are what we have done [in fantasy] to the object," which implies that we can derive from the object only that which we accord it. Such an object, freed to be, can have a place as an other in our inner world, rather than, let us say, adhesively pasted on, addictively amalgamated, or automatically split off. Of course, it might not follow my wishes or respond to my needs, might let me down, or drop me. Truth is a key and often overlooked ingredient in the development of a sense of safety, trust, and therapeutic alliance. Nonetheless, this "setting free" still engenders profound anxiety. No doubt the surround plays a key part, but so does the patient.

Our intrinsic roots in "mutuality and dialogue," as René Spitz calls them, hinge on this unconscious choice. Attendant on this leap into unknown waters is the capacity to mine life's psychic riches, in contrast to walking through minefields; to play in the gap rather than plastering over gaping holes; to creatively "space out" rather than falling forever through the cracks into bottomless space. Freedom to free associate implies freedom to be deeply "associated" with our psychic sources, to recognize and take pleasure in intrinsic "associatedness."

Carla

Carla is a bright, attractive, cooperative patient who is being seen at a low fee. She accrues a large bill. We explore some of the dynamics and meanings involved. Is she inducing in me the experience of deprivation and helplessness that she experienced with her mother? As I wrestle with and learn about this firsthand, an internal shift occurs, which I do not fully understand, but which I recognize as I bring up the issue in a new way for our mutual consideration. As we explore her reaction to my beginning to speak differently, it seems that she recognizes what has been going on and that I have become more able to deal with it. Unconscious material seems to show, and through the interpretive dialogue she says that she perceives me as more capable than she is (and was) of dealing with this dilemma constructively—not just as having this capacity, but using it. She seems to begrudge me this learned capacity. She conveys that I should remain as helpless as she feels and not cope better than she does. She wants to make me and her internal others pay. She cannot "give me this"—not payment of the outstanding bill, but the fact that I somehow found a "solution" more in accord than she, for the time being, can. This "good" patient is bitter and envious, and she tries to spoil the analysis. Spite predominates.

Later, Carla confides that she sits dreamily with her new baby in the waiting room after the hour has ended, not only looking to see who else comes to meet with me but also taking in from afar, through "osmosis," something generative from me. It terrifies her to let this happen in the consulting room and unfortunately in her life as well. She does not want to "take anything from me which she hasn't put there herself."

Martin Continued

Now back to Martin—in one sense far more difficult to work with since he enacts extremely obstructive transferences—who reacts differently to the dilemma in question. After many rounds of exploring and interpreting his cutting me off, I spontaneously say "My turn," as he begins his interruption. He is shocked, baffled. Then he laughs. Gradually, he becomes able to play with it. Sometimes he jousts, "No, my turn!" I laugh and continue. When he interrupts or obstructs, I repeat quietly but firmly, "My turn now." And, usually he gives me my say. Turning toward the lifegiver, he gives me my turn, my place. A tyrannical toddler, he is learning to take turns. The word "illusion" comes from the Latin *ludere*, to play. Truth and illusion interpenetrate: The play of illusion needs truth as a marker; illusional play leads to realization of deeper truths; these truths, as capacities, in turn inspire creative uses of illusion.

I went through months wrestling with this, many cycles of getting lost and confused, thinking I saw some clarity, struggling some more and getting lost again. My response arose spontaneously and was not defensive, although I was preserving myself and the therapy. Martin sensed a shift, which must have reflected an inner movement in him and between us as well. Perhaps, we had each freed ourselves through a shift in truth. My statement and the playful new learning it set in motion followed naturally the breakthrough that had already happened.

In another example, Martin takes a tissue, cleans his glasses, and throws the tissue some distance into the wastebasket. He repeats this periodically. Many meanings of this activity develop, some we come around to, some not. Among them were that he is breaking the flow of the session, distracting us, dissipating a painful or potentially painful moment, peeing into the basket and on our work, and playing at being Michael Jordan, "scoring" and having me adore his prowess. Once, after I remembered that I had, earlier in our work, cleaned my own glasses as he entered the consulting room, I saw that he was also identifying with me as being more interested in my clean glasses than in "giving it up for him" as he entered, and that he was giving me a taste of my own medicine.

This activity continued despite our exploring it and my interpreting. If he missed his "shot," he usually would get up, pick up the tissue, and place it in the basket. Once, he left it on the floor during the session and picked it up and deposited it as he left. He did this again another day. Then, one day he did not pick up the tissue either upon missing the basket or as he exited the office. I felt rather soiled. The next time this happened, as he was getting ready to open the door to leave, I found myself saying, "It's okay for you to shit on my floor, but it's not okay not to clean it up." He laughed in recognition, turned back, picked up the tissue, placed it in the basket, and left, shaking his head. I was not trying to be provocative; it turned out that the exchange was evocative.

Martin's reactions to my comments showed, I believe, that he was relieved that I responded as I did. How would I handle what he called being "truncated?" How would I manage feeling shit on, having my face rubbed in it, and having no help sorting through and making sense of it—like his childhood experience of various early traumata? In some such instances, he surprisingly did not begrudge me the fact that I could survive, save myself, and navigate these straits. He let me know that it was meaningful to him and seemed to take in this capacity to some degree. He responded to my comment about the tissues by saying, "I'll give you this much, you stood up." Several months of intense and dense material regarding anality followed. During what was, in one sense, a "pissing contest," Martin was also learning to "give a shit" and, through this, to "give and take."

Paul

Paul, a recovering addict, cannot let anyone get close or help him. He offloads emotions. Bit by bit, year by year, he discloses additional addictive behaviors, like compulsive stealing and womanizing, episodes during which he feels completely entitled, vengefully self-righteous, and entirely without guilt or conscience. These disclosures bring in their wake the most intense shame. I begin to see that in such states others are eradicated, as are the effects of his actions. He painfully comes to see how self-centered he has been, and for the first time, he cries as he begins to fathom some of the damage he has done. For each step he excruciatingly takes toward letting me in, toward letting himself experience the truth of his own emotions and actions and becoming a subject responsible for them, in inverse proportion he fights, every step of the way, terrified of being controlled, of losing control, of acknowledging warm, loving feelings and needful longings. Exquisitely wary, he wants to terminate at a most vulnerable, exposed point. Somehow, we are able to work through the anxieties, and he continues on.

After five years of intensive therapy, we agree to terminate. As we wind down, Paul says, "I will miss you." This carries a shocking authenticity. I feel the milk of human kindness rise in my breast and feel genuinely warm toward him. In our final session, I am stunned when he gives me a book, *Tuesdays with Morrie*. The subtitle is, *An Old Man, a Young Man, and Life's Greatest Lesson*. The lesson, it turns out, is saying goodbye. But, before he gives me the book, a visible giving that has impact only in that it embodies a not-visible, true inner giving, he hands me a card. The title, on top in gothic print, which looks like a headline from an old newspaper, reads "Laugh in Time." The caption just below is, "Lottery Winner says: It will not change my life." Below this, taking up most of the card's cover, is the picture of a dour, hard-looking peasant woman, clad in black with white babushka and apron, standing in the doorway of her simple dwelling.

For an instant I see his alcoholic, traumatizing, foreign-born mother and his identification with her. I laugh aloud. It is a wonderful gift, a stunning admission. He joins in, and we share a long, heartfelt laugh. After a while, he says, "That's not me, that's what I was." I know this is only half true. What is most dear to me is his simultaneous recognition and expression of what he received, along with his consciously disavowed admission of the ongoing struggle to let change be, to give me that, to give himself that. That was the real gift.

Challenges in Embodying Zen Realization

In Zen practice, we vow to "save all beings."[5] Save here connotes protecting and nourishing as well as helping liberate. It does not imply converting or proselytizing. From the beginning, "all beings by nature are Buddha." The Dalai Lama told a group of Western Buddhist teachers, "When you speak about helping, it sounds a bit like a one-way street, you helping others. In Tibetan the word 'compassion' has no direction, it is omni-directional." So, compassion includes myself, the agent of compassion, a point in the multicentered Net of Indra. Consider this from Robert Aitken:

A friend once inquired if Gandhi's aim in settling in the village and serving the villagers as best he could were purely humanitarian. Gandhi replied, "I am here to serve no one else but myself, to find my own self-realization through the service of these village folk."

In the Introduction to this book, I write about the Bodhisattva ideal:

I used to believe the conventional wisdom that bodhisattvas forswore their own complete enlightenment until all beings were free. . . . now I see it is a mistaken belief. Someone who sees deeply, in this very moment, that his own happiness develops in concert with the happiness and liberation of others—and whose actions arise from the ground of this realization—such a person is an awakening being, a bodhisattva. As the other blossoms, I blossom and find joy. As I deepen, the other benefits.

However, there have been many instances over the past thirty years when Zen teachers' conduct has not benefited and even harmed others. While at Tassajara Monastery in 1983, I noticed some curious social goings-on unrelated to the seminar I was attending with Thich Nhat Hanh. I was not surprised when a scandal regarding boundary violations and abuses of power on the part of the monastery's then-Abbot soon erupted into public knowledge. It rocked the San Francisco Zen Center and spawned some useful self-examination in the Zen community. Examples of similar boundary violations emerged in other Zen lineages, in other spiritual traditions, and recently within the Catholic

Church. Similar misconduct on the part of psychotherapists is, of course, unfortunately not uncommon: Sometimes skilled, humane, beloved teachers, supervisors, and therapists violate the basic trust of their healing craft. Years later, similar issues visited our own Zen lineage when concerns surfaced regarding a fellow teacher, which were categorically denied. A panel composed of some of the most experienced Buddhist teachers, from outside the lineage—several of whom were also experienced psychotherapists—was convened. In the face of a direct personal accounting of violations, the denials continued. Some of those looking into the matter were shocked. Their astonishment and dismay made me even more curious about the disjuncture between practice and insight, practice and conduct (or character). Why would it, why should it be such a jolt, especially to the therapists among them? Some were friends of the individual, and that contributed to the difficulty. If even experienced, deeply respected, clinically experienced Buddhist teachers were surprised, then perhaps we were all missing something.

The reasons since given for this alleged and other acknowledged boundary violations, run the gamut: lack of awareness of sex and power issues, unexamined early trauma, psychological problems such as undiagnosed depression, and attachment and personality disorders such as malignant narcissism. We could add an undeveloped, distorted, or perverted ethical sense, sociopathy, compartmentalization, and dissociated functioning to the list, and it still would not be complete. These examples of Zen teachers' misconduct, and the pain they generated, have spurred me to examine the scope of Buddhist practice, realization, and awakened conduct and lay the groundwork for an integral narrative of liberation drawing from the "gold" of Zen and psychotherapy alike. I see boundary violations and teacher misconduct as subsets, and perhaps symptomatic, of a more elusive and extensive disconnect.

This disconnect manifests often in relationships, especially group and organizational settings. In one Zen tradition, teachers were gathered with the founding senior teacher of the lineage; the senior teacher was preparing to retire. "There will be no pope," he said. That meant no single successor to the head of the tradition and no hierarchy, as is often the case, but rather a loose affiliation of teachers and centers. The meeting proceeded, and although there was some conflict between two teachers, it seemed thoroughly resolved in the context of a good group discussion.

All ended apparently well. Within days, schisms erupted, threatening to fragment the group. That there would be no pope did not keep there from being a battle for overall succession, although nobody saw or acknowledged the dynamic at play.

During a conversation with the head of a respected monastic lineage about personal and emotional issues in Buddhist practice, I mentioned humorously that in contrast to lay Buddhist traditions where members are mixing it up in the nitty-gritty of day-to-day work and family obligations and pressures, the monks and nuns at the monastery might not be as subject to roiling interpersonal and emotional issues. His long, full-bellied, and rollicking laugh pierced the quiet of the meditation center where we were meeting, and he replied, "We live in a Petri dish. The interpersonal strains are even greater!" He went on to discuss how monastery residents had benefited from consultation with a group therapist to try to address some strained relationships. In our own lineage, as well, we experimented for a time with group discussion meetings in the 1970s and brought in a therapist to consult with us. Although useful for a while, it did not become part of our culture and did not prevent various painful and disturbing conflicts and schisms. Coincidentally, psychotherapists too are coming to see how subject they are to unconscious emotions, how these can undermine the learning in various settings, including psychoanalytic training programs. More attention is now being given to group process. But, I think the early Zen experiments and the new institutional ones for those in psychoanalytic training, while useful, do not go deep enough. They may also be, in one sense, a way to "do something" without fully grokking just how impactful our unconscious emotional activity can actually be.

After nearly forty years in both fields, I believe that Buddhists can benefit greatly from understanding *unconscious* emotional communication in the relational field. I think this is the key element, the "gold," that psychotherapy brings to the partnership with Zen. In contemporary Western Buddhism, we are now quite aware of emotions, and Theravada and Vajrayana schools have honed methods for working with afflictive or destructive emotions. We have read about emotional intelligence and social intelligence and have become aware of the need to address interpersonal stresses and strains, harnessing nonviolent communicational methods. In some contemporary Zen teachings, becoming aware of and working with emotions as they arise in the body, as well as the tendency to avert from and cling to certain emotional experiences, form the very core of the practice. In one such tradition, the founding teacher broke from traditional emphases on *kensho* to teach precise in-the-moment awareness of shifting emotional and self-states and how our predilection for, even cultivation of, the very ones we claim to want to be liberated from cause us further suffering. Yet, recently there was a schism in this lineage triggered by the founding teacher removing one or more respected teachers' permissions to teach, something that was "out of character" for her and caused widespread distress in the community.

In another case, a highly respected teacher known for teachings on peace and reconciliation apparently seemed to also act out of character and out of alignment with his own teaching when his representatives abruptly and unilaterally disempowered the group of helpers and teachers that had helped spread the teachings far and wide. These eruptions of interpersonal and group anguish are not the result of poltergeist, bad karma, or a dybbuk but rather unconscious and unacknowledged emotional forces at play among people.

Zen teachers are human, and we might say that these accounts demonstrate the obvious. It has also been argued that students overidealize their teachers and need to get real. However, I think the ideal of alignment of dhyana, prajna, and sila as a core element of Zen practice remains a worthwhile one—not perfection but harmony, integrity, and acting in accord with circumstances, especially turbulent ones, for the benefit of all. Zen and other Buddhist teachers and religious leaders ideally walk the talk, embodying their own ideals. They teach by example without trying to be role models. Ideally, their practice distills into their living, as does their insight. Their teaching is their life, their presence, and the quality of their day-to-day interactions with students and all beings. So, these disjunctures, which continue despite the considerable influence of Western psychology, have convinced me that these are not simply isolated instances of misbehavior in a new cultural setting. There is a piece missing in the underlying narrative, myth, and process. I think Western culture, with its psychological bent, can make a real and needed contribution, without risk of throwing out the proverbial baby with the bathwater.

This reminds me of Krishnamurti's response to philosopher Jacob Needleman, who, while interviewing Krishnamurti, was needling him to get the scoop on his enlightenment experiences. After several minutes of deferring, Krishnamurti finally blurted out, "Sir! First be good, then be wise." This had a profound impact on me when I first listened to it on tape in my room adjacent to the Peahi Nursery School in 1973. That Krishnamurti himself was human and unable to live this ethical teaching himself I learned from Radha Rajagoal Sloss in her book, *Lives in the Shadows with J. Krishnamurti*, which details in a balanced and thoughtful way in the context of his life, the disjunctures between his deep insight and teachings and his conduct. There is a Yiddish saying—*"Zi ken nicht zein zi eigene hoiche,"* which means "You can't see your own hunchback." Maybe it is like the title of the rhythm-and-blues song, "Blinded by the Light." We may think that, by virtue of being a nondual experience, enlightenment shines the "light," dispelling darkness forever. And, indeed, it seems to, especially since in *kensho* there is no past, present, or future. Perhaps, in "translation"—the transition back to conventional living—illumination does, indeed, by its very nature cast a shadow that, again, by nature we are unaware of it. One meaning of the word *dukkha*, or suffering in Sanskrit (and the First Noble Truth of Buddhism: "There is suffering"), is being "out of joint" or out of alignment. Unconscious emotional communication in the relational field can cast "a ray of darkness" that helps dispel "the light" that can throw us "out of joint" and generate suffering.

An example of putting an emancipatory experience and teaching at the service of something else occurred at a meeting of Zen teachers when the group was discussing ethics and ethical boundary crossings and violations. A teacher who is also a psychotherapist said, "Precepts are just guidelines, they are not rules. You can never predict, you never know what the real situation is." He went on for a time like this. In one sense, it made me think of the teaching of a Korean master on "don't know mind": "Only don't know, just go straight, only don't know!" But it also made me uncomfortable. I felt that he was conflating a deep truth of Zen, psychotherapy, and living with ethical relativism, implying that maybe, in some conditions, it is okay to violate boundaries. As I listened, it seemed like he was also conveying that he was above the law, not subject to the same ethical boundaries as others. He was in a stream of

Zen whose founder has been associated with boundary violations over the years, and I should not have been surprised, but I was. Maybe it was because he was a therapist. There is a crucial developmental achievement implied in a mature not-knowing—a "no-ing" that prevents it from collapsing into anything goes. The "no" was in the wrong place; instead of this implied developmental "no," there was a defiant refusal to accept a boundary and, with it, limitation and difference. "No" provides safe, containing relational conditions that are the crucible of transformation. I felt that this teacher needed to learn "the power of 'no'" rather than a distorted, relativistic "now." No means no, but not when buttressed by this disavowal of boundaries based on a perversion of not-knowing and of the spontaneity of Zen.

Change of Heart

The psychotherapeutic process and Zen practice each offer an opportunity for an ethical "turning" or change of heart for both therapist and patient. Symington once said to me that there was a difference between being selfish and self-centered. This was a kind of psychoanalytic koan for me for years; I could not fathom it. In retrospect, I guess it had to be "been." One day, all of a sudden, it dawned on me. Of course: selfish, like elfish or reddish. Not just "like" an elf or the color red, but expressing elfness and redness—*being* it. Expressive of self, true self-ish. One does not keep one's attributes all to oneself, but lives them expressively, thus giving them to others. One gives of oneself, "gives it up." Self-centeredness is indeed in stark contrast to this. This must have reflected an internal shift in which the perceived dichotomy between being myself and being in touch with others fell away—ephemeral and needing integration, to be sure—nonetheless, this was a freeing change.

Truth is not something we can attain or patch on. It is something we realize with a start, as if we had always known it, as our self-protective delusions fall away as we give them up. Turning toward truth, not just absolute truth but also emotional truth about ourselves and our relationships with others, can "rock our world" and reveal hidden self-deception. Marion Milner, painter, British Independent psychoanalyst, and "natural mystic," writes:

Until you have, once at least, faced everything you know—
the whole universe—with utter giving in, and let all that is "not
you" flow over and engulf you, there can be no lasting sense of security. Only by being prepared to accept annihilation can one escape
from that spiritual "abiding alone" which is in fact the truly death-
like state.

While painful, it is also liberating and brings a certain joy. This joy
asks of us "not less than everything," as T. S. Eliot writes. It is the gift
inherent in the sacrificial yet enjoyable attentiveness of the psychotherapist. It is this ongoing engaged relinquishment and the empty but fertile
ground charged with potential that is its source that provides the corrective to the therapist (or Zen teacher) who might impose his own problems and agendas on the patient through forced "neutrality," opaqueness,
or self-conscious and often anxiety-driven "self-disclosure."

Stephen Applebaum's words echo my thoughts:

> The heart of the ability to be evocative is heart. You have to be, not
> act to be. To care to engage one's feelings with those of another, to
> enter one's experiential world, to face the frightening warding off
> with determination and skill—all these are acts of love, and are
> experienced as such by the patient.

Acts of love co-arise with gestures of truth. As my patient Martin
helped me see, they pass from "giving a shit," to giving of oneself in creative abandon from the spacious ground of intrinsic affinity. Embodying this capacity is perhaps the most profound and elusive freedom of
all. It opens the door to "the dearest freshness deep down things."

Chapter 7, "The Bliss Body and the Unconscious," pulls together the
main themes of the book and examines the "golds" of each path, their
alchemy, and how they contribute to an integrative narrative of
liberation.

The Bliss Body and the Unconscious

Freud thinks that we have been dealt "severe blows to human self-love" by three revolutions in human thought. First, Copernicus discovered that the earth is not the center of the universe, and neither is man. Then, Darwin showed that humans are subject to the same laws as microorganisms, so we are not so special after all. Finally, Freud's elaboration of the unconscious added insult to injury by demonstrating that we are not in control of even our own self-experience. "The ego," he writes, "is not master in its own house." And what about the Buddha? He invites us to discover that our house is not what we thought, that what and whom we take as real may be a case of mistaken identity. We may be more vast and more interconnected than we ever imagined—and less substantial.

Buddhists tend to cringe when they hear about the unconscious. I ran the possible title of this chapter by a longtime friend, Buddhist teacher, and psychotherapist whom I respect deeply. Her response was, "I like the bliss body part." It made me laugh, and when she asked why I was laughing, her question reinforced why I was writing the book. Perhaps, it confirmed Freud's "not master in our own house" hypothesis. Another Buddhist teacher friend, a fellow basketball fan, finds it easy to speak about Michael Jordan or other superstars being "unconscious" or "in the zone" during a game, but he also refers to moments of being unreflective as being "unconscious." On the other hand, psychoanalysts have been known to speak of "getting unconscious together" when describing a supervision group in which the dynamics of a case are explored in the context of the shared reverie of group members. Grotstein suggests that we "cast a ray of darkness" into perplexing clinical material because attempts to consciously understand sometimes yield only predictable formulations of limited value. Both not-knowing and becoming aware of not knowing have value. Bion urges clinicians to listen without memory, desire, or attachment, to welcome the selected fact of a session in a way that lets it rise to the surface. Of course, there is an interplay between not knowing and knowing, translating the fruits of reverie into metaphor and usable, eventually verbal, form. In common parlance, we speak of becoming more "conscious" or aware about a particular automatic behavior or habit, and Freud writes about making the unconscious conscious.

I have come to believe that Buddhist meditators tend to overprivilege conscious introspection, and for that matter consciousness. They think the unconscious is still just the id, the repository of forbidden sexual and aggressive wishes that reduces humans to a bundle of blind impulses. It gets under their skin. I do not think most appreciate just how far the unconscious has come. That is not to say that Buddhists do not repress sexual and aggressive urges—of course we do. Ideally, we sublimate and channel these urges, and when we do give them expression, we try to do so in a creative and life-giving way, rather than inducing misery in ourselves or others. But, then again, we are human, and thoughts of sexuality and aggression can frequently engross and sometimes capture us as we practice attentiveness on the cushion or when we reveal ourselves in the course of psychotherapy. But, in recent decades, a great deal more has come to light about what the unconscious is and how it works. I briefly summarize a few ways to think about unconscious experience, describe what I mean by "the Bliss Body," and then explore how their alchemy might lead us toward a more integrated view of human experience.

Unconscious Experience

Freud's dynamic unconscious is characterized by sexual and aggressive bodily based drives, primary process thinking, and conflict and repression. The therapeutic focus of many in the United States who ascribe to this view is on interpreting defenses, resistances, and wishes. Klein's view is anchored in bodily based fantasies that drive a series of intersecting internalized object relations. Splitting, rather than repression, is privileged, and the analyst focuses on the patient's leading anxiety about these internalized object relations and interprets it in the transference in order to develop the patient's awareness of split-off parts of the personality and foster reparation and reintegration so healthy parts of the personality can grow. Bion's view is radical within psychoanalysis and in some ways akin to Zen. For him, the basic ground of psychoanalytic therapy is not the unconscious at all but rather infinity. Instead of focusing on repressed or split-off content, he emphasizes containing and metabolizing function necessary to transform raw sensory input into materials to be stored and worked over so they could be thought, felt, and dreamed. The therapeutic task is not to listen for derivatives of unconscious conflict or split off parts of the personality but to listen unsnagged by memory or desire or theory.

The Chilean psychoanalyst Ignacio Matte Blanco is concerned that psychoanalysis is "wandering away from itself" and tries, through his innovative formulations about an unconscious not founded on repression, to recover the essentials of Freud's contribution and extend them. Building on Freud's primary and secondary processes, Matte Blanco describes an unrepressed unconscious characterized by two kinds of propositions or types of logic: asymmetric and symmetric. Later, he writes of these modes as thinking and feeling and adds a third—being. Here, Matte Blanco uses an allegory to describe the ubiquitous activity of the unconscious. He remembers the story of a man who enters a bar and begins to walk up the vertical wall, arriving at the ceiling. He walks along it, head down, and asks for a whisky mixed with beer. People are astonished. When he finishes drinking, he pays and repeats the same journey in the opposite direction. When he leaves and closes the door, someone observes, "What a strange man, to drink whiskey mixed with beer!" Unconscious activity is so much a part of our life, we tend to miss it. It is like a fish asking what water is or where the sea is. As Matte Blanco expanded his view of the unrepressed unconscious to include our very *being*, Rodney Bomford, retired Anglican cannon, mathematician, and Matte Blanco scholar, makes a case in his book, *The Symmetry of God*, for the unconscious itself being a close equivalent of what we consider the sacred.

Bollas describes an unrepressed unconscious that he calls the "unthought known" and an emotional field so interconnected that it is the analyst who sometimes receives the patient's free associations before the patient is aware of them. His notion of self-experience, most of it unconscious, is intrinsically interactive with "objects" in the outside world. We each, he writes, have our own distinctive idiom, a personal and aesthetic signature that pre-dates the environmental influences in our upbringing. We seek, again unconsciously, external objects and interactions that will release this personal idiom. A simple example might be how one child is drawn early on to sounds and then to musical instruments and conducting, while another cannot get enough of throwing balls, then street games, and goes on to professional sports. Building on the Freudian concepts of condensation and displacement, Bollas describes how unconscious experience collects and comes together not only in our sleeping dreams, but also in our waking life in powerful moments of psychic intensity, powerful felt senses that are multiply determined and full of possible meanings. By freely associating to these experienced intensities, we crack them up, and their meanings are disseminated into the interpersonal and cultural commons to seed further condensing and dreaming. More recently, Bollas has spoken about how, when he listens to the unconscious, certain words or phrases or intonations may strike him while he is in a receptive state. Those moments can indicate unconscious emotional communication between him and his patient. Simply "echoing" the word or phrase can often spark a fruitful exchange if what struck a chord in Bollas did indeed represent unconscious communication.

Psychoanalysis has evolved from a one-person psychology to a two-person psychology; today, some at the frontier of research and practice find that a living systems perspective best describes the psychotherapeutic process. So, in addition to the differences between the repressed unconscious and the unrepressed unconscious, there are differences in perspective between an individually oriented unconscious that describes the singular psyche and an intersubjective unconscious, which has more affinity with unconscious emotional experience in the relational field.

Psychoanalytic thinkers describe unconscious emotional communication differently depending on their working theory about basic human connectedness and separateness. I remember a seasoned psychoanalyst I liked who supervised a group of supervisors. He had an ego psychological orientation, and he would speak about externalization rather than projection and projective identification; it blurred the boundaries of the self too much for his taste. Others like Green and Ogden write about a third area of experience created between patient and analyst, in which we can "catch the drift" of cocreated unconscious experience. This concept builds on and extends D. W. Winnicott's notion of a transitional or intermediate area of experience as well as Freud's preconscious. Freud wrote early in his career that we do indeed communicate unconsciously, and directly, without conscious mediation, but he did not follow up on this idea. Schore, with his groundbreaking neuroanalytic research documenting the extensive work on right-brain-to-right-brain communication and regulation of affective states, intriguingly develops, extends, and perhaps confirms Freud's idea. From another angle, Lisby Mayer's book, *Extraordinary Knowing*, also pursues this idea and explores how much we know, often quite accurately, about people, places, and things without knowing how we know it. The book *Blink* by Malcolm Gladwell popularizes just how much of our daily information processing and decision making is accomplished outside awareness, often with uncanny efficiency and insight. And, from cognitive neuroscience and other fields has come the idea of implicit or procedural experience and memory. These terms refer to both nonconscious and nonverbal experiences of repeated and mutually engaged interactional patterns. In the final phase of writing this book, a colleague, reading the manuscript, found herself associating to an intriguing formulation of Ferro, an Italian psychoanalyst. Ferro views the unconscious that emerges in an analytic session as a continually transforming, cocreated holographic field consisting of "characters" whose cultivation by the analytic pair grows the capacities to think, feel, and dream. Developing these capacities takes precedence over focusing on dynamic content. Each statement, each action of the patient or psychotherapist is heard as an expression of the shifting resonances of the emotional field, which itself seeks representation. I am in turn reminded of the *gatha*, or verse, we recite when we put on the *okesa*, the biblike garment that represents the Buddha's robe, which we sew ourselves as we study and prepare to accept the sixteen precepts[6] in our lineage in the ceremony called *Jukai*: I wear the robe of liberation / the formless field of benefaction / the Tathagata's true teaching / Save the many beings.

This rather dry summary of course does not include all the approaches to the unconscious or convey the excitement in this multidisciplinary endeavor to plumb our psychic depths. I was once wondering why I liked the Bourne film series. Then, one day I slowly pronounced the protagonist's name, Jason Bourne. This time, "J Son Born" is what I heard, and it had great impact. Although language is only one way the unconscious expresses itself, here is another similar example, involving two people: A patient was speaking about someone and could not remember if the person's name was Irene or Ilene. She went back and forth about it. I listened for some time. Then, a light went off, and I slowly said to my occasionally rather concrete patient (not to resolve her dilemma), "Ilene." *I lean* surfaced for us both to see, with all the overtones about frightening yet desired dependence. The unconscious surprises, informs, and amuses; it also shocks and destabilizes. It throws us off our (conscious) game and—although it is an element of our own psyche whose feedback we do well to attend to and integrate—it is, at the same time, "other." Unconscious experience is a force to be reckoned with. One moment, it can be a source of creativity, even wisdom, and in the next feel like a persecutor. Psychoanalysis did not invent the unconscious any more than the Buddha invented essential nature. They are two deep overlapping streams that cannot be grasped but are lived every moment.

In Chapter 6, "Knowing the Truth," I explained how clinical experience with a dissociative patient led me to view our communications as a process of unconscious interactive resonance. I think we are always impacting one another emotionally, moment to moment, in a shifting series of interpersonal configurations. Sometimes, we experience not only a fantasy about what the other's experience is but also a direct imprint of it. We may not know if it is ours or theirs, and we may interpret or ascribe our own incorrect meaning to it, but I believe emotional states can be transmitted directly, outside conscious awareness. Such intimacy is not always comfortable or beneficial. Bion writes that when we meet someone there is an emotional storm. Stern spoke at a recent conference about initial connections involving being "captured" by the new emotional configuration, and Symington wrote earlier in his career about a kind of corporation that is formed when two people meet. His article, "The Analyst's Act of Freedom," describes how he became aware of these forces in a therapeutic relationship and how his struggle to internally free himself had a liberating effect on the clinical work and eventually on his patient. I recalled recently that in 1983 in Plum Village Thich Nhat Hanh spoke about how important it was to keep our mind from being colonized by external elements such as hyperconsumerism as well as certain internal states of mind. I thought his choice of words was dramatic: "colonized." I was confident of meeting anything and tackling it head-on. Now, I appreciate the word and the teaching.

Part of psychotherapy involves coming to accept and appreciate and play in the fertile connectedness—conscious and unconscious—that links us and to use it to examine and remove obstacles to full aliveness. Many, however, find it difficult to accept that unconscious processes even exist, and only with great difficulty come to let them in, not to mention welcome them, as both resource and ally.

Here is an imaginative description by Edelman and Tononi that captures something of what happens when unconscious emotional communication in the relational field is working in an organizing and mutually enriching, rather than in a dysregulating, way:

> Imagine a peculiar string quartet in which each player responds by improvisation to ideas and cues of his or her own, as well as to all kinds of sensory cues in the environment. Since there is no score, each player would provide his or her characteristic tunes, but initially these various tunes would not be coordinated with those of the other players. Now imagine that the bodies of the players are connected to each other by myriad fine threads so their actions and movements are conveyed back and forth through signals of changing thread tensions that act simultaneously to time each player's actions. Signals that instantaneously connect the four players would lead to a correlation of the sounds; thus new, more cohesive, and more integrated sounds would emerge out of the otherwise independent efforts of each player.

Such intricate coordination, with no conductor, is quite akin to Buddhism. Physicist Michio Kaku speaks about resonance on another register:

> Matter is like tiny notes on tiny little vibrational strings. The laws of physics are the laws of harmony. When the strings bump into each other they create chemistry. Chemistry is the melodies played out on these strings. The universe is a symphony of strings. The mind of God that Einstein wrote about is cosmic music or resonance.

When dysregulated, the result is not sweet, spontaneous, harmonious communication (music) but rather more a painful cacophony or perhaps deadening silence. Notice how Edelman and Tononi's and Kaku's language fleshes out and adds dynamism to the metaphor of the Jeweled Net of Indra.

The Bliss Body

> Chao-chou asked Nan-ch'uan, "What is the Tao?" Nan-ch'uan said, "Ordinary Mind is the Tao."
> Chao-chou asked, "Should I try to direct myself toward it?"
> Nan-ch'uan said, "If you try to direct yourself you betray your own practice."
> Chao-chou asked, "How can I know the Tao if I don't direct myself?"
> Nan-ch'uan said, "The Tao is not subject to knowing or not knowing. Knowing is delusion; not knowing is blankness. If you truly reach the genuine Tao, you will find it as vast and boundless as outer space. How can this be discussed at the level of affirmation or negation?"
> With these words, Chao-chou had sudden realization.

What did Chao-chou realize? Consider this comment from Yasutani Rōshi:

> Bright, bright, clear, clear, naked and splendid.
> The great earth, mountains and rivers, the uncovered womb.

There are flowers and the moon—who is the Master!
Spring, Autumn, Winter, and Summer compete with new
    garb.

Here is the Bliss Body—suchness, the way things are, beyond dualistic construction. Intrinsic to it is the Jeweled Net of Indra, the seamless-
ness of singularity and interconnectedness that emerges vividly as we
slough off and relinquish self-preoccupation through focused meditation. If mutual affective resonance describes a central element of
psychoanalytic intersubjectivity, the Jeweled Net of Indra conveys our
fundamental existential interdependence. Emotions make us human
and are the stuff of human communication. Unconscious communication in the relational field puts human flesh on the filaments of Indra's
Net. In the psychotherapeutic register of connectedness, emotions are
the catalyst, the glue, and simultaneously the transmitter, the receiver,
and the "stuff" that is transmitted and received. The process is much
faster and more seamless than this unwieldy language conveys. Buddhists do well to learn about how instantaneous this process is, for it can
help us make sense of what otherwise seem like disconnected events:
eruptions of interpersonal anguish that tear asunder the *sangha*, out of
apparently peaceful circumstances.

For psychotherapists, patients, and others, the connections here are
not only emotional ones—which rise and fall, come and go—but also
fundamental representations of a container more vast than interpersonal relations, and without circumference, center, or diameter. In 1984,
during the last of his 14 two-week yearly visits to Maui, our Japanese
teacher, Yamada Rōshi, called senior students in one at a time for *dokusan*. He had usually been rather grandmotherly in dokusan with us, but
on this occasion it was a classical Zen "examination in the room." He
asked each of us, "What is the mind?" I responded, he challenged my
response, I responded again. We went back and forth, and I could not
gauge "where we were." Then, he asked me to ask him the same question,
"What is the mind?" I asked and waited. He gathered himself and
responded, "The mountains, the river and the great earth, the moon, the
sun, and the stars." Now, these were the words that served as the catalyst
for his own enlightenment experience decades earlier and had been
written up in *Three Pillars of Zen* as the experience of a Japanese

businessman. But, as he spoke, there was no there and then or here and now. There was no right and wrong response, good or bad student, or master for that matter, no feeling of confidence or inadequacy. He was presenting what we would call the bare essential fact of existence, and it echoed with a vastness that was palpable.

Thich Nhat Hanh is from Vietnam, the only country where Theravada and Mahayana traditions developed seamlessly in concert. As we have seen, he likes to speak about a piece of paper and how it owes its very being, its "paperness" to all things nonpaper: the sun, the earth, the rain, the lumberjack, the truck driver, and the paper factory employees. He looks at the piece of paper and sees that fundamentally there is no such thing as paper apart from its constituents. It is void of self-identity, yet we know and use it and its qualities. It is literally made up of non-paper elements. An experience such as Flora Courtois's awakening, described in Chapter 1, "Coming to Life," is not adequately captured on the interpersonal affectively embedded register alone.

Emotions in Context

Emotions are one constituent element of what makes us human. In Zen, we speak about the five *skandhas*, or bundles: form (body and breath), feeling (sensation), perception, mental reaction (formation), and consciousness. They interact and, moment to moment, come together in clustered arrangements to give us the experience that there is a "there there"—a solid person. Yet, moment to moment they are dissolving and rearranging themselves.

As with identity, emotions too can be deceiving. A Buddhist-inspired bumper sticker reads: "Don't believe everything you think." We could say the same for emotions: be discerning with what you feel—you may be deluding yourself. We know how compelling feelings can become and how convincing the truth value of our perceptions can be when colored by powerful emotion. We just know, say, that we are on the right side of an argument because the feeling of being wronged tells us that our perceptions are correct. We feel we *know* that the driver in front of us is purposely making us late for a most important appointment—until, that is, we are able to see that two cars ahead of

him, traffic is stopped because a driver who wants to turn right is waiting for a mother, toddler in hand, walking in the crosswalk on the way
to preschool. Emotion, like all experience, can deceive and awaken,
depending on how we use of it. "At the service of what?" is a question
we would all do well to ask regarding our experience. Once I told my
analyst that I was unsure whether what I was talking about was defending against some other feeling or was an authentic experience. I "knew"
of course that it could be both and could switch from one moment to
another. I enjoy remembering his response, "Let's see." We don't know,
we need to listen to the context, the harmonics, the impacts that ripple
and radiate in multiple directions. We await the voice of, and consultation from, our resonating unconscious—the other and the intersubjective echo—and, of course, we stay alert to the behavioral harvest. This
tracking is a critical element in an integrated narrative or archetype of
liberation. No matter the number of enlightenment experiences we
have had; the koans we have passed, our status as teacher, therapist, or
guide; or the years of therapy or analysis—we must understand that
there are impacts we are creating and energies and qualities we are actually conveying and about which we don't have a clue. Our pets and our
loved ones may actually have a better seat. It is not for want of interest
or practicing awareness, but rather in large part because that is the way
unconscious emotional communication in the relational field works.
Bollas provides a wonderful metaphor for thinking about the impacts
we generate. He suggests we imagine watching someone moving
through space in a room full of people, then imagine that we cannot
see the person's body but only the effects of his actions. It is as if the
person is a ghost. It is like the old TV show *Topper*. What impacts do
we leave in our wake?

I now develop a series of interconnected ideas that bring together the
Buddhist notion of cause and effect with unconscious motivation,
intention, presence, the Bliss Body, the nature of reality, the act of perception, and an integrative myth, ideal, or "dream." I gather together
these and other strands we have been exploring into a narrative or praxis
of liberation. But, first, some personal stories, which may help illustrate
and connect the integrative "model" I want to convey.

The Unconscious and the Bliss Body in Action

In the recent past, I worked for several years with teenagers and young adults in the juvenile justice system in San Mateo County, California. I was asked to supervise second-year graduate students who were providing individual and group mental health services to high-risk youth in a variety of settings—from residential camps, to jails, to community-based schools within a school—within the context of a private nonprofit agency. At the time, I was busy starting up Deep Streams Institute and teaching Zen and psychoanalysis and practicing both, and I agreed only because of a long-time connection with the person who asked. However, this work turned out to be extremely compelling. I decided to sit in with my supervisee in group therapy sessions. In short order, we realized that traditional psychodynamic group process would not work, and that we needed to be more interactive and become more "real objects" than traditional therapists to these people whose lives were in such a state of chronic crisis. After a few meetings, I happened to ask the group what mattered most to them in their lives. This thought generated much discussion as few adults had ever asked them such a question with real interest. What really matters, why do you think it matters, how do you know it matters, and how did it come to matter so much? As the students came to trust us, they began to lay it out: conquering girls, "bling," lots of money, their "Moms," how many guys they could beat up, hanging with the coolest guys, and so on. As time passed, they began to include other things, like happiness, making a difference in someone's life—more altruistic and even existential matters. One of the questions I asked that facilitated reflection was what happened when they acted out of what mattered to them. It began to dawn on me that I was asking about motivation, intention, core values, internal working models, and philosophies of living, although I did not use these words. When you are driven by having to have lots of bling and wanting to be the top dog, or belonging to and being taken care of by the top dog, where does that lead you? What are the results? What fuel are you using to power your "ride," and what are the effects? We would discuss it, without moral lessons or judgments. I recalled Freud's early energic model and wondered about psychic fuels and energies, not simply unconscious wishes, dynamics, and conflicts. What emotional fuel is driving your behavior? What these students valued and held most dear sponsored certain emotional qualities that drove and informed their behavior and then led to certain results. Mostly, it worked unconsciously—meaning, here, without reflection.

I began to see that we were also discussing cause and effect, the law of *karma*, or action, a key teaching in classical Buddhism but relatively underprivileged in Zen and generally not considered directly at all in psychotherapy. It is not only our outer behaviors but also our inner intentions that determine what unfolds from a certain state of mind, action, or interaction. The impacts from our intentions radiate far and wide in visible and invisible ways that last a long time. But, how can we truly determine an intention given that motivations are multiple and unconscious? The road to hell is paved with good intentions. I was initially skeptical of practices such as metta, or loving kindness meditation, that sought to consciously generate particular beneficent spiritual qualities of mind and heart. My concern was that such practices could obscure a possible conflicting unconscious inner motivation or affective state. Within the history of Zen Buddhism, however, the critique may have been that, when these practices were used to generate merit, they reinforced dualistic thinking and even ego aggrandizement. Zen may thus have tended historically to deemphasize these classic practices.

By way of example, the emperor of China is reputed to have asked Bodhidharma, the fierce legendary Zen monk, what the first principle of Buddhism was. "Vast emptiness, nothing holy," Bodhidharma replied. (Notice the difference from the earlier Dhammapada, "We are what we think, having become what we thought.") The emperor asked, "I have built many temples and sponsored many monks, what is my merit?" Bodhidharma said, "No merit at all." "Who is this standing before me?" the emperor asked. Bodhidharma's reply, "I don't know," was not the response of someone in an identity crisis. He was speaking, we could say, from the essential, absolute, or dharmic perspective, where the process of becoming does not arise, not to mention operate as a focus. In this book, I also explore what we call the phenomenal, relative, or karmic dimensions. I also want to illuminate their interpenetration, and what gets "lost in translation" between realization (in which the universal and particular are inextricably interwoven) and personalization (by which we bring to life and apply that realization in the particulars of our daily living).

In my work with the high-risk youth, I began to see that the energies driving these young men and woman were in turn determining their fates: scores of their homeboys and homegirls injured or dead, family members caught up in gang violence, pregnancies that brought children they could not care for, fine minds wasted. The cause-and-effect relationships were clear. I developed the notion of psychic fuels (similar but not reducible to unconscious motivation and intention)—energies outside our awareness that inform, drive, and infuse our behavior. They are also transmitted (communicated) through our interactions, no matter what we said, meant, or felt. They have resonating impacts that ripple across the filaments of Indra's Net and continue reverberating in unpredictable ways for a long time. Insight here was less crucial than fundamental presence. It was like what Murray Stahl, my freshman psychology professor, told us about parenting: "It's not what you say but who you are." A series of humbling and illuminating experiences with my own body and how it moved in space also became a laboratory for studying and driving home how this operated: an "up-close and personal" experience of Indra's "emotional" Net at work.

After playing tennis for many years, I began, as a young man with thick, inflexible leg muscles, to do yoga and approached it ambitiously. The result was an injury to my hip capsule that spawned other joint injuries and early-onset osteoarthritis. For a few years in my late twenties, I could not walk very well, and this was alarming and depressing. Muscle groups throughout my body had compensated for the original injury, and although I exercised, I was stiff, out of balance, and unable to do activities I enjoyed, like playing tennis, because of the resulting inflammation. A side effect was not being able to sit in the lotus or half-lotus position, the most stable of the meditation postures. Some years later, a chiropractor suggested I consult with a physical therapist, which had never occurred to me. She began to mobilize the joint. She didn't just give me exercises to do; she worked hands-on. Gradually, I put my trust in her and her approach, which was quite painful. She was reviving a frozen joint, frozen functioning, and it took a while to come to life and for range of motion to improve. My gait was completely off kilter, and I needed to learn to walk again. I was banging into things as I wobbled at home. Things would feel more stable, a new normal set in, then more gains and release would prompt another destabilization, and I was again thrown off balance. This cycle continued, but the valleys and troughs evened out, and I came to feel in a new normal kind of body. It passed through my mind how analogous this was to protecting an emotional or psychic wound or trauma. Then things got really interesting.

When I bumped into something, it would hurt, throw off my balance, and things would slide into their old twisted configuration. Suffice it to say that I was highly motivated to look at what was going on. I had a general sense that I was hurling my body, throwing it, and hurtling through space. Perhaps I was defying the effects of injury, acting as if I were that 18-year-old again, competing in a tennis match. But there was more. As I really slowed down the reel and focused in, I thought I observed a whiff of anger in the movements, something that had completely escaped me. Was I banging into something to feel its presence, like an adolescent might interact with parental limits? The psychodynamics were less intriguing again than the quality of energy, the psychic fuel that seemed to be driving the movement. I mustered up all the mindfulness I could, but it was hard to catch in action. It happened beneath the threshold of awareness—but it was not classically unconscious, that is, repressed or split off. It was like trying to catch a daydream or a reverie in the twilight area between waking and dozing off.

Eventually, I could observe things more clearly, some mechanical and some emotional. I noticed that when I moved abruptly in certain ways and in certain directions, things would become out of balance. One area of my lower back had compensated for the injury to the opposite hip and just did not want to bend at a certain angle. I developed a "workaround" and practiced body mechanics like a new religion, and the slips back into the "old normal" decreased dramatically. There were things I could do; I was not being condemned to a life of infirmity. I also came to notice that anger was occasionally driving my body movements. It was as if I were using my body to deliver a blow or emphatically punctuate a just-beneath-theradar inner dialogue with a "humph" kind of movement, in which a foot would hit the table leg or my shoulder an open door. At other times, I realized I was in the midst of a movement, say toward the stove, and would pivot in midstream toward the refrigerator, leaving muscle groups going in two directions at once, throwing things out of whack. Economy of movement and mindfulness in motion became the order of the day.

Each action was driven by and had the operational quality and effect of a particular psychic fuel. This fuel engendered impacts that indeed radiated far and wide and for a long time, in my body, in ways I did not like, and that motivated me, as suffering is wont to do, to have a closer look. I learned that something I thought was completely outside the realm of my control could be influenced by mobilizing, not only my joints, but also my attention, and in ways I had learned to do on the cushion and on both sides of the couch. To a Zen student in the sudden awakening tradition, this was a gradual awakening of great importance to my well-being. It was like Paul Ekman discovering microemotions, but here they were in play in physical movement. All this arose in conjunction with the unearthing of a hidden self-concept.

It dawned on me at the time that I was not caring for my best emotional interests very well, and there might be something of a closet samurai in me. This was new information since I had always been quite sensitive to my feelings and to the feelings of others. Within my original Zen community and later in my own Zen teaching, I would speak of the importance of opening to, rather than shutting down, our emotional life. But, as life events and circumstances revealed another layer of emotional vulnerability, even fragility, and the need to care for and protect my emotional well-being, I realized that I had been a kind of emotional samurai. I prided myself in meeting each thing, event, or feeling "just as it was," reflecting of course both the Zen and the psychoanalytic spirit, but simultaneously concealing a lack of acceptance and respect for the real impacts of certain qualities and certain emotions. I realized that qualities, emotions, psychic fuels, and spiritual qualities *really mattered*. The categories of positive and negative emotions never held much sway for me, but I came to appreciate what classical Buddhism calls the afflictive and wholesome emotions and their impacts. As a young Zen student, I recall my teacher saying that when we were not feeling compassionate we should act with compassion. This rankled me: Why should I pretend? I had extended the teaching of when tired, sleep; when hungry, eat; when feeling anything, just feel it, meet it head-on. But, I had unconsciously put this teaching, however well internalized and expressed in the Zen training setting, at the service of something else. It had become a banner behind which I remained unaware of the impacts of some emotional events, occasionally self-generated.

A non-life-threatening but annoying arrhythmia was another frequent teacher about the interplay among thoughts, feelings, and bodily happenings and the powerful impact of primary emotional states. At first, a physician told me there was no emotional contribution, but I knew there must be because factors were at play at the time that were heartbreaking and outside my control, and I was feeling both despairing and helpless. Over the years, I have become more able to track powerful emergent emotional states and the initial rumblings, the precursors of the arrhythmia. The hallmark of trauma is a strangled scream, a suffocated sob, something like Munch's painting by the same name. For two years, I have provided support for an event honoring parents whose children were killed in Iraq and Afghanistan. Witnessing a hundred tables on which parents lovingly placed their child's things, vivid expressions of his or her whole life, evokes such a feeling. One evening, I awoke with such a powerful emergent sob, fueled this time by an old trauma coming to life. When the arrhythmia kicked in, I made the connection. Since then, a new surgery and, who knows, perhaps this kind of deepening self-observation have contributed to the arrhythmia abating.

Emotional and personal growth continue throughout life, at least they had better, for spiritual teachers and psychotherapists. Some think that those who are truly spiritually adept achieve a state that is permanently resistant to affliction. But, the people to whom they ascribe this state, such as the Dalai Lama, categorically deny it and are the first to discuss their human afflictive emotions such as anger, frustration, or a sense of failure. I do not think that such a person is happy when their strategy for their country's liberation does not work. It saddens them deeply. They do not take it personally, but they do take responsibility, as H.H. has done for "the failure" of his policy of nonviolence. Rather, whatever emerges, a spiritually evolved person is able to fully experience its impacts and meet them with equanimity. His or her response is generally a skillful and compassionate one that prevents further harm and creates a good chance of results that benefit all. The long view, based on understanding the impermanence of all things, also helps. I was struck by H.H.'s response to a question about the state of Tibet. After acknowledging his grief and upset and concern, someone asked why he did not advocate taking up arms. Wasn't this making the plight of his people worse? "When I feel most despairing," he responded, "I think, let's see what evolves in 100 years." I have heard it said that certain spiritually evolved people say they experience the full range of human emotions, but those who know them well know otherwise: They are permanently in another register of existence, and afflictive states do not even visit such individuals. Perhaps, but this view might also reflect a persistent clinging to an ideal of how such an evolved individual should be.

The Alchemy of Zen and Psychotherapy

So, what is the upshot? What is the alchemy that these "golds" of Zen and psychotherapy, the Bliss Body and the unconscious, generate? In the film *What the Bleep Do We Know!?* a quantum physicist makes two statements: One, from the beginning, essentially there is nothing; two, we create reality as we know it by how we connect the dots of the data we receive on multiple channels. In Zen, we call it *shunyata*, the fertile void. It is not something called "nothing." D. W. Winnicott's phrase, "potential space," is perhaps a better term. The basic ground is vast, boundless, timeless, measureless potential space. I think we have little control over our emotions. Likewise, I think pain is part of life, but anguish is optional. How we respond to our emotions and our pain and to afflictive situations and life circumstances is where we have a measure of control. But, these two statements in the film jolted me into awareness of a new possibility. It is that, prior to responding, in our very act of apprehension—how we construe a certain situation by connecting the dots of sensory and affective data—there may be some play in determining how and what we experience. Our uptake in turn has impacts on the others involved and perceived and so "constructed." We know that the brain is actively constructing models of reality moment to moment and readjusting these based on new data. It is not that we "choose" or "dial up" whatever reality we want, carte blanche. Rather, our assimilated internalized and personalized insights develop, through ongoing attentional "practice," a kind of *dhyana*. They shape our very perceptions (not solely our responses to perceptions and affective experience) and so have influence over what realities, both psychical and material, emerge.

We see this in terms of expectations: Students who are expected (and perceived) to be capable of success are more likely to succeed. Experiencing a drug addict sprawled out on the street as a child of God, a Buddha, a human being with basic dignity, rather than a bum will not only affect our response to that person but also affect and create that person. A documentary about hunger and homelessness, *You Call Me by My Name*, asks, "Does our own internal sense of desperation or psychic hunger causes us to blind ourselves to what confronts us in the street? In protecting ourselves, do we deny the personhood of those truly in need?" The film's title is taken from a statement of a homeless person, who said: "You saw me, you called me by my name." Jean Sanville thinks that a self (or we might say a mind) is "born of illusion because mother and father believe that a self is there and call it into being by their own responsiveness." Fonagy likewise found that developing a mind of one's own depends on being perceived and understood as someone with thoughts, feeling, intentions—in brief, personhood and a mind. We could say that as we connect the dots of our sensory visual and other experience and bring forth a person (or other being) with dignity, we help liberate that "other" from "other" status so he, she, or it can realize and share intrinsic awakening or liberation.

Many in Buddhism and psychotherapy focus on seeing things as they "really are." But perhaps our perceptions, on the one hand, and "what is," on the other, co-arise: We awaken to what is as we perceive and create it. Our perceptions are infused and informed by a guiding myth, a dream, a philosophy of living. In Zen, no matter our *kensho*, no matter the "transmission outside of words and letters," no matter our presentation of koans, the proof of the pudding is in the eating. How does insight manifest? How is it cultivated and disseminated into the world of action? Some may counter, "Why these are dualistic categories; it is one movement, not 'even one.'" Since words can be put at the service of different functions, this may be so, and it may also be so much hot air. "By their fruits ye shall know them." We need to track those fruits, understand that they often differ from what we think, realize that it takes other skills to do this tracking, and keep learning.

In accord with what understanding, motives, psychic fuels, energies, spiritual qualities, are we connecting the dots, making links, deriving meanings, acting on them, perceiving? Aitken Rōshi says that we live Buddha's dream. We live it out and create it moment to moment. It is the same with the psychotherapeutic dream of fully welcoming the disparate and disowned parts and experiences, making space for them as we widen our tent of the self, the space of the heart. Dylan writes: "You can be in my dream if I can be in yours." We are by nature in one another's dream; we are moment to moment dreaming one another. It behooves us to cultivate a mutually beneficial dream.

Nanao Sakaki has a poem: "I sit down quietly in lotus position, / Meditating, meditating for nothing / Suddenly a voice comes to me: / "To stay young / To save the world / Break the mirror." Can we break the self-absorbed mirror and painful storyline that we construct and sustain? Currently, many say, "It's just your story, let it go." But it is our story, our dream—what drives us, what we live and stand by, what actually gets communicated in our moment-to-moment interactions, no matter what our conscious intention, how we connect the dots—that makes all the difference in the world. This story is not ego aggrandizement; it is what we live by, how we live, and what we leave in our wake.

Dream

Ideals cut different ways. They can inspire, and they can tyrannize. Each path, Zen and psychotherapy, has them: archetypes, myths—stated and unarticulated. They are the dreams that animate the practice. They work behind the scenes as guides to live by. No matter how useful, however, it is important to stay open to revising them and to learning from experience. How would a fully functioning human being live? In *Mahayana* Buddhism (great vehicle), it is the *Bodhisattva*, in *Theravada* Buddhism (school of the elders), the *Arhant*. Mahayanists used to refer to Theravadins as the *Hinayana* (lesser vehicle) school. But, all vehicles shall be towed, at owner's expense. Since alignment and integrity are important to me, I have thought of suggesting the mensch as a possibility.

When I was a young adult, before I began to practice Zen, I had the experience that I describe in the "Introduction," of wondering what it would be like if thought no longer shaped our perceptions of the world. A space opened. Later, I read the following line from the *Dhammapada*: "We are what we think, having become what we thought." One question opened the universal dimension. The other helped me appreciate how things work in the karmic or relative dimension. (Please remember—they are not two, not even one!) The first speaks to "letting go," realization, *prajna*; the second, I believe, more to "coming forth," to personalization. Both questions, both dimensions are crucial.

Here is a dream: In baseball, the ideal is a five-tool player: The player can hit for average, hit for power, throw, field, and run. Some have deep insight, some highly focused zazen, some follow the precepts and understand them deeply. But, can we be three-tool players? Can we develop and integrate dhyana, prajna, and sila so that they are in alignment and naturally potentiate one another? There is the experience of the Bliss Body and the insight it provides into our essential nature and that of all beings (prajna). There is strong attentional practice on the cushion (dhyana), turning toward truth, opening, not just to the pure suchness of the birds and clouds, but to what comes forward from unconscious emotional communication, from intimate and other relationships. We continue to refine the jewel, both through zazen and koans that refine the enlightened eye (prajna) and by refining our personal and interpersonal being-in-the world. When we ask, "At the service of what?" and "How and to what ends am I using the treasure?" we are acknowledging that we do not know, and we are open to using data from interactions and relationships to shine a ray of darkness into the matter. We consult not only with the unconscious impacts of our actions and the psychic fuels they convey, data that can be sometimes available in somatic experience; we also check in with our pets, our intimates, and track the *après coup* fruits, the traces we have left in our wake. *Sila*—enlightened activity, ethical conduct, goodness, mutual benefit—is both a result and an engine of this activity. As psychotherapists, we can imagine the analogues in our practices and lives.

Here is Zen master Dogen: "To be enlightened by the 10,000 things is to free one's body and mind / and those of others. / No trace remains / and this traceless enlightenment / is continued forever." Do not suppose that this amounts to riding off into the sunset in perpetual liberation. This no-trace that is continued forever needs maintenance and refinement.

There is a risk that "arriving," described as a relief in the introduction, can calcify and lull us into thinking "we're there" and there is literally nothing to do. Is genuine curiosity and learning by experience operating? Or, has realization become a stale, lifeless artifact? Suzuki Rōshi once responded to a questioner, "Yes, we are perfect just as we are. And we all can use a little improvement." This speaks to what we call the essential and the training levels in Zen.

I believe that the continuing education of both the Zen and spiritual practitioner, and the psychotherapist and patient, should ideally include the kind of "tracking the traces" that I am describing, which requires an understanding and appreciation of unconscious emotional communication in the relational field. Even though psychotherapists may understand unconscious emotional communication, and Zen practitioners may have experienced the Bliss Body, each element operates only as it is activated and expressed moment to moment. Since the universal and the personal "inter-are," opening to the unconscious relational field of emotions enriches our enlightened eye, makes us more discerning, and brings us into alignment. It opens the gate of wisdom, for right conduct is the living expression of emptiness, completely in accord with our insight into our fundamental insubstantial and intimately interconnected true nature.

Although many emphasize the "mind training" element of Buddhist meditation, our practice, Zen or psychotherapy, is not just a technique, a means to an end—it expresses the universe, and it calls it into being. We are responsible for our impacts in the world, intentional and unintentional. At the end of the film *Black Orpheus*, two young boys call up the sun with their guitar playing. Like them, we are bringing forth the universe in every act, every perception. Is this myth, or is it reality? Can we trust that what we call up, name, perceive, and thereby bring forward into the universe will be of benefit to all as well as to ourselves? Nyogen Senzaki, whom we heard from earlier, has left us words of instruction: "Trust your own head / Do not put on any false heads above your own / Then moment after moment follow your steps closely / These are my last words to you."

In Zen, we sometimes use the term *person of no-rank*. Such a person responds freely, in accord with circumstances, unfettered by concepts such as gain and loss, enlightened and deluded, subject and object. His or her actions do not come from a formula, a cookie cutter, and they may therefore seem contradictory. But, this spontaneity ideally is not random or chaotic but infused with prajna—thorough-going, internalized understanding of our empty and interconnected nature—and responds in accord with the situation at hand. This wisdom must be lived and personalized in the crucible of daily relational living, through practice, or dhyana. How is Zen, as Yamada Rōshi said, "the perfection of character"? The Bliss Body is a direct, unmediated experience, part and parcel of a narrative of liberation. From the beginning, things just as they are—standing up, sitting down, laughing, weeping—nothing is missing and nothing left over. How does this penetrate into our everyday conduct, our relationships? The upwelling of compassion that comes with realization wanes as we resume everyday life. Continued clarification of enlightenment through koan study and mindfulness in everyday moments can help. But, mindfulness needs to be complemented, not only by awareness of emotional and social intelligence or by new ways of thinking about trauma in the body but also by unconscious emotional communication in the relational field, awareness of how we are using our experience, what "fuel" we are utilizing and conveying, and what unconscious rippling impacts we are generating.

In Zen, there is a purification chant in which we acknowledge the harmful effects our actions have had on others, effects wrought by greed, ill-will, and delusion. In some traditions, we develop ways to work with the precepts and with the paramitas[7] to bring home their relevance in daily living. But, chanting and working on a conscious level with ethical guidelines go only so far. I want to say that the process of purification, refining what Aitken Rōshi calls the "agent of compassion," can stand to benefit from awareness of unconscious emotional communication in the relational field. The person of no-rank trusts his or her own mind, head, heart, and realization. But, we need to "trust and verify." Why? Because unconscious experience happens, and all of us are, as Sylvia Boorstien says, "just a moment away from a meltdown," from delusion.

As these understandings and practices become more integrated within us and in our behavior, a "new normal" develops. We observe how things work, the impacts of our actions—inner and outer, conscious and unconscious—on our own well-being as well as on others. If we are "turning toward truth," we learn from experience. There is another question that can arise: How much "truth" can we take? It is one thing, in circumscribed settings, such as the consulting room or the dojo or the dokusan room, to feel "together," to welcome all manner of experience in a more accepting way, and to act in an integrated way. It is quite another to come face to face with ourselves and our impacts in daily relational living in real time, or après coup. Sometimes, it can be more than we can handle. But, this capacity can grow, and with it we can have many moment-to-moment awakenings to what is really happening. "Just this" moments characterized by deep suffering require contact with something that is "not suffering" in order to metabolize the pain and awaken to the moment's immanence. The Bliss Body is not always blissful. It has no permanent absolute substance and cannot be bought or sold. It is not respectable, and has no meaning and no particular "use." Yet, its "marvelous functioning"—eating, sleeping, falling down, getting up, laughing, weeping, grieving, rejoycing, being born, dying—never ceases.

Flora Courtois and I were each gazing, she at a desk and I at a photo on a book cover. Gazing freely, as the painter Bonnard describes it, reflects and generates liberated attention. We open ourselves to learning from the depths, now the universal, now the personal. There are moments when both dissolve, others when they interpenetrate. We cultivate openness to the impacts of living. Neville Symington says that personality organizes around the "beestings" of relational living. They hurt; it is pointless to pretend that they feel good. The capacity and the ongoing, freshly generated willingness to bear and transform them is crucial. This is the "standing" we spoke about that co-arises with understanding.

With the ever-renewing "new normal"—physical, emotional, or spiritual—we become more resilient, less subject to insults and injuries, more naturally restoring and self-righting. We can "trust our own heads" (and hearts and minds and bodies) not only because we follow the precepts, not only because we have internalized a sense of ethics, but also because we are, moment to moment, experiencing, tracking, and refining our "impact in the world"—and feeling the sting as we wake up to things that unsettle and trouble us. We also wake up to the other side: how certain fuels and actions generate mutual benefit in their wake. This entire movement, this entire function requires us to be multilingual. The two paths not only contain and hold us as we change, they also restrain and temper us with their respective vernacular and their discipline.

We live more freely, peacefully, and ethically, creating in an unforced way more buoyancy, aliveness, and true contentment and less pain and harm for all. As an emotional samurai who prided himself on nondualistically meeting whatever emerges head-on, I once found this hard to accept. But, we can also practice selectively focused attention (without being Pollyannas and Goody Two-shoes) so that we "water" and amplify those tendencies that lead to mutual benefit and restrain ourselves from acting on afflictive psychic fuels, greed, ill-will, and delusion. We stop, look, and listen; reflect on our experience; pick up cues when things are awry and out of alignment; stay open to unconscious emotional communication in the relational field; ask "at the service of what?" and become aware of how we are "turning toward truth"—until it becomes second nature. Then, we again take a sounding of the entire field and keep "following (the impacts and ripples of) our steps."

In Chapter 8, "Forging Integrative Learning," I talk about refraining from neglecting, minimizing, overriding, disavowing, rejecting, or simply denying the realm of the personal and its transformative and integrative possibilities.

CHAPTER 8

Forging Integrative Learning

In previous chapters, I discussed the interplay of the universal and the particular, a subset of which is the personal. How do these play out in psychotherapy training and practice? In Zen training and practice? In this chapter, I examine these questions using as a starting point my own experience of psychoanalytic training and then expand their relevance to my experience of Zen training. In both practices, I explore the conditions for integrative learning and examine the disavowal of the emotional and personal dimensions and how this "turning away" can eviscerate the learning process. I also present integrative ideas differentiating the person from the personality, incorporating the work of Winnicott, Matte Blanco, Bion, infant research, and neuroscience.

Forging Psychotherapeutic Learning

Many years ago at a psychoanalytic conference, the presenter asked if there were any more questions. Up to that point, the exchanges had been quite theoretical. "Do you have your hand up?" he asked someone sitting in front of me. The person said timidly, "Well, I *had* a question, but," and then she hesitatingly and apologetically continued, "it's personal." There was dead silence in the hall. Then, the presenter replied, "Is there any *other* kind?" I breathed a sigh of relief: Maybe I, too, could pipe up.

Why examine this subject at all? Isn't the personal much ado about nothing? Some think that psychoanalysis is the method of choice for exploring internal experience. Wouldn't inviting the personal into seminars and case conferences cause analytic training to devolve into group therapy or an encounter group? Doesn't it risk candidates using the setting to trumpet and impose their unresolved personal issues, obstructing group process and "real" learning? Won't it jeopardize privacy and confidentiality? Doesn't the personal reflect our self-centered individualistic culture? There is a natural trajectory in any apprenticeship—first you learn the basics, then you practice them, then they become second nature. Shouldn't we put aside what we already personally know to take in the new, master it, practice it, and then transmit it? Or, is there an important missed step in this schema of the transmission of psychotherapeutic knowledge and skill?

The most difficult part of analytic training was the courses and case conferences. I enjoyed the readings, the case material, and many of the teachers. Individually, candidates were highly experienced clinicians and bright and decent people. Transferences between all of us, however, were extraordinarily powerful yet rarely unacknowledged. There developed what felt to me like an exclusive and elitist group identity that, while denied, bred arrogance. Although I respected and admired class members individually, I came to find the atmosphere we cocreated stifling.

Thankfully, I was at the same time participating in a supervisors' conference at another institution. We met on a weekly basis for four years. The facilitator, a senior clinician, was a gruff, funny, and oddly tolerant man. During the group's four years together, meeting once a week, a remarkable thing happened: We became a work group. It crept up on us. Safety and trust developed. We provided one another acceptance and support. We created an intellectually stimulating atmosphere without feeling like we had to walk on eggshells or tiptoe around differences. Alternative perspectives were welcome. The sharing was heartfelt and personal as well as clinical, and we laughed, often at ourselves.

At the final meeting of the supervisors' group, I wondered aloud, "If only we could bottle what we've developed." We had all learned so much—about supervision for sure, but also about ourselves, one another, psychotherapy, and the process of psychoanalytic learning. We had enjoyed ourselves and each other. What if we could apply this to settings that tended to be intellectually and emotionally stultifying, such as psychoanalytic institutes? The group leader did not think it could be done. When I asked why, he said there was too much anxiety; others were monitoring your progress; you needed to get a stamp of approval; you had to meet certain criteria; it was a different situation. I was saddened by his response, and I am not sure I agree with him.

The last year of training was the best. Difficult transferences begin to lift like a veil. Some of my own ideas came together. I found an analytic voice and, with it, became aware of my internal working models of the analytic process. Theory, practice, my beliefs and values, my personality, my life, began to feel more of a piece. I didn't just study and learn, say, Bowlby—I had my own ideas *about* Bowlby. "Bowlby" became "*my* Bowlby."

Getting Personal

For many, "personal" seems to connote "personal issues." And, personal issues are best kept in one's own therapy. We often forget that it is through the personal that we integrate the theory and the practice and weave them together in our professional and personal lives and identities. I think best in a setting that feels safe, where I trust others and am in turn trusted by them—where we entrust one other with our personal responses to the material we study and our efforts to grapple with it, where we integrate and "create" it as our own, and risk being known. I learn best when there is acceptance of differences in how we think and process information and affect, where we can associate to material freely, use our imagination, make connections freely and follow them up: remembering this story, this movie, this quote, this personal experience, and yes, if we choose to share it, a particular exchange in our own analysis. Bion writes that knowledge is a link, an *emotional* link. I learn when affect is alive and allowed—where privacy is respected, of course, and there is no coercion, but where affect is not stifled, where we do not worship at the shrine of disembodied abstract cognition in a hyperintellectualized "muscle beach" atmosphere.

I was once driving Neville Symington to his hotel after a public dialogue with his late cousin, San Francisco psychoanalyst Lisby Mayer, on spirituality and psychoanalysis. In the car, he shared some uncertainty with me about preparing to present Bion's ideas to a group he heard had not had much exposure to Bion. I suggested that he had lived with Bion for some time now, and that he might want to share with the group *his* Bion. He wrote back a few weeks later that the talk had gone very well, and that my comment had been helpful. How I learn, I found, is not very different from how others learn, be they candidates or seasoned psychoanalysts.

Why is it so challenging to create the relational conditions in group learning settings for this kind of work-play with the ideas and case material we encounter during our psychotherapy training? We understand more today about the therapeutic process as it unfolds in the consulting room, about the supervisory process, and about the factors that promote good-enough human development itself. My sense is that our experiences in our analyses and supervisions—one to one, protected settings—are usually stimulating, encouraging, progressive, and occasionally healing and transformative. Why then the frequent disconnect when it comes to learning in class, case conference, workshop, conference, and other communal spaces? Ignorance and inattention to unconscious emotional communication in the relational field is one reason. The unconscious repudiation of the personal is, I think, a second element.

Psychoanalysis is in heavy company here. While classical psychoanalytic formulations saw the personal as uncontrolled primal impulses (the id) or as the regulating function itself (the ego), organized religion tended to associate the personal with pride, impurity, and desire—factors that impeded living a godly life. Curiously, although the scientific method developed in opposition to religion, aspiring to free humanity from the tyranny of blind belief, science took a similar position—relativity theory and quantum mechanics notwithstanding—by traditionally viewing the personal as a contaminating interference in the process of achieving objective knowledge. The scientific lens, like the religious heart, needed to be purified and the personal expunged. The "I" was excised from Freud's writing by Strachey's translation and replaced with the term *ego*, reflecting a pseudoscientific prejudice, more unconscious today perhaps than in Freud's time. Knowledge here requires antiseptic, sterile, "objective" conditions. Contrast this with the view of Schlein, a humanistic researcher in the 1970s who said that the best knower is the one closest to the data.

Now, one might say that psychoanalysts make plenty of room for the personal in the training analysis required of candidates. But, there is an odd fragmentation here: We *assume* that there is a cross-fertilization, a "transfer of training" among the three segmented compartments: the analysis, the supervision, and the course work. But, does this actually happen? I'm not so sure. When it does, it often seems to be *in spite* of training and can require some unlearning.

I see the personal as neither self nor not-self but rather the living creative activity of *personalization*. Unlike narcissistic self-aggrandizement, it cannot be adequately described or grasped, yet it is active, idiomatic, and without self-consciousness. I am contrasting the personality with the *person-in-action*; the latter includes reflecting, thinking, feeling, creating, imagining, intuiting—not to mention standing up, sitting down, laughing, and weeping.

Many years ago, I noticed a mother on the beach with her toddler. Her toddler began wailing after another child took her pail away. The mother scolded the toddler, "Don't say *mine*, it's everybody's." This story took place in 1970s Maui and reflected the Age-of-Aquarius mores of the era. I cringed then as I cringe today, telling it, acutely aware of just how contemporary the vignette is.

My thesis is this: To help another transform, we ourselves must be in transformation, not bandying about dead words and thoughts, or dueling with inert theories. Information is useless unless it is worked over, transformed, and authored—unless it is passed through a forge and becomes our own. In training as a psychotherapist we learn by repeated, playful, creative engagement with intriguing, confusing, often painful, sometimes conflictual emotional material. We do this by free association, imagination, metaphor, meaning making—by dream work—in the presence of facilitative others. For Freud, this process was governed by condensation and displacement, working over prohibited and inhibited emotional material. Bion called this activity "dream work alpha" and saw it as our bread and butter, our daily mental activity, an achievement-in-progress that enables us to digest, transform, and integrate the flood of raw sensory material into usable emotional experience.

Personalizing Knowledge

There is awesome risk in personalizing knowledge. In Winnicott's imaginative telling, the infant has the marvelous and crucial experience of creating the nourishment that is provided by virtue of the mother's attunement. The infant creates or finds the object, magically, a creative omnipotence. There is also a ruthlessness we must pass through where we destroy the object, in fantasy, without concern for its protection and survival. Winnicott called this *object usage*: an all-out, no-holds-barred use through which we create the object as objectively perceived and place it outside the sphere of omnipotent generation. Then, we are capable of entering the fray, making use of people, places, and things, and letting ourselves be made use of. Ogden describes the crucible, as it plays out intersubjectively, when talking about the relationship of himself, the reader, and his book:

> This book will not be "understood" by you; you will not simply receive it, incorporate it, digest it, or the like. To the degree that you will have anything at all to do with it, you will transform it. (The word transform is too tepid a word to describe what you will do to it.) You will destroy it, and out of that destruction (in that destruction) will come a sound you will not fully recognize. The sound will be a voice, but it will not be one of yours that you have heard before, for you have not previously destroyed me as you will encounter me in your reading of this book.

We all want to bring forth something—a voice—that gives us pleasure while contributing to others. We want and need to be able to make use of others in the world and be made use of, hopefully in mutually beneficial ways. Marge Piercy expresses this in poetry:

To Be of Use

The people I love the best
jump into work head first
without dallying in the shallows
and swim off with sure strokes almost out of sight.

They seem to become natives of that element,
the black sleek heads of seals
bouncing like half-submerged balls.
I love people who harness themselves, an ox to a heavy cart,
who pull like water buffalo, with massive patience,
who strain in the mud and the muck to move things
forward,
who do what has to be done, again and again.
I want to be with people who submerge
in the task, who go into the fields to harvest
and work in a row and pass the bags along,
who are not parlor generals and field deserters
but move in a common rhythm
when the food must come in or the fire be put out.
The work of the world is common as mud.
Botched, it smears the hands, crumbles to dust.
But the thing worth doing well done
has a shape that satisfies, clean and evident.
Greek amphoras for wine or oil,
Hopi vases that held corn, are put in museums
but you know they were made to be used.
The pitcher cries for water to carry
and a person for work that is real.

In Winnicott's telling, first there is total subjectivity, then passage through a forge. To make knowledge real, it must become "mine." To become mine, the infant paradoxically creates it as the first not-me object and so constructs a transitional or intermediary space. Paradoxically mine and not-mine, me and not-me playfully intertwine in the space where the (m)other refrains from asking for an answer to the question, "Is the Teddy real or made up?" To be of use, we must be able to fully use. Just as ego capacities do not equate with ego aggrandizement, so the personal, brought forth and disseminated freely, shared with people on the way, can express the truest gift. It all depends on how we are using it, at the service of what.

Fonagy speaks about mentalization; Bion about reverie and *alpha function*, metabolizing *beta* into *alpha elements*; Grotstein about "autochthony" or authorship; Milner and the British Independents about imagination; Spezzano about getting excited. I believe these and related formulations describe different facets of a similar process: how we create living usable knowledge. Of course, we cannot control, predict, or hurry the learning curve, but without active engagement with the materials, as a baker with the dough or a potter with the clay, I do not believe integrative, usable learning can happen.

As I discussed in the Introduction to this book, in the early 1970s I founded the Peahi Nursery School on Maui, the kind of learning environment I would have liked to be part of as a young child. I read Dewey on learning by doing and Montessori, for whom play represented children's work, then Piaget and Winnicott. "Provide the relational conditions and they will learn." I lived in a room adjacent to the school. On weekends, I would see children driving with their parents on their way to town or the beach. More than one would exclaim, "That's my school!" This gave me no small satisfaction.

One of the capacities psychotherapists develop is linking and thinking (thinking that includes feeling and somatic awareness). I did not enjoy early school experiences much until I realized that disparate things, like a civilization's art, history, politics, economy, religion, and so on, evolved in concert and mutually influenced one another. If psychotherapy is not linked, not part and parcel of the tapestry of human life, it becomes cultish. When as a psychoanalytic candidate I would occasionally wonder out loud during class about how psychoanalysis, like Buddhism, is a way of responding to suffering, I had the feeling I was crossing a line. Maybe it was seen as mixing church with state, bringing "God" into a secular discussion, evoking a threat to people's freedom to think. For me, it was fascinating to compare these two responses to suffering: how they conceived of it, how they envisioned the challenges of being human. Seeing the psychoanalytic project comparatively within the larger context of human healing responses to suffering was exciting and useful. It helped me clarify what psychoanalysis brought to the table that was unique. It connected up with art, religion, myth, philosophy, ethics, and existence itself. My beliefs and assumptions about human nature, about pathology and healing snapped into focus as I saw a "bigger picture." Somehow, though, it was as if this alive personal link was experienced as a distraction from the pure "gold" of unalloyed psychoanalytic theory and technique. It was only as I came to understand the implicit and preconscious theoretical underpinnings of the various clinical theories, each with its implicit storylines regarding development, pathology, therapeutic action, the therapeutic relationship, and so on, that I became "free to think," in and out of the consulting room, something one of my supervisors had exhorted me to do.

As psychotherapists, we need to develop a personal relationship with psychotherapeutic thinkers. It was freeing for me to see that there were multiple Winnicotts—Ogdens, Rodmans, Eigens, Sanvilles, Phillipses, even Winnicotts—among them. I wrote an article on Winnicott and mysticism some time ago. Afterward, I realized that I had digested some essential things and could express and play with the ideas, creating something original. This creation was my Winnicott. I was freed up and able to teach an enjoyable and successful course on the thinker and the man.

Linking is not easy and brings up many anxieties, from the primitive to the more evolved. One patient, after years of terror, finally comes to articulate that she is afraid that "Ideas will have a life of their own." If she says them, or even thinks them, they will gallop out of control, take over, happen—without her okay. Anxiety was also, for this patient, as for many—and I find that this too often goes unmentioned in clinical writing—a sign of a pleasurable "learning curve ahead."

When the material that arises, in class-space as in therapy-space, is brought into fruitful "relations" with our internal world—out of this creative intercourse deep learning can emerge. Our idea-babies come forth alive, if at times unformulated and unrefined. New understandings, links, associations, thinking about thinking, integrations, distinctions, insights become possible in us and in the patient as the relational field becomes fertile and potent. More important, it is from personal engagement, conscious and unconscious, that our capacity *to live this process as a way of life* accrues. This capacity is rooted in our continuing emotional growth and work-play. It is tested, lived, and becomes the source of *conviction*—one of our best allies in analytic work. Dry theory is the straw. We *spin it into therapeutic gold* only by bringing it into intimate relation with our personal internal world. Unlinking the personal from the study of psychotherapy inhibits this process.

What are the conditions that facilitate transformative learning? The role of safety as described by Bowlby and others cannot be overstated.

Safety helps us manage inevitable anxieties and take personal risks, which in turn support and sponsor our own and others' creative expressions. Fonagy's work teaches us that to become able to think there must be an other who holds us in mind as someone with a working mind. Benjamin and others present spoke about the role of "primary recognition." Trust and mutual respect as well as welcoming and encouraging differences are key. Motivation, of course, is central. And, not least, our suffering impels us in psychotherapy and Zen alike.

Emotion versus Intellectualization in Training

I want to briefly address the suspicion of emotion and the overprivileging of intellectualized thinking in seminar and case conference settings. I have often wondered why I responded to some teachers more than others. I have come to see that there is a certain quality of affect in their thinking that I find congenial. For me, the personal is interwoven with affect-in-thinking. This idea leads me to follow up on the work of Ignacio Matte Blanco, the Chilean psychoanalyst who extended Freud's work on the unconscious. Matte Blanco wrote that he developed his theories because, although he was an emotional person, in his family he showed another side; his nickname as a boy was "little nitpicker."

Matte Blanco saw the unconscious as comprised not by blind conflictual impulses but rather by propositions. These propositions were characterized by a logic all their own, in fact, by two logics. He named these logics "symmetrical" and "asymmetrical," and they have, respectively, characteristics of Freud's primary and secondary processes. (Later, Matte Blanco expanded "logic" to mean core ways of thinking, feeling, and being.) Simplifying shamelessly, symmetrical logic characterizes deep feeling states, while asymmetrical logic is associated with discursive, linear thinking. Matte Blanco discovered that there is some thinking (asymmetry) in all, even the deepest, most symmetrized emotional experience. Likewise, in all thinking there was some measure of feeling (symmetry). So, these two logics and modes of unconscious experience coexist and, I think, need one another. In group learning spaces in analytic training, can we allow enough affect and the associated metaphorical, emotionally colored, subjective experience and communication, such that they enrich and sharpen our thinking? Can we allow enough thinking in our feeling so that our feeling and associative capacities, imagery, metaphors, and so on stay grounded and in touch? I believe we can learn much from Matte Blanco's work about the optimal unconscious environments for deep learning.

Here are two examples of how these processes played out during training: In the first, I was presenting in a case conference. The patient, a woman who had just gotten pregnant, was experiencing terrible anxieties about the potential reaction of her mother. After some input, I felt the atmosphere take on a persecutory quality. Now in principle, this could be an important learning moment: for my work with the patient, for the learning and exchange in the class, and for me personally. But, it was not; the space did not feel emotionally safe to "go there." "My Matte Blanco" would say that there was not enough constructive symmetry—felt affective connection and trust—for us to make hay with this material, to think fruitfully with the requisite asymmetry about these emerging deeply symmetrized clinical, personal, and group phenomena.

In the second example, an analyst originally from a non-Western culture came to teach a weekend class. He immediately sensed the anxiety in the class and our compensatory moves: a disengaged quality, the withdrawal of affect and aliveness, and a kind of intellectual arrogance. It took him about ten minutes to make his "diagnosis": "Well," he said, "I see . . . now let's all try something different, not business as usual. Why don't you each share with the group something about yourself that you would not usually think to say in this setting." As he spoke, his affect was so bright, so encouraging and engaging, so warm, that the chilling current that had coursed through the room upon hearing his invitation dissipated in short order, and the entire atmosphere was transformed. Within minutes, we were chattering like long-lost friends. This scene reminds me of the astonishing transformation and coming to life in the film *Awakenings*. Regretfully, it was also just as short-lived. As our next weekly class meeting began, there were two short references to the weekend. Then, as if nothing had ever happened, the atmosphere became chilly, impersonal, and hypertheoretical. There were no further references to the weekend thaw. The playful, warm interactions facilitated by the bright, affect-laden, playful personality and the sure diagnosis and prescription of the good doctor, were—not repressed, not split off. What happened to them? Disavowal is one possibility.

What are some implications of weaving the personal into psychoanalytic training? In a climate where creative risk, associative thinking, imagination, and intuition feel unsafe, anxiety, competition, inauthenticity, and isolation tend to prevail. Theory is dry and lifeless—we don't play with ideas but rather shoot around dead objects, jousting to see who can catalogue them best. Unpersonalized theories are like plastic doughnuts: They don't nourish, and they don't satisfy—they make us sick—but we continue to pass them around. Opportunities for cultivating curiosity, creativity, integrated knowing, healing, and transformation are lost. In so doing, we risk becoming technicians rather than healers who "walk the talk," whose personal and psychoanalytic identity cross-pollinate.

How might the personal connect up with therapeutic action? I do not believe that patients respond magically to the content of an interpretation. Rather, we take in, bit by bit, the increasingly fertile, mutually responsive give and take of the therapeutic couple, beginning with the transformative capacities of the therapist. This generates what Bion calls a "commensal relationship," which he defined as "a relationship in which two objects share a third to the advantage of all three"—a relationship of an oedipal couple, capable of bearing pain, being curious, making new links and leaps, linking and thinking, not-knowing, creating new, satisfying, and pleasurable possibilities for mental and emotional life.

If the therapist is proffering unmetabolized and disconnected bits of informations—curiously cathected and identified with, yet unanchored to and incongruent with his own deep personal experience and professional identity—what kind of transformation is possible? Deep learning implies less a disembodied technology the therapist is performing on the patient than a way of being that the therapist lives with the patient. This therapist the patient can make use of. This living a bit of life together, as D. W. Winnicott calls it, offers the patient another way of being in the world, of being with himself, of being with another. This relationship is what transforms, not medically dosed interpretations. Of course, there are interpretations, clarifications, confrontations, and more: moments of special impact. But, these are exchanged and occur within the context of a lived relationship with someone who has distilled the "teachings" into a way of living that works, a way of being human in the world, with him- or herself, and with others. This way of being cannot be taught or learned in the atmosphere permeating some psychoanalytic training institutes today, where the emphasis seems to be just on the opposite: getting the technology just right and saying the right thing at the right time.

If I am personally involved with the material I am learning, then I continue to grow. I think this may be a hidden element in therapeutic action. Does the patient sense that the analyst is also learning? Not simply that he or she "self-discloses," but rather, in the everyday work, are the patient and analyst collaborators, *partners in liberation*, constructing and embodying a way of learning and being together? We cannot suddenly become capable of this in the consulting room if we have not begun in the classroom. For transformative analytic workplay, our personal identities and professional identities must cross-pollinate. We must *be* the collaborative, healing influence we hope to bring about—from the generative commensal relationship within ourselves. How can we do so when we cut off a leg or an arm—the emotional, personal, symmetrical, imaginative, intuitive, creative relations with our material? When we become barren by evacuating the personal and the affective?

The patient comes to know us much more deeply than we imagine. This factor in healing again has nothing to do with purposeful self-disclosure. There is a certain intrinsic authority of the analyst, a beneficent way in which patients contact and learn from our unarticulated beliefs, values, visions, hopes, and philosophy of living. Especially if they can sense that these have been developed over time and form a sense of lived knowledge and conviction, and if they are still being recalibrated and continue to develop in the analysis. While in training, we can begin to grow this capacity for fertile and integrative ongoing deep learning relations with ourselves, with others, and with the world, rather than five to twenty years after, and in spite of, training. It is crucial that we develop an internal working model of psychotherapy and of life, a philosophy of living, a set of core values, and that we recognize that these core values are implicitly active. We should not be afraid to have them seep out and indirectly inform our analytic conduct, without, of course, indoctrinating the patient.

In this way, we can begin to heal the split between our quasi-religious theoretical loyalties and our own deep structure. We integrate theory and practice on a daily basis, testing the mix in the crucible of our own lives, which includes the analytic space. What shakes out, the precipitate, is our own distinctive distillation: a living, related psychoanalytic and personal identity, voice, and philosophy of living. We become the author and so find the source of psychoanalytic authority. It is not having power over the patient or replacing the patient as author of his or her emotional experience. We are just another person, yet a unique one: an analytic person! One who learns from experience and lives this in the consulting room. In this way, we can, as therapists, help the patient—and as teacher help the candidate or student—become the author of his identity and develop analytic conviction and authority. We cannot do this by passively holding the "teachings" as if they are wisdom received from on high and, only later, often years or decades later, subject them to reflection. Recall: when asked why he served the people tirelessly and sacrificed so much, Gandhi replied, "I am here to serve no one else but myself, to find my own self-realization through service to these village folks." We can, from the beginning, bring what we learn into relation with our insides so that we might enjoy and use it more freely, for our own benefit and the benefit of others.

The Forge of Zen Practice

Even if, in order to make progress, you sorted out all the Chan (Zen) teachings with their thousand differences and myriad distinctions, your mistake would still consist in searching for proclamations from other people's tongues.

... There must be a real man in here! Don't rely on some master's pretentious statements or hand me down phrases that you pass off everywhere as your own understanding!

This man or woman, this "person of no-rank" comes forth afresh in each moment of life, now shopping, now making love, now brushing his teeth, now listening, now dreaming, responsively in alignment with circumstances. The person emerges from and expresses his no-self nature in the particulars of daily life. His distinctive idiom comes forward as well, unique one person from the other, but it has nothing to do with self-expression and is not in the register of self-confidence or self-esteem. It reflects a sloughing off rather than a patching on or building up. The exchanges in the *dokusan* room between teacher and student or in daily life dialogues, or *mondo*, demonstrate each person coming forth completely, not holding anything back (similar to the psychotherapeutic idea of two fully evolved subjectivities interacting). But, in Zen, it expresses the fruit of deep inquiry and penetration into the existential questions, "Who is the subject?" "Who is the one who hears?" "Who is the dreamer that dreams the dream?" Until this becomes clear, we are, in Zen parlance, ghosts clinging to bushes and grasses.

In the account of the Chinese emperor's exchange with Bird's Nest Rōshi, we heard from Po-Chu'i that a child of six may know it, but a man of sixty cannot live it. Here is an example of two people of quite different ages in Dharma play, holding back nothing. One is the renowned elder, Layman P'ang:

> One day the Layman saw a herdboy. "Where does the road go?" he asked. "I don't even know the road," replied the herdboy. "You cattle-watcher!" exclaimed the Layman. "You beast!" retorted the herdboy. "What's the time today?" asked the Layman. "Time for planting rice," replied the herdboy. The Layman laughed heartily.

In Zen practice, we bring forward realization of the essential matter freely, with maximal aliveness, without thought of protecting others, including our teacher—ideally. But, there are certainly struggles along the way. Anxieties akin to those that emerge in a deep psychotherapy: competitive anxieties and concerns about being seen, recognized, liked, hurting the teacher, and so on. It can surprise the student to find that these can operate in two directions. Ideally, the teacher wants to see the student surpass him in insight, practice, and awakened expression in the dokusan room and in daily life. But, unconscious emotions in the relational field can obstruct, and sometimes it takes a village to shine a ray of darkness into the matter in the relational field. There are psychological, emotional, and developmental elements to freeing up the (no-self) person of no-rank to fully come forward and share his or her particular gifts. (One of the Buddhist precepts is not to withhold the Dharma assets.)

In Zen as in psychotherapy practice, the aim is never to eliminate rich and distinctive personality traits, but to help relieve the person's suffering, to enhance expression of life-giving elements. I once asked a psychoanalyst after a talk she gave on the topic of transference and transcendence whether she could imagine the absence of transference. She replied that in her experience there is always a trace of transference. Zen realization contains no transference or countertransference. In our subsequent refractions, we personalize and we let go of our experience and our attachments to it. It is not so much that a trace of transference remains. Rather, our actions are always emerging through the personal idiom. The personal is the impersonal and boundless expressed in material and emotional particulars, most of them unavailable to us as we live. That is why we need understanding and awareness of unconscious emotional communication in the relational field. No only do we "enact," to use a term from psychotherapy, unconscious emotional trauma, we also enact or present the Dharma. And, sometimes, when we enact both, disentangling and addressing them can take some doing.

Spiritual teachers of all stripes are human; we develop personal problems. The remarkable master Hakuin Zenji—renowned for his brilliant insight and expressive and artistic capacities and for reviving, reforming, even refounding the Rinzai School of Zen—writes about what he calls a "Zen sickness" and how he dealt with it. Krishnamurti, while not a Zen teacher, would go through serious disabling troubles that those who cared for him called "the process." I see these experiences through a psychospiritual lens: They represent not only a function of how the individual teacher is implementing the practice but also periods of intense personal emotional crisis and turbulence and, in some cases, disorganization. Enlightenment and strong *zazen* do not provide an exemption from the realm of the personal (and the interpersonal), a "get-out-of-jail-free card." We have examined examples of boundary violations and other "acting out of character" on the part of Zen teachers. These violations exist on a continuum: On one end is a Buddhist teacher, not in the Zen tradition, who knew that he had the AIDS virus and knowingly had intercourse with his students. In one accounting, this teacher poignantly describes how convinced he was that because he was enlightened he was exempt from the laws of biology. The realization that the universal and person co-arise can be dangerous if hijacked unconsciously and placed at the service of ego aggrandizement. How much here has to do with psychopathology and how much has to do with inflation and a distortion of elements within the teachings of his lineage that cast the guru as a being on a level higher than ordinary humans I leave for another writing.

On the other end of the continuum is an example that illustrates an underdeveloped degree of personalization less dramatically than the previous tragic story. A teacher is delivering a *teisho* (a presentation of Zen, not a lecture, literally the roar of the Dharma) at a meeting of Buddhist teachers. As I listen, something sounds "off"; I can't connect with what is being said. There is an unreal, as-if quality. I become sleepy. I try to reflect. The tone of voice goes up and down hypnotically. It feels as if this teacher is in a cocoon, and the words are like an induction, like a mother's lullaby, but oddly couched in the delivery of a "tough" Zen master. Then, I recall hearing the teacher's teacher give a teisho a long time ago. I have an image of this person having taken in their teacher whole hog; it seems like the teacher is "channeling." I begin to tune out; there is something inaccessible, and I can't find a way in. I notice a smile on the teacher's face, but as I look closer, it seems more like a smirk. I recall seeing such an expression on the face of the teacher's teacher. My experience is of someone in a role bubble, acting the part of Zen master. Unlike the previous teisho, and the one that followed, there is dead silence afterward. Finally, apropos, someone asks a rather formulaic question.

There is nothing objective about this account—it was my subjective experience. I recall a similar dynamic when I began to teach. I would catch myself speaking like Aitken Rōshi. I recall one student who needed quite a bit of time and patient listening. I felt that I was "a Zen teacher," not here to do "supportive therapy." Where were the existential questions? When would we get down to the "real work" on the essential level? This student taught me a great deal about teaching and about allowing the two streams to comingle within me such that I could be of help. Similar to Ogden's (2009) "dreaming the patient" while the patient cannot yet do so, as I settled in and "lived a bit of life together" with the student, over several years her capacity grew to use her Zen practice in new and beneficial ways.

Over the years, both psychoanalysis and Zen have privileged not only classical versions of understanding but also the authority of the analyst and Zen master. One interpretation does not a valuable analytic process make. Interpretation and developing usable internalized understanding are part of a jointly regulated, if asymmetrical, interactive process. In

Zen teaching, likewise, I am coming to see that koan study and kensho, while valuable and sometimes transformative experiences, are also part of a broader, more inclusive process of unfolding in the teacher–student relationship, in one's Zen training, and in the "continuing education" of teacher and student alike.

The foundational Zen story tells how the Buddha, after weeks of sitting under the Bodhi tree inquiring into the roots of human suffering, opened his eyes one morning to see the morning star. Recall that he exclaimed, "Now I see that all beings by nature are enlightened from the beginning. It is only because of their ignorance and attachments that they cannot bear witness to this." What did the Buddha realize when he saw the morning star? How would you respond? Although I do not discount direct understanding, I want to offer an alternative narrative of awakening. The Zen master may not actually enlighten the student, as many Zen stories convey. As concerns the *process*, Zen dialogue may be similar to how transformative experience is intersubjectively generated in psychotherapy. What if, rather than enlightening the student, it worked like this: The Zen teacher "holds in trusteeship," as Grotstein says, the transformative understanding of the identity of *samsara* and *nirvana*—form and emptiness—a realization the student cannot yet "dream" or realize for him- or herself. In time, as the student's practice deepens, he unconsciously begins to convey via unconscious communication in the relational field a growing "readiness." Then, at an opportune moment, the teacher, intersubjectively moved, intuitively in sync with the student, says a word or makes an action that helps reveal to the student what has been all the while apparent but unavailable.

Lifelong Learning

> Do I contradict myself?
> Very well then, I contradict myself.
> I am large, I contain multitudes.
> —WALT WHITMAN, *Song of Myself*

Watching our steps closely, as Sensaki Sensei encourages us to do, involves stopping, looking, and listening—taking a sounding of the echoes, the ripples of our actions omnidirectionally. We listen, consciously and unconsciously, and track the impacts and resonance of thoughts, emotions, perceptions, psychic fuels, intentions, motivations, reactions, bodily sensations, and movement—on verbal and nonverbal registers. Is this dualistic? Yes, but it is in the service of alignment and mutual benefit. Our needs for connection, ongoing learning, and life-giving attachments continue to evolve over our life spans, including Zen teachers and psychotherapists. As Suzuki Rōshi said, "We are all perfect as we are. And we can all stand a little improvement."

The Dance of the Universal and the Personal

I begin this closing section with several stories about my teachers, some recent personal discoveries of my own, and musings about what they might mean for Zen and psychotherapy, the dance of the universal and the personal, and an integrative narrative of liberation.

I vividly recall the emotional impact on Aitken Rōshi when he discovered he had another family, in Polynesia, that his father had not told him about. Visiting and spending time with this new-old family, their warmth and openness, seemed to transform him. His becoming a grandfather recently has had a similar effect: emotional ripples coursing through Indra's Net. I also recall the tremendous impact on a Buddhist teacher friend who discovered that he had a son he did not know about and with whom he has developed a close relationship.

The famous Zen scholar D. T. Suzuki was once spotted at a conference at Columbia University in animated conversation with a proponent of psychic powers, something Buddhism tends to look askance at. When asked why, he replied, "Because it's so interesting." Once when Yamada Rōshi was asked about reincarnation, he replied, "There's always the phenomenal world." In the essential world, birth and death are so many concepts, like clouds floating across a vast, bright, and empty sky. There is no coming and going; no success or failure; no enlightenment or delusion; no past, present, or future; no Buddhas or ordinary folk. Maybe Rōshi was saying something like "In the relative world, on the register of coming and going, being born and dying, you never know." It intrigued a number of his students, given how firmly rooted he was in his own distinctive essential nature and how disinclined most Zen teachers are to comment directly about the matter. He also said that if he were reborn, he would like to be a big shade tree offering protection and rest for travelers on the way. He also would wish that his wife be reborn as a tree, right alongside him, their roots entwined in the earth below, both offering shelter and rest. At a talk he gave at a Bay area Zen temple, Robert Thurman spoke about the Tibetan view that in some past life we have each been one another's mother. When challenged by several people in the audience about the empirical validity of past lives and the political uses they were possibly being put to, he said the main purpose of the teaching, whatever its veracity and related politics, was to impress upon us, to shock us into appreciating, just how intimately connected through space and time we and all beings are.

With research still evolving, and advances in genetic tracing, we are coming to see that this general idea—that we are indeed connected in ways previously unimaginable—may be gradually coming to have some scientific backing. And with the new field of epigenetics, we are learning that cracking the genetic code is not the alpha and omega. There are factors that turn on and off certain genes, activating or inhibiting certain potentials, that we might never suspect. Such factors might include our states of mind and ways of being, *across generations*. As the science develops, this may take the psychoanalytic idea of the intergenerational transmission of trauma to another level. It may also confirm the activity of the law of cause and effect in Buddhism—the sometimes subtle but profoundly resonating impacts of what we actually transmit by the quality of our presence and psychic fuels.

Getting Personal

Lately, the phrase "I belong to the world" has been welling up from time to time. I am not sure what it means, but I sense life expanding. Our Coming Home Project with veterans, families, and care providers, bringing together the spiritual teacher, psychotherapist, and community organizer in me, is quite satisfying and seeing how it helps people especially so. Part of this involves certain elements of my identity that continue to come to light and unfold in ways I had not imagined.

I begin with, "What's in a name?" It dawned on me some time ago that my "spiritual parents" (Robert Aitken and his remarkable wife,

Anne) were Robert and Anne A, while my biological father was Robert Bobrow (Robert B), and his wife, whom I met with him in 1973, was Ann B: Robert and Anne A and Robert and Ann B. Some years after I met my biological father, I legally changed my name to "Bobrow." People at the time would say, "Joe you seem different . . . in a good way." I didn't know what they were talking about until a friend suggested it might have to do with my taking my original surname. I learned that Bobrow came from Bobrov, a common Russian name. Later, after I became a father, my son became friends with two Russian Jewish boys who lived downstairs from us, and they would spend hours with us in our flat. When we would occasionally have dinner with their family, the boys' mother would ask me if I was Jewish. I would reply, "Yes." Then, she would say that Bobrow is a Russian name, and again I would reply in the affirmative. One day, as we went through this yet again, I became slightly annoyed, and I repeated her words. Through her reactions, I realized it: Bobrow was a Russian, *not* a Jewish, name. How could this be? I wondered—both my parents were Jewish. I asked my sister from my father's side and learned that neither Bobrow nor Bobrov were my real names. For a Zen teacher who practices seeing through "name and form," *these* names and forms meant quite a bit to me. She told me that my paternal grandfather had, out of fear of his family being killed in the pogroms, changed the family name to Bobrow. The original name was Handleman, which means "tradesman." This was a letdown. After a year or so, I thought to ask her what my paternal grandmother's maiden name was. She said it was Luria.

I didn't make a big thing about names. When people mispronounced Bobrow, I would often joke "Boh-brow, Baa-broh, Barbero—just don't call me late for dinner." But Luria, that rang a bell. It was a family of scientists and psychologists that could trace their forebears back to pre-Inquisition Spain, an era I had always loved, a place where philosophers, religious teachers, artists, and writers from different ethnicities and orientations coexisted and flourished. And, there was Isaac Luria, the famous Kabbalist. The strands of identity began to feel more woven. I had read a few stories about the Hasidic masters who in spirit resembled the old Zen worthies. Later, however, I was helping a friend with her dissertation by participating in a series of interfaith Buddhist–Christian groups. Once she asked us each to make a kind of diorama, using a variety of natural and other materials, that represented our view of spirituality. When we went around and shared our impressions about one another's work, everyone laughed and pointed out the Tree of Life I had created. I was surprised and also delighted; here was another register of meaning and identity. There was the big tree, with apples hanging from the branches, complete with sun and moon—nary a Buddhist wheel in sight.

A few months ago, I was browsing through a local bookstore and came upon a major new translation of the *Zohar*, the primary text of the Kabbalah, by Danny Matt, a scholar of Jewish mysticism who had taught a seminar on the Hasidic masters that I attended. I opened the first pages and saw the Tree of Life, with the tree's branches—the Sephirot—which I had glanced at briefly years earlier. But this time, there were old testament names associated with each of the Sephirot. The myth of Joseph and the coat of many colors had always resonated, but the impact in this moment was palpable. I discovered that the name "Joseph" is associated with the Sephirah Yesod and with Tsaddiq. There is a range of meanings here, from righteous one, covenant, to phallus and originator. I have two Zen names, conferred by Aitken Rōshi. One, given upon taking *Jukai* (accepting the Buddhist precepts) is Seikai, or True Sea. The second, upon receiving Dharma Transmission (independent teacher status), is Gen'un, Source Cloud or Cloud of the Origin. I have always been interested in origins: Who was my father? Where did I come from? What is the nature of reality? Mine has been a story of working with pain and loss rooted in part in unrighteous behavior. Yesod is also sexuality, purified over time, cultivated in restraint, the procreative life force of the universe, a transmitter of energies from Ayin—the origin, primal no-thingness—on through to a midwife-like presence, Shekhinah. I have been a disseminator by nature, interested in integration and in integrity. I also learned a bit more about Isaac Luria and lurianic Kabbalah, with its guiding myths of contraction or withdrawal, shattering, sparks, liberating the sparks, and repair. I resonated with this. It sent currents, frissons resonating through me, across the hidden tracks of my generational sensibilities.

It was a *Nachträglichkeit* moment that organized and set in motion a slew of memories and connections, an *après coup* "tracing of my tracks." I wondered, could I have been, as Bollas describes, unconsciously selecting objects to represent my idiom and, simultaneously, tracing out connections in some of my early travels and my "pilgrimage" that are transgenerational and defy our conventional sense of time? I knew that I was connecting dots, and yet it felt like *unearthing*, as well as revising, a personal narrative.

My friend Haru, a Buddhist priest in another tradition, has heard this story, and he is not surprised. He sees it as a transgenerational transmission, something he and those in his Buddhist tradition believe in. In his view, the mechanism works via our DNA. Bion thinks that we came into life with "pre-conceptions"; Bollas thinks our idiom pre-dates environmental influences and needs interactive elaboration and dissemination. I had never allowed for such a dimension of influence in my sense of who I was. This experience fleshed out the growing feeling that somehow I belonged to the world. Dualistic as the notion is, the world draws me in, makes a claim, and unbeknownst to me, perhaps I have been tracing the tracks of the world "calling." The point was that my personal history is not simply *mine*—elucidated, worked over, and as much as possible, transformed and healed. My history is intrinsically part of our cultural, racial, biological, spiritual, intellectual history. Similar to Indra's Net, but with a difference—more like a net of Indra's *within* the interconnected point that is "Joseph."

I associated to the Tree of Life and recalled how immersed I became in big trees in Hawaii as I turned the ripe old age of thirty. I thought of Yamada Rōshi's desire to be reborn as a big sheltering tree alongside his wife. I felt like part of a much deeper and wider story. Isaac Luria also lost his father as a child. The Jews were expelled, twice, and exterminated. Although I had no relatives in the Holocaust, I have always felt this tragedy deeply since a young child. This was not a matter of transcending my personal pain and identity through discovery and embodiment of no-self. The life stream plunges deep, ranges far and wide. Thich Nhat Hanh captures it in his way, in the present moment, horizontally, via his distinctive vision of *paticca samupaddha*, or dependent co-arising. But, the vertical time dimension felt different. It created a deepening conviction that I am indeed vast and contain multitudes, horizontally and vertically through space and time, part of an incredibly interconnected web of affinities. The personal story, the personal identity, is but a part of a much wider, deeper more interconnected tapestry. I do not mean that "everything is everything," as Marvin Gaye sang. Unconscious emotional communication in the relational field puts flesh on the filaments of the Jeweled Net of Indra. This felt like another layer of connective tissue that resonated with my interest in the karmic, relative, or personal dimension, as well as the universal, and in their intricate interplay.

Why do I share all this? I hope it conveys why we must not minimize or discard the personal—how it too can be a doorway to liberation. This personal dimension not only embodies our essential nature it also helps us feel rooted as we root around, feet planted in the great stream of life. The personal dimension not only reflects the self-centered obsession of our contemporary culture, or clinging to the known, to "our story," but also can reveal how we are already part and parcel of the story of stories, of intertwining strands of history. My story is the story of life.

Classical Buddhism, not just Tibetan Buddhism, talks about reincarnating to finish our development. I do not know about past lives; I haven't experienced them. And, I am not sure about the finishing part; it seems so ongoing. But, there is a sense of my life being the life of the history of the world. Attachment to constriction and pain is resolved and relinquished not only by transcendent experience or by healing our personal stories, but also by finding and confirming and affirming our participation and belonging in the great family of man and the family of all beings. Our identity expands in the container made by the multiple intersecting crisscrossing identities through time.

A central thread of my personal pain has been the feeling of being a patchwork quilt. Held within the container of human history (as well as *shunyata*, or vast potential space) there is the joy of discovering that this patched-together quilt is a tapestry of the world and its history: ghosts become ancestors. The alchemy of transforming ghosts into ancestors occurs in part through these increasingly internalized recognitions of cradled and expanding registers of belonging and historical identity. I used to wonder if this ongoing personal work was a distraction from Zen practice. I don't anymore. As I wrote in Chapter 2, "It *takes* a (distinctive, personal) self to fully *embody* our essential (no-self) nature. And as one unravels, experiences, and realizes the empty, multi-centered nature of all beings and of consciousness itself, the (particular, personal) self and its unique qualities are potentiated, brought to life and fruition."

So, the partners in liberation are not solely the unconscious and the Bliss Body, psychotherapy and Zen, or even spiritual practice and emotional growth. The marriage is between the absolute and the relative, the boundless impersonal and the personal register. It is expressed in the dance of the universal and the particular—shifting forms, proportions, and emphases—intercourse indeed: shunyata (or its Kabbalistic counterpart, *Ein Sof*) and our everyday humanity. In Kabbalah, it is the marriage of Tif'eret and Shekhinah, brought to fruition through Yesod. Who knew that Yamada Rōshi's fraction—where all phenomena can be the numerator and empty infinity is the denominator—would bear such resemblance to my other native tale of the marriage of the universal and particular? All this was poignant and sweet and made me feel full and happy for a few days. Then, like all things, it ebbed. As Yasutani Rōshi said, "Your practice begins today."

On September 11, 1989, Yamada Koun Rōshi, leader of the Sanbo Kyodan School of Zen Buddhism, died at his home in Kamakura, Japan, after a long illness. He was the Dharma successor to Yasutani Haku'un ("White Cloud") Rōshi. The teacher name given to him by Yasutani Rōshi, Koun Ken, means "House of Cultivating Clouds." In 1969, along with his wife, Yamada Rōshi established the Sanun Zendo, "Zendo of the Three Clouds." The first of this group of three great teachers was Yasutani Rōshi's teacher, Dai'un ("Great Cloud") Harada Rōshi. Yamada Rōshi became Robert Aitken's teacher and the head teacher of the Diamond Sangha from 1971 to 1984, when Aitken Rōshi received transmission.

Yamada Rōshi was also a teacher of mine. He came for *sesshin* yearly from 1970 to 1984. This is a story of his final visit to the Maui Zendo. On the eve of his departure early the next morning back to Kamakura, on January 10, 1984, following evening *zazen*, students gathered in the commons room at the Maui Zendo. After having tea with us and answering questions for well over an hour, he said:

Now I will say my last words. The last word, you know, that is a koan. I will say the last word, ha! Earlier, Joe pointed to that picture over there, and asked if I knew that person [a picture of a young Yamada Rōshi in robes, holding the flower he was given as he stepped off the plane in Maui for the first time]. I asked him,

"Do you know him?" Joe replied, "I do not know him." I too said that I didn't know him at all. I am afraid to have to tell you that what I have said this evening has been deceiving, that I have deceived all of you [laughter]. And I must say that I have deceived myself too [more laughter]. But you know [pointing to his own head], I like him [even more laughter]. And we need him, we cannot do without him. This afternoon at Iao Park, I was reading a poem of William Merwin's in a book he gave to me. This!—is it the words I say, or is it the poem of William's? I do not know. It is like a dream. That is all. Sayonara. It is time to go to bed.

To realize this dream, this laughter, and with it our own true face and that of all beings is the discipline and the joy of Zen practice. The roots run deep. We tap into them each time we exhale, laugh, cry, diaper the baby, write a letter, or pull some weeds. I close with a New Year's greeting I addressed to Aitken Rōshi, Yamada Rōshi's Dharma heir, in 1985:

We come thinking you have the key to the vault. You send us on a treasure hunt and even assist us in the search. And you rejoice with us when we return, having finally gotten the great joke. Then, you help us learn how to erase our tracks, unload the loot, and seeing that the whole thing is a dream, become fluent in the language of poverty. Totally subversive.

Afterword:
At the Heart of the Matter

A Zen ancestor said,
"Everything flows from your own heart."

Today I will speak about heart and integrity. Is there common ground? What is the relation of an unburdened heart and the heart of wisdom? Typically, when we think of matters of the heart, we think of romance, melodrama, and sentiment. But the Heart Sutra is not necessarily about those things. So why do we call it the "Heart" Sutra? The heart of wisdom knows that there is nothing at all. Nothing to defend, protect, improve, or conceal. Nothing to attain, or mess up. It is unfettered by craving, self-preoccupation, fixed, narrow, restrictive views, or compulsive modes of living. Because the heart of wisdom is self-reflexive, it can discover and express its own insubstantiality. Fa-Yen calls it, "The fresh breeze that rises when the great burden is laid down."

Because there is nothing absolute and permanent, the heart touches down and finds itself as myriad beings. It realizes its identity with the Jeweled Net of Indra. By what are we confirmed?—"Hoooo!"—By the Hoot Owl, did you hear it this morning? By my child's homework assignment or the illness of a loved one.

A wise-hearted one lives joyfully because she knows that she doesn't have to take herself seriously. And *that* is a matter of utmost gravity. (Of course this does not mean ignoring what's going on—to the contrary.)

The Heart Sutra is about realizing the heart of the matter for ourselves. Where do we find it? How do we come to this "place"? The heart is not circumscribed by the chest cavity or adequately described as a chakra. Its "turf" is spacious and boundless in harmonious interplay, at the heart of the matter. How is it actualized? Realization is not only the experience of *kensho*. It means making real. In each moment, we bear witness. It's made real when we enlighten this moment's activity, when we contact the many beings, when we enter the Dharma gates of ordinary living. It's made real by each inhale, each exhale. It comes into life with each mindful step, with each task. A sanctified action is a mindful action. We are in attendance; there is no gap between the action, the actor, and that which is acted upon. We peel away, see, acknowledge, and penetrate deeply. And relinquish. Letting go is not getting rid of. We turn away from the veils of delusion generated by self-centered, protective strivings, and we turn toward and take refuge in things as they are. We catalyze this heart of wisdom and open ourselves to its teachings.

At the heart of the matter there is nothing absolute at all, and so we are connected beyond concepts. The sounds of the children playing in the schoolyard arise in, and as, my own body, and simultaneously each and every being is completely unique and sacred just as it is. We are at home here, *at play in the fields of the Lord*. We open to the singing of the birds, the rumble in our tummy. It's not a matter of sentimentality, respectability, or politeness. It co-arises with clear seeing. Wisdom and compassion are unleashed only as we come to grasp directly and immediately who we are and what our fundamental relationship is to the world and its beings. "Immediate" doesn't only mean "sudden." It means "without mediation." So, if the heart is incalculably wider and deeper, more alive and vivid than we ever imagined, where is it realized? Where is it practiced? Although it's not enclosed by the rib cage, still we have to bring things home. Hakuin says it succinctly, "This very body is the body of the Buddha."

Now what are the qualities of the unburdened heart, free of self-preoccupation, free of the need for self-improvement and redemption? They are exemplified in the Four *Brahmaviharas*, the qualities of an awakened one, one who is alive at the heart of the matter. *Metta* is loving kindness. *Karuna* is compassion. Each of these is preceded by the word "boundless." They are without self-imposed limits, free flowing, extending everywhere. Boundless loving kindness, boundless compassion, the third vihara, or abode, is *mudita*, or joy in the joy of others. *Upeksha*, boundless equanimity, is the fourth vihara. *Metta* is kindness, imbued with love, which naturally characterizes our conduct and our life when we are in touch with our self just as we are—intrinsically intimate with the world and its beings just as they are. Its expression is kindness. *Karuna*—what a wonderful sounding word. Compassion arises and flows naturally when I see that from the beginning the world and I are not divided, and I cultivate this connectivity in my daily life. This truth is not realized secondhand; it is personal, vivid, and in the particulars. More than simply an attitude or an approach, *compassion* means "to suffer with" and "to suffer as." Please don't get snagged on fixed ideas about compassion. Don't think it has a particular content. Don't equate it with being "nice." The skillful, timely, sometimes persistent "No" of a parent is crucial to the child's development. With mudita, joy in the joy and the liberation of others, the awakened heart sees that all things from the very beginning, just as they are, are the Buddha-nature, itself. Acting in accord with this experience, we appreciate and take pleasure in the nourishment, growth, and surprising unfoldings of another. That person is, from the beginning, none other than a Buddha, a jewel, just as they are, in all their distinctiveness, with all their qualities, whatever they may be. Equanimity, upeksha, arises directly from the perception and deep acceptance that all things are fundamentally empty. As Martha and the Vandellas sang, "Nowhere to run to, baby, nowhere to hide." All attempts to fill it up or block it out come to naught. There is a gospel song, "Rock My Soul in the Bosom of Abraham." It goes, "So high, can't get over it—so low, can't get under it—so wide, can't get around it—oh, rock my soul." There's nothing to attain, nothing left unattained. Just as I am, just as you are, there is not a hair missing, not a drop left over. This equanimity is not simply the result of training, of techniques for calming the mind. That helps, but these qualities are rooted in the unburdened heart that sees deep and clear, that loves boundlessly, in particulars.

Remember Te-shan and the old woman selling *monju*? *Monju* are soft rice cakes, the really sticky ones sometimes filled with sweet soybean paste. "Full of arrogance, Te-shan went south to extinguish the doctrine of a special transmission outside the sutras." Although the particular banner we carry may vary, who does not recognize himself in Te-shan? So very certain and therefore so self-righteous. He had not yet been energized by ambiguity. He stops to ask for "refreshment" (which also means "to punctuate the mind"). The woman inquired what he was carrying in his pack. "Notes and commentaries on the Diamond Sutra," he replied shortly. In the spirit of *mondo*, or everyday Zen dialogues, she said, "I want to ask you a question. If you can answer, I will serve you without charge. If you cannot answer, then I won't serve you at all." Te-shan agreed, and she lowered the boom: "I hear the Diamond Sutra says, 'Past mind cannot be grasped, present mind cannot be grasped, future mind cannot be grasped.' Which mind does Your Reverence intend to refresh?" In this encounter, Te-shan got more than he asked for, and less. His Zen study had begun.

So, what refreshes? It's a pause that refreshes, Coca-Cola notwithstanding. Our parents were right to tell us, "When you cross the street, stop, look, and listen." For the practice of Zen, to enter the great stream of life and death, it cannot be business as usual. The self and its preoccupations are apparent *and* hidden, and it is the hidden ones that really get to us. If our self-centered cares, worries, projects, and machinations are in fact what burden, bind, and constrict us, and if our search for safe refuge itself can create imprisonment and turn us unintentionally away from the source of nourishment, what is the antidote? Awareness. Awareness. Awareness.

The first awareness is on the cushion and with ourselves. The second awareness is in action. Awareness in the hurlyburly of daily activities brings learning that practicing solely on our cushion in a sacred but circumscribed setting cannot. The third awareness might be called awareness-in-relation. That means attentiveness in relationship to my teacher, my child, my wife, my boss, my supervisees, my cat. Of course, each of these modes of awareness interpenetrate, but for learning purposes we can examine them separately. Each requires attention and acceptance, compassion and penetrating understanding. So, if our heart's burden is the maintenance of the self as separate, then our attempts to prop it up, rationalize, defend, and justify it; conceal, expiate, redeem, and rehabilitate it, ad infinitum, only tighten the noose—and keep our torturous activity hidden, our actual emotional activity, inner and outer. What a price we pay. We read in the *Song of Enlighten-*

ment, "What could be better than the true way of the Absolute? Cut through directly to the root of it all. I don't want to hear about the leaves and branches." This is our way.

But, caveat emptor. Our human psyche has the distinct ability, even tendency, to split off certain of its activities, so we can *appear* whole, appear *alive*, as if we really grokked something. When, in effect, simultaneously we are actively maintaining other activities of a completely different nature, in the basement, so to speak, unaware. We all know examples from our own lives and examples from our Zen and Buddhist *Sanghas* and the wider religious landscape. The thread that runs through the mundane examples and the more serious boundary violations involving money, power, and sex is the split between the public, respectable, "enlightened," and the private. This brings us into the realm of character. Insight and character go hand in hand. We can develop authentic awareness and deep insight within a sacred but very circumscribed field—on the cushion, in the dokusan room, the dojo, public talks—and still not be whole people. We have not integrated the internal factors that actually fuel our delusions. Dismantling delusions— that is an aspect of Zen practice. We see into, realize, and embody, more and more deeply, our essential nature. But it is not a cultist trick. Delusion is not an abstract philosophical event. Enlightenment is not an aesthetic pursuit. Koan study is not literary interpretation. Delusion is in the particulars, and the particulars have a personal context.

I have told this story to some of you. In one of my first serious relationships, I thought I was flexible and non-defensive. She could tell me anything, no problem, I'd hear and contain it, and we could talk it out. But when she implied that I wasn't committed or caring enough, the floodgates opened, and she never heard the end of it. How dearly I cherished that identity. And how privately superior it made me feel. Yet, I was blind to this data, such was my reactive immersion in it. I couldn't see and really reflect on it.

Others have told their own stories. For one person it's one thing, for another it's a different buried, cherished self-image that is nursed. For years, I thought I was a very peaceful person. Others would tell me, "You seem so mellow." Sure I'm mellow. Most of the time. But one day it dawned on me, "The reason you are here, dummy, practicing Zen, is because you have a busy mind. And you're a very complex person." That may be why I didn't begin by studying Tibetan Buddhism, although I valued the teachings. The practices seemed busier than what was already going on in my mind.

So, what refreshes? The monju woman didn't talk about refreshment—she provided it, and she presented it. She showed, directly, that reforming any mind, rehabilitating past, present, future is pointless. Her question to Te-shan went right to the heart of the matter. But sidestepping or leapfrogging character, which is an unrecognized motivation that actually brought many of us to Zen, has its drawbacks. So, the way to true refreshment is through this ongoing bringing to light, through the three kinds of awareness—bringing to light; sloughing off the burdensome and protective self-activity that is informed by mistaken views of self and other, of reality, of the world, and motivated by self-preservation; and the denial of *dukkha*. It is like a stone on our hearts. This is how we purify our motivation.

You know, in Zen we have a tradition of working toward awakening. While devotion and focus are still critical, thankfully it has become less of a G.I. Joe, samurai type of affair. Awakening to essential nature unfolds out of persistent mindful practice, unhitched from the fruits of our efforts. If we can practice like this, and none of us can do so perfectly all the time, then the perennial experience of enlightenment that we read and hear about, that we sometimes can sense in another, may emerge. In the *Song of Enlightenment* we read, "In speech you hear its silence." Dogen writes that "body and mind fall away." Wu-men said it was like having a dream and knowing it for yourself but being unable to speak about it. This perennial experience develops naturally with deep curiosity and purpose and right effort.

In some traditions, that's it, it stops there, with a sacred vision. But in our tradition, we take to heart Lin-chi's injunction, "Not enough, not enough yet." We keep going. And perhaps we encounter "the fallen away body and mind," our own boundless nature, in vivid particulars. Having done the work not only of focused concentration but also of awareness, this perennial experience is less likely to be placed at the service of preserving and protecting the hidden self. See, that is the problem. Enlightenment is the unbidden result that reveals the way it is from the beginning. We cannot make it happen any more than we can make our son into a daughter or bring out the sunshine when it is raining. It is the result of this ongoing wrestling with facing, bringing to light, understanding, working through, integrating the varied dimensions of our practice and our lives, of what is so, of the way it is. Not only is it the natural result, like the pear falling from the tree, but it is also a cause of rejoicing for all beings, the fundamental refreshment and flowering at the heart of all things. The hidden knots and attachments to conceptual structures that we have constructed to protect us in reaction to the inevitable suffering of life, and that end up driving us, unravel and lose their grip.

So the unburdened heart—deep peace, self-acceptance, and love—finds common ground with awareness and insight into our true nature. The method, the goal, or foundational reality—and the practitioner herself—all fall away and so come into alignment. Not three, not two, they are not even one.

What is the upshot? I said I'd speak about integrity, but it would be brief. Because that's our very practice, here on retreat and in our daily, relational lives. Integrity and virtue are the natural result. Not just method, not just skills—integrity and virtue cannot be manufactured. They come unbidden and accrue silently, benefiting all beings, as we walk this arduous and joyous path together.

Acknowledgments

How to begin to thank those who have given of themselves and so contributed to this book? You are family, friends, colleagues, patients, teachers, students; more than I can recognize here.

To my patients, psychotherapy and Zen students, and recently the veterans, service members, families and care providers who are part of the Coming Home Project: You have taught and inspired me more than I can say.

I drew a sense of camaraderie from psychoanalysts who were interested in spiritual experience: Jerry Fogel, Michael Parsons, Michael Eigen, Jim Grotsein, and Neville Symington. I appreciate new friendships with Ted Kenney, John Briere, Mark Epstein, and Christopher Bollas. Charles Spezzano and Jerry Garguilo took a chance on an unpublished author in 1994. Jean Sanville and Hedda Bolgar shared their hearts and minds, and the harvest inspires and nourishes. Roy Schaefer had lunch with a young therapist many moons ago and encouraged me to put my interdisciplinary ideas into words. Lifetime friendships with Susan Kerman and David Moltz, my first supervisors at Morrisania Hospital, are a blessing. My early mentor Ted Reiss said I'd make a good psychologist, and professor Murray Stahl captivated a teenager with tales of the unconscious and introduced me to Krishnamurti.

The bond with Zen friends from the early days of training in the Diamond Sangha in Hawaii remains strong. Regular gatherings over many years with fellow teachers and Dharma buddies Norman Fischer, James

Baraz, and Jeff Kitzes have been an important source of support, learning, and friendship. Teaching with Ajahn Amaro has been lively and enriching. I'm grateful for the Dharma friendship with Trudy Goodman; our paths have crisscrossed throughout our adult lives. Good discussions with Haru Inoye and Liane Louie Badua allowed me to articulate what I hold dear. Allan Finlay helped at workshops and by transcribing ideas.

Thanks to my sisters Lucy, Rosy, and Susan and my nephew Demian for your interest and encouragement, and to Rosy for the final proofreading.

Greg, your generosity helped get Deep Streams off the ground. Esalen Institute kindly invited me to spend a month as spiritual teacher in residence.

My experience living with the residents of Plum Village for two summers, in 1983 and 1984, provided seeds that continue to sprout. With gratitude to my teachers, including Anne Aitken. With appreciation to Tom Rosbrow for his support.

Notes

1. Case 55 of the *Blue Cliff Record* (Cleary & Cleary, 1979a, 1979b), a major collection of Zen koans, describes the following encounters: Tao Wu and Chien Yuan went to a house to make a condolence call. Yuan hit the coffin and said, "Alive or dead?" Wu said, "I won't say alive, and I won't say dead." Yuan said, "Why won't you say?" Wu said, "I won't say." Later, Tao Wu passed on. Yuan went to Shih Shuan and brought up the foregoing story. Shuang said, "I won't say alive, and I won't say dead." Yuan said, "Why won't you say?" Shuan said, "I won't say! I won't say!" At these words, Yuan had an insight (Cleary & Cleary, 1977b, p. 365).

2. The first treasure is the Buddha. This refers to Shakyamuni, the founder of Buddhism, as well as all other Buddhist teachers and ancestors. It also refers to a deeper dimension where all beings by their original nature are Buddha. Realization of this is awakening. The Dharma is the second treasure. It is boundless, void of anything permanent or absolute, and simultaneously full of possibilities. Dharma also means phenomena, the truth of Buddhism, and the Buddhist teachings. It is represented in Chinese and Japanese with the ideograph "law." So, another meaning is "the way things are," the Tao. The Sangha originally referred to the community of renunciates who studied with the Buddha. It has also come to mean religious fellowship or community, monastic and lay, and more fundamentally, the intrinsic interconnectedness of all beings.

3. As if one body were not enough, in Mahayana Buddhism there are the metaphorical Three Bodies of the Buddha: the *Dharmakaya*, the *Sambhogakaya*, and the *Nirmanakaya*. The Sambhogakaya is called the body of bliss or the body that experiences the fruits of Buddhist practice. It is sometimes explained as the communion of the absolute (*Dharmakaya*) with the relative (*Nirmanakaya*), where the relative body experiences the joy of realization of the absolute. The three bodies of the Buddha are also three aspects of awakening that are embodied in our daily experience. The Nirmanakaya presents absolute uniqueness, represented in

infinitely rich variety, the Dharmakaya clarity-emptiness, and the Sambogakaya interdependence-oneness.

4. Psychotherapy has a parallel dimension with several similar characteristics—the unconscious. Some—Bomford (1999) and Grotstein (2007) among them— equated the Unconscious with God.

5. "Great Vows for All": Beings are numberless, I vow to save them / Greed, hatred and ignorance arise endlessly, I vow to put an end to them / Dharma gates are countless, I vow to wake to them / The Buddha Way is endless, I vow to follow through (*Deep Streams Zen Institute Sutra Book*).

6. These are the Ten Grave Precepts: Not Killing, Not Stealing, Not Misusing Sex, Not Lying, Not Giving or Taking Intoxicants, Not Discussing Faults of Others, Not Praising Yourself While Abusing Others, Not Sparing the Dharma Assets, Not Indulging in Anger, Not Defaming the Three Treasures. The following are the Three Refuges: I take refuge in the Buddha, I take refuge in the Dharma, I take refuge in the sangha. The Three Pure Precepts are as follows: Renounce all evil; practice all good; keep your mind pure—thus all the Buddhas taught. The Mahayana version drops the final line and rewrites the third: Renounce all evil, practice all good, save the many beings

7. In Mahayana Buddhism, the Lotus Sutra lists the Six Perfections as (original terms in Sanskrit): *Dāna paramita*: generosity, giving of oneself; *Śīla paramita*: virtue, morality, discipline, proper conduct. *Kṣānti* (*kshanti*) *paramita*: patience, tolerance, forbearance, acceptance, endurance; *Vīrya paramita*: energy, diligence, vigor, effort; *Dhyāna paramita*: one-pointed concentration, contemplation; *Prajñā paramita*: wisdom, insight. In the Ten Stages (*Dasabhumika*) Sutra, four more paramitas are listed: *Upāya paramita*: skillful means; *Praṇidhāna* (*pranidhana*) *paramita*: vow, resolution, aspiration, determination; *Bala paramita*: spiritual power; *Jñāna paramita*: knowledge.

References

Aitken, R. (1978). *A Zen wave*. New York: Weatherhill.

Aitken, R. (1982). *Taking the path of Zen*. San Francisco: North Point Press.

Aitken, R. (1984). *Mind of clover*. San Francisco: North Point Press.

Aitken, R. (Ed. & Trans.). (1990). *The gateless barrier* (Wu-men Kuan). San Francisco: North Point Press.

Aitken, R. (1992). *Zen talks, essays and prefaces*. Honolulu, HI: Honolulu Diamond Sangha.

Aitken, R. (1993). *Encouraging words*. New York: Pantheon.

Albom, M. (1997). *Tuesdays with Morrie*. New York: Doubleday.

Alvarez, A. (1992). *Live company*. London: Routledge.

Applebaum, S. (1999). *Speaking with the second voice: Evocativeness*. Unpublished, unpaginated manuscript.

Arden, M. (1999). *The peacock's tail and the emperor's new clothes*. Unpublished manuscript.

Bachelard, G. (1960). *The poetics of space*. Paris: Presses Universitaires de France.

Balint, M. (1968). *The basic fault: Therapeutic aspects of regression*. Evanston, IL: Northwestern University Press.

Batchelor, S. (1990). *The faith to doubt*. Berkeley, CA: Parallax Press.

Beck, C. J. (1989). *Everyday Zen*. San Francisco: Harper and Row.

Benjamin, J. (1982). Jessica Benjamin. *Psychoanalytical Review*, 69, 158–162.

de Bianchedi, E. T. (2001). The passionate psychoanalyst. *fort da, The Journal of the Northern California Society for Psychoanalytic Psychology*, 7(2), 19–28.

Bick, E. (1987). The experience of the skin in early object relations. In *Collected papers of Martha Harris and Esther Bick*. Pertshire: Clunie Press. (Original work published 1967)

Bion, W. R. (1961). *Experiences in groups*. London: Tavistock.

Bion, W. R. (1962). A theory of thinking. *International Journal of Psychoanalysis*, 43, 306–310.

Bion, W. R. (1970). *Attention and interpretation*. London: Tavistock.

Bion, W. R. (1977). *Seven servants*. New York: Aronson.

Bion, W. R. (1984a). *Learning from experience*. London: Karnac Books. (Original work published 1962)

Bion, W. R. (1984b). *Transformations*. London: Karnac Books.

Bion, W. R. (1987). *Second thoughts*. London: Styllus.

Bion, W. R. (1989). *Two papers: The grid and the caesura*. London: Karnac Books.

Bion, W. R. (1992) *Cogitations* (F. Bion, Ed.). London: Karnac Books.

Bion, W. R. (1994). Making the best of a bad job. In *Clinical seminars and other works*. London: Karnac Books.

Bion, W. R. (1997). *Taming wild thoughts* (F. Bion, Ed.). London: Karnac Books.

Blake, W. (1995a). Auguries of innocence. In *Poems of William Blake*. Guernsey, UK: Guernsey Press. (Original poem written in 1805)

Blake, W. (1995b). The little black boy. In *Poems of William Blake*. Guernsey, UK: Guernsey Press. (Original poem written in 1787)

Bobrow, J. (1997). Coming to life: The creative intercourse of psychoanalysis and Zen Buddhism. In *Soul on the couch: Spirituality, religion and morality in contemporary psychoanalysis* (C. Spezzano and G. Garguilo, Eds.). Northvale, NJ: Analytic Press.

Bobrow, J. (2001, January). Reverie in psychoanalysis and Zen: Harvesting the ordinary. *Journal of Transpersonal Psychology*, p. 165–175.

Bobrow, J. (2002). Psychoanalysis, mysticism and Winnicott's incommunicado core. *fort da, The Journal of the Northern California Society for Psychoanalytic Psychology*, 8(2), 62–71.

Bollas, C. (1989). *The shadow of the object*. New York: Columbia University Press.

Bollas, C. (1998, December). *Differences between classical and Kleinian technique*. Presentation at Herrick Hospital, Berkeley, CA.

Bollas, C. (1992). *Being a character*. New York: Hill and Wang.

Bomford, R. (1999). *The symmetry of God*. London: Free Association Books. Boorstein, S. (2004, June). Dharma talk. Presented at Buddhism and Psychotherapy Retreat, Deep Streams Institute, Santa Rosa, CA.

Bowlby, J. (1982). *Attachment and loss* (Vol. 2). New York: Basic Books.

Cleary, T. (1983). *Entry into the inconceivable*. Honolulu: University of Hawaii Press.

Cleary, T. (1990). *Transmission of light (Denkoroku)* (T. Cleary, Trans. & Ed.). San Francisco: North Point Press.

Cleary, T., & Cleary, J. C. (1977a). *The Blue Cliff record* (Vol. 1). Boulder, CO: Shambhala.

Cleary, T., & Cleary, J. C. (1977b). *The Blue Cliff record* (Vol. 2). Boulder, CO: Shambhala.

Coltart, N. (1996). Buddhism and psychoanalysis revisited. In *The baby and the bathwater*. London: Karnac Books.

Cook, F. (1977). *Hua-yen Buddhism*. University Park: University of Pennsylvania Press.

Courtois, F. (1971). *An American woman's experience of enlightenment*. Los Angeles: Zen Center.

Dalai Lama. (2000, June 20–24). Presentation at the Buddhist Teachers in the West conference at Spirit Rock Meditation Center, Woodacre, CA.

Deikman, A. (1982). *The observing self*. Boston: Beacon Press.

Dhammapada. (P. Lal, Trans.). (1974). London: Noonday Press.

The Dharma Rag. (May 2008). 11(5), http://www.smzen.org/dharmarag/TheDharma RagMay2008.pdf

Dithrich, C. (2001). Discussion of Elizabeth T. de Bianchedi's "The passionate psychoanalyst." *fort da, The Journal of the Northern California Society for Psychoanalytic Psychology*, 7(2), 29–37.

Dylan, B. (1963, May). The talking WW III blues. On *The freewheelin' Bob Dylan*. Columbia Records.

Edelman, G., & Tononi, G. (2001). *A universe of consciousness: How matter becomes imagination*. New York: Basic Books.

Eigen, M. (2001, September 21). *Damaged dreamwork*. Paper presented at the Northern California Society for Psychoanalytic Psychology introductory event, San Francisco.

Ekman, P. (2003). *Emotions revealed*. London: Weidenfeld & Nicolson.

Eliot, T. S. (1942). Little Gidding. In *Four quartets*. New York: HarcourtBrace.

Eliot, T. S. (1971). *Four quartets*. London: Harcourt Brace Jovanovich, p. 59. (Original poem written in 1943.)

Eliot, T. S. (1999). Inventions of the March Hare. In *Poems 1909–1917*. New York: Houghton Mifflin Harcourt.

Engler, J. (1986). Therapeutic aims in psychotherapy and meditation: Developmental stages in the representation of the self. In K. Wilber, J. Engler, & D. Brown (Eds.), *Transformations in consciousness*. Boston: Shambhala.

Epstein, M. (1995). *Thoughts without a thinker*. New York: Basic Books.

Erikson, E. (1966). *Gandhi's truth*. New York: Norton.

Fa-Yen. (1996). In N. Foster & J. Shoemaker (Eds.), *The roaring stream*. Hopewell, NJ: Ecco Press.

Fisher, C. (1992). Beyond identity: Invention, absorption and transcendence. *Adolescent Psychiatry*, 18, 448–460.

Fogel, G. (1991). Transcending the limits of revisionism and classicism. In G. Fogel (Ed.), *The work of Hans Loewald*. Northvale, NJ: Aronson.

Fonagy, P. (1995, May 20). *The capacity for understanding mental states*. Paper presented at the Los Angeles Institute and Society for Psychoanalytic Studies and the Psychoanalytic Center of California.

Fonagy, P. (2000). Attachment and borderline personality disorder. *Journal of the American Psychoanalytic Association*, 48(4), 1129–1146.

Freud, S. (1895). Project for a scientific psychology. In J. Strachey (Ed. & Trans.), *The standard edition of the complete psychological works of Sigmund Freud* (Vol. 1, pp. 295–397). London: Hogarth Press.

Freud, S. (1896). The aetiology of hysteria. In J. Strachey (Ed. & Trans.), *The standard edition of the complete psychological works of Sigmund Freud* (Vol. 3). London: Hogarth Press.

Freud, S. (1900). The interpretation of dreams. In J. Strachey (Ed. & Trans.), *The standard edition of the complete psychological works of Sigmund Freud* (Vol. 4). London: Hogarth Press.

Freud, S. (1907). Obsessive actions and religious practices. In J. Strachey (Ed. & Trans.), *The standard edition of the complete psychological works of Sigmund Freud* (Vol. 9). London: Hogarth Press.

Freud, S. (1912). Recommendations to physicians practicing psychoanalysis. In J. Strachey (Ed. & Trans.), *The standard edition of the complete psychological works of Sigmund Freud* (Vol. 12, pp. 109–120). London: Hogarth Press.

Freud, S. (1914). Remembering, repeating and working-through. In J. Strachey (Ed. & Trans.), *The standard edition of the complete psychological works of Sigmund Freud* (Vol. 12, pp. 147–156). London: Hogarth Press.

Freud, S. (1915). The unconscious. In J. Strachey (Ed. & Trans.), *The standard edition of the complete psychological works of Sigmund Freud* (Vol. 14, pp. 161–204). London: Hogarth Press.

Freud, S. (1916). Introductory lectures on psycho-analysis. In J. Strachey (Ed. & Trans.), *The standard edition of the complete psychological works of Sigmund Freud* (Vol. 16, Part 3). London: Hogarth Press.

Freud, S. (1918a). A difficulty in the path of psychoanalysis. In J. Strachey (Ed. & Trans.), *The standard edition of the complete psychological works of Sigmund Freud* (Vol. 17, pp. 140–143). London: Hogarth Press.

Freud, S. (1918b). From the history of an infantile neurosis. In J. Strachey (Ed. & Trans.), *The standard edition of the complete psychological works of Sigmund Freud* (Vol. 17, pp. 7–122). London: Hogarth Press.

Freud, S. (1920). Beyond the pleasure principle, group psychology, and other works. In J. Strachey (Ed. & Trans.), *The standard edition of the complete psychological works of Sigmund Freud* (Vol. 18, pp. 1–64). London: Hogarth Press.

Freud, S. (1923–1925). The ego and the id. In J. Strachey (Ed. & Trans.), *The standard edition of the complete psychological works of Sigmund Freud* (Vol. 19, pp. 1–308). London: Hogarth Press.

Freud, S. (1961). *The future of an illusion.* New York: Anchor. (Original work written 1927)

Fromm, E. (1960). Psychoanalysis and Zen Buddhism. In E. Fromm, D. T. Suzuki, & R. De Martino (Eds.), *Zen Buddhism and psychoanalysis.* New York: Harper.

Gabbard, G. (1997). A reconsideration of objectivity in the analyst. *International Journal of Psycho-Analysis, 78,* 847–850.

Gazzaniga, M., & Bizzi, E. (2000). *The new cognitive neurosciences* (2nd ed.). Cambridge, MA: MIT Press.

Gladwell, M. (2005). *Blink: The power of thinking without thinking.* New York: Little, Brown.

Green, A. (1975). The analyst, symbolization and absence in the psychoanalytic setting. *International Journal of Psycho-Analysis, 56,* 1–22.

Grotstein, J. (1995, April). *Psychoanalytic technique.* Seminar taught at the Psychoanalytic Institute of Northern California, San Francisco.

Grotstein, J. (2000). *Who is the dreamer who dreams the dream?* Hillsdale, NJ: Analytic Press.

Grotstein, J. (2002). "We are such stuff as dreams are made of": Annotations on dreams and dreaming in Bion's works. In C. Neri, M. Pines, & R. Friedman (Eds.), *Dreams on group psychotherapy: Theory and technique* (pp. 110–145). London: Kingsley.

Grotstein, J. (2003). East is east and west is west and ne'er the twains shall meet. Or shall they? In J. Safran (Ed.), *Psychoanalysis and Buddhism—An evolving dialogue.* Boston: Wisdom.

Grotstein, J. (2007). *A beam of intense darkness—Wilfred Bion's legacy to psychoanalysis.* London: Karnac.

Hamilton, V. (1982). *Narcissus and Oedipus.* London: Routledge and Kegan Paul.

Hamilton, V. (1996). *The analyst's preconscious.* New York: Analytic Press.

Huxley, A. (1945). *The perennial philosophy.* London: Chatto and Windus.

James, H., & Besant, W. (1885). *The art of fiction.* Boston: DeWolfe-Fiske.

Jones, E. (1946). A valedictory address. *International Journal of Psycho-Analysis, 27,* 7–12.

Kabat-Zinn, J. (1990). *Full catastrophe living.* New York: Dell.

Kaku, M. (2005). *Parallel worlds: The science of alternative universes and our future in the cosmos.* New York: Allen Lane.

Kapleau, P. (1980). *Three pillars of Zen.* New York: Rider.

Keats, J. (1970). Letter to George and Thomas Keats. In W. R. Bion, *Attention and interpretation.* London: Tavistock. (Original letter December 28, 1817)

Kernberg, O. (2004). *Aggressivity, narcissism, and self-destructiveness in the psychotherapeutic relationship.* New Haven, CT: Yale University Press.

Kim, H. J. (1980). *Dogen Kigen—Mystical realist.* Tucson: University of Arizona Press.

Kinnell, G. (2001). *A new selected poems.* New York: Houghton Mifflin Harcourt.

Klauber, J. (1987). *Illusion and spontaneity in psychoanalysis.* London: Free Association Books.

Klein, M. (1940). Mourning and its relation to manic-depressive states. *International Journal of Psycho-analysis, 21,* 125–53.

Klein, M. (1946). Notes on some schizoid mechanisms. *International Journal of Psycho-Analysis, 27,* 99–110.

Klein, M. (1975). The origins of transference. In *The writings of Melanie Klein. Volume 3: Envy and gratitude* (pp. 48–56). London: Hogarth. (Original work written in 1952)

Klein, M. (2002). *Love, guilt and reparation—And other works 1921–1945.* New York: Simon and Schuster.

Krishnamurti, J. (1973). *Dialogue with Jacob Needleman, Krishnamurti Foundation* [audio tape]. Ojai, CA.

Krishnamurti, J. (1975). *The first and last freedom.* New York: HarperCollins.

Lifton, R. J. (1999, November 2). *Evil, the self, and survival: Conversations with history*. Interview of R. J. Lifton by Harry Kreisler at the Institute of International Studies, University of California at Berkeley.

Loewald, H. (1980). *Papers on psychoanalysis*. New Haven, CT: Yale University Press.

Macy, J. (1995, Spring). Interview. *Inquiring Mind*, 11, 2.

Maezumi, H. T. (1978). *The way of everyday life*. Los Angeles: Zen Center of Los Angeles.

Maezumi, H. T. and Glassman, B. T. (1977). *The hazy moon of enlightenment*. Los Angeles, CA: Zen Center of Los Angeles.

Matt, D. (1987, March). *Hasidism*. Seminar taught at Peninsula Temple Sholom, Burlingame, CA.

Matte Blanco, I. (1988). *Thinking, feeling and being*. London: Routledge.

Matte Blanco, I. (1998). *The unconscious as infinite sets: An essay in bi-logic*. London: Karnac Books.

Mayer, E. L. (1996). Changes in science and changing ideas about knowledge and authority in psychoanalysis. *Psychoanalytic Quarterly*, 65, 158–200.

Mayer, E. L. (2007). *Extraordinary knowing*. New York: Random House.

McDonald, M. (1995, Winter). Of mud and broken windows: Teaching the wounded soul. *Blind Donkey*, 15, 2.

Meltzer, D., & Harris Williams, M. (1988). *The apprehension of beauty*. London: Clunie Press.

Milner, M. (1969). *The hands of the living God*. London: Hogarth Press. Milner, M. [also known as Joanna Field]. (1981). Discovery of the "Other." In *A life of one's own*. New York: Tarcher/Putnam.

Milner, M. (1987a). The concentration of the body. In *The Suppressed Madness of Sane Men* (pp. 234–240). London: Routledge.

Milner, M. (1987b). *The suppressed madness of sane men*. London: Routledge.

Mitchell, S. (1993). *Hope and dread in psychoanalysis*. New York: Basic Books.

Montessori, M. (1964). *The Montessori method*. New York: Schocken Books.

Neil, A. S. (1995). *Summerhill School*. New York: St. Martin's Press.

Nim, Soen S. [also known as Seung Sahn]. (1976). *Dharma* talk. Talk given at Zen retreat, Providence, RI.

Ogden, T. (1989). *The primitive edge of experience*. Northvale, NJ: Aronson.

Ogden, T. (1994). *Subjects of analysis*. Northvale, NJ: Aronson.

Ogden, T. (1999). *Reverie and interpretation: Sensing something human*. London: Karnac Books.

Ogden, T. (2001). *Conversations at the frontier of dreaming*. Northvale, NJ: Aronson.

Pagels, E. (1979). *The gnostic gospels*. New York: Random House.

Parsons, M. (1986). Suddenly finding it really matters. *International Journal of Psychoanalysis*, 67, 475–488.

Piercy, M. (1973). To be of use. In *Circles on the water*. New York: Knopf. Exact quote: http://www.northnode.org/poem.htm

Rayner, E. (1991). *The independent mind in British psychoanalysis*. London: Rowman & Littlefield.

Reps, P. (1957). *Zen flesh, Zen bones*. Rutland, VT: Tuttle.

Rilke, R. M. (1986). *Letters to a young poet* (S. Mitchell, Trans.). New York: Vintage.

Sakaki, N. (1987). *Break the mirror*. San Francisco: North Point Press.

Sanville, J. (1991). *The playground of psychoanalytic psychotherapy*. Northvale, NJ: Analytic Press.

Sartre, J. P. (1981). *The family idiot: Gustave Flaubert* (Vol. 1). Chicago: University of Chicago Press.

Sasaki, R. F. (Trans.). (1971). *The recorded sayings of Layman P'ang*. New York: Weatherhill.

Schore, A. (2003). *Affect regulation and the repair of the self*. New York: Norton.

Senzaki, N. (1973). *Last words* [Original calligraphy]. Maui, HI: Maui Zendo.

Shibayama, Z. (1974). *Zen comments of the Mumonkan*. New York: Mentor.

Sloss, R. R. (2000). *Lives in the shadows with J. Krishnamurti*. Universe.

Spezzano, C. (1993). A relational model of inquiry and truth: The place of analysis in human conversation. *Psychoanalytic Dialogues*, 3(2), 177–208.

Spezzano, C. (1995). *How psychoanalysts learn*. Paper delivered at the What Is Contemporary About Contemporary Psychoanalysis? symposium at the Psychoanalytic Institute of Northern California, San Francisco.

Spitz, R. (1983). *Dialogues from infancy* (R. N. Emde, Ed.). New York: International Universities Press, 1983. (Original work published 1963)

Stern, D. (1993). *Psychoanalysis: Diversity and integration*. Panel discussion panel at American Psychological Association, Division 39 annual meetings, New York City.

Stevens, W. (1972). Tea at the Palaz of Hoon. In H. Stevens (Ed.), *The palm at the end of the mind: Selected poems and a play* (p. 54). New York: Vintage. (Poem originally published 1921)

Suzuki, S. (2006). In P. Chodron, *Practicing peace in times of war* (p. 31). Boston: Shambhala.

Symington, N. (1983). The analyst's act of freedom as agent of therapeutic change. *International Review of Psycho-Analysis*, 10, 283–291.

Symington, N. (1993). *Narcissism: A new theory*. London: Karnac Books.

Symington, N. (1994). *Emotion and spirit*. New York: St. Martin's Press. Sullivan, A., & Gilbert, W.S. (2005). The complete annotated Gilbert and Sullivan (Ian C. Bradley Edition). London: Oxford University Press.

Thurman, R. (2005, May). *On making the world we want*. Talk at Green Gulch Zen Farm, Stinson Beach, CA.

Volkan, V. (1996, January 15). *Psychoanalytic treatment of narcissism*. Seminar taught at Psychoanalytic Institute of Northern California, San Francisco.

Whitman, W. (1855). Song of myself. In *Leaves of grass* (51:1320). Self-published. Retrieved from http://www.bartleby.com/142/14.html

Winnicott, C. (1978). A reflection. In S. A. Grolnick & L. Barkin (Eds.), *Between reality and fantasy*. New York: Aronson.

Winnicott, D. W. (1958). Mind and its relation to the psyche-soma. In *Collected Works: Through paediatrics to psycho-analysis*. New York: International Universities Press. (Original work published in 1949)

Winnicott, D. W. (1964). *The child, the family, and the outside world*. London: Pelican.

Winnicott, D. W. (1965a). Communicating and not communicating leading to a study of certain opposites. In *The Maturational Processes and the Facilitating Environment*, Madison, CT: International Universities Press.

Winnicott, D. W. (1965b). Ego distortion in terms of true and false self. In *The maturational process and the facilitating environment*. Madison, CT: International Universities Press. (Original work published 1960)

Winnicott, D. W. (1968). Fear of breakdown. In *Psychoanalytic explorations*. Cambridge, MA: Harvard University Press.

Winnicott, D. W. (1971a). Mirror-role of mother and family in child development. In *Playing and reality*. London: Tavistock.

Winnicott, D. W. (1971b). Transitional objects and transitional phenomena. In *Playing and reality*. London: Tavistock.

Winnicott, D. W. (1971c). The use of an object and relating through identifications. In *Playing and reality*. London: Tavistock.

Winnicott, D.W. (1975). Metapsychological and clinical aspects of regression within the psychoanalytic set-up. In *Collected Works: Through paediatrics to psycho-analysis*. New York: International Universities Press.

Wunder, J. (2008). *Hermeticism and the secret societies*. Farnham, UK: Ashgate.

Yamada, K. (1973). *Zen teisho*. Talk given at Maui Zendo, Maui, HI.

Yamada, K. (1979). *Gateless gate*. Los Angeles: Zen Center of Los Angeles.

Yasutani Haku'un Rōshi. (1975). In Dharma talk by Robert Aitken Rōshi, Maui Zendo, Maui, HI.

Yasutani Rōshi. (1973a). Last poem (Aitken Rōshi, Trans.). *Journal of the Diamond Sangha*, No. 2.

Yasutani Rōshi. (1973b). Last poem. *Journal of the Zen Center of Los Angeles*, Summer/ Fall 1973.

Yoshizawa, K. (2009). *The religious art of Zen master Hakuin*. Berkeley, CA: Counterpoint.

Yunmen (1994). In U. App (Ed.), *Master Yunmen*. New York: Kodansha America.

Credits

CHAPTER 1

The first half of chapter 1 is adapted, with permission, from Bobrow, J. (1997). Coming to life: The creative intercourse of psychoanalysis and Zen Buddhism. In C. Spezzano, and G. Garguilo (Eds.), *Soul on the couch: Spirituality, religion, and morality in contemporary psychoanalysis* (pp. 109–46). London: The Analytic Press.

CHAPTER 2

Chapter 2 is adapted, with permission, from Bobrow, J. (1998). The fertile mind. In A. Molino (Ed.), *The couch and the tree: Dialogues in psychoanalysis and Buddhism* (pp. 307–20). New York: Farrar, Strauss and Giroux.

CHAPTER 4

Chapter 4 is adapted, with permission, from Bobrow, J. (2004). "Presence of mind: On mentalization, mindfulness, and no-mind." *Int'l Journal of Applied Psychoanalytic Studies.*

CHAPTER 5

Chapter 5 is adapted, with permission, from Bobrow, J. (October 2002). "Psychoanalysis, Mysticism, and the Incommunicado Core." *fort da, Journal of the Northern California Society for Psychological Psychology*, Division of Psychoanalysis, American Psychological Association.

CHAPTER 6

Chapter 6 is adapted from Bobrow, J. (2003). Moments of truth—Truth of moments. In J. Safran (Ed.), *Psychoanalysis and Buddhism: An unfolding dialogue.* With permission from Wisdom Publications, 199 Elm Street, Somerville, MA 02144. Wisdomexperience.org.

CHAPTER 8

Chapter 8 is adapted, with permission, from Bobrow, J. (April 2007). "The disavowal of the personal in psychoanalytic training." *Psychoanalytical Review* (pp. 263–77).

AFTERWORD

This Afterword is based on a talk as a *teisho* during sesshin. *Teisho* is a Dharma presentation, literally "roar of the Dharma." *Sesshin* is an intensive retreat, literally "to touch the Mind, to convey the Mind."

Index

About the Author

Joseph Bobrow is a psychologist-psychoanalyst, Zen master, and the author of three books: *Zen and Psychotherapy: Partners in Liberation*, *Waking Up from War: A Better Way Home for Veterans and Nations*, and *After Midnight*, a collection of poems. He is the founder and roshi of Deep Streams Zen Institute in Los Angeles, which offers Zen practice, interdisciplinary education, and community service. Joseph has long been bringing together the best from Buddhist and psychodynamic traditions in his community work to alleviate individual and collective anguish. Most recently, he developed integrative retreats for military veterans, their families, and care providers, which help heal the unseen wounds of war.

What to Read Next
from Wisdom Publications

Psychoanalysis and Buddhism
An Unfolding Dialogue
Jeremy Safran

"An extraordinary book. Safran deserves much praise."
—Mark Epstein, MD, author of *Thoughts without a Thinker*

Ending the Pursuit of Happiness
A Zen Guide
Barry Magid

"In an era dominated by the pursuit of quick fixes and the growing medicalization of the mental health field, this book provides a radical and vitally important challenge to the prevailing cultural ethos."
—Jeremy D. Safran, PhD, professor and director of clinical psychology, New School for Social Research, and editor of *Psychoanalysis and Buddhism*

Ordinary Mind
Exploring the Common Ground of Zen and Psychoanalysis
Barry Magid

"Exciting and hope-inspiring work. The very reading of this book is in itself therapeutic."—James S. Grotstein, author of *Who Is the Dreamer Who Dreams the Dream?*

The Gateless Gate
The Classic Book of Zen Koans
Koun Yamada

"Yamada Roshi's straightforward commentary on the *Wu-men kuan* (*Mumonkan*) is again available in this new edition, and I'm delighted."
—Robert Aitken, author of *Taking the Path of Zen*

Nothing Is Hidden
The Psychology of Zen Koans
Barry Magid

"A nuanced, sensitive, and compassionate analysis. This book can help point toward more honest introspection that will yield healing and acceptance."—*Publishers Weekly*

Bearing the Unbearable
Love, Loss, and the Heartbreaking Path of Grief
Joanne Cacciatore

"Simultaneously heartwrenching and uplifting. Cacciatore offers practical guidance on coping with profound and life-changing grief. This book is destined to be a classic . . . [it] is simply the best book I have ever read on the process of grief."—Ira Israel, *Huffington Post*

About Wisdom Publications

Wisdom Publications is the leading publisher of classic and contemporary Buddhist books and practical works on mindfulness. To learn more about us or to explore our other books, please visit our website at wisdomexperience.org or contact us at the address below.

Wisdom Publications
199 Elm Street
Somerville, MA 02144 USA

We are a 501(c)(3) organization, and donations in support of our mission are tax deductible.

Wisdom Publications is affiliated with the Foundation for the Preservation of the Mahayana Tradition (FPMT).